TOP TRAILS™
San Francisco Bay Area

Written by
David Weintraub

Series edited by
Joseph Walowski

🐾 **WILDERNESS PRESS** · BERKELEY, CALIFORNIA

Top Trails San Francisco Bay Area

1st EDITION May 2004

Copyright © 2004 by David Weintraub

All photos, except where noted, copyright by David Weintraub
Maps by Ben Pease, Pease Press and Fineline Maps
Cover design: Frances Baca Design and Andreas Schueller
Interior design: Frances Baca Design
Production and additional design: Ben Pease, Pease Press
Book editor: Joe Walowski

ISBN 0-89997-348-5
UPC 7-19609-97348-5

Manufactured in the United States of America

Published by: **Wilderness Press**

1200 5th Street
Berkeley, CA 94710
(800) 443-7227; FAX (510) 558-1696
info@wildernesspress.com
www.wildernesspress.com
Visit our website for a complete listing of our books and
for ordering information

Cover photos: Summit Trail on San Bruno Mountain; Mariposa lily

SAFETY NOTICE: Although Wilderness Press and the author have made every
attempt to ensure that the information in this book is accurate at press time, they are not
responsible for any loss, damage, injury, or inconvenience that may occur to anyone while
using this book. You are responsible for your own safety and health. The fact that a trail
is described in this book does not mean that it will be safe for you. Be aware that trail
conditions can change from day to day. Always check local conditions and know your
own limitations.

The Top Trails™ Series

Wilderness Press

When Wilderness Press published *Sierra North* in 1967, no other trail guide like it existed for the Sierra backcountry. The first run of 2800 copies sold out in less than two months and its success heralded the beginning of Wilderness Press. In the past 35 years, we have expanded our territories to cover California, Alaska, Hawaii, the U.S. Southwest, the Pacific Northwest, New England, Canada, and Baja California.

Wilderness Press continues to publish comprehensive, accurate, and readable outdoor books. Hikers, backpackers, kayakers, skiers, snowshoers, climbers, cyclists, and trail runners rely on Wilderness Press for accurate outdoor adventure information.

Top Trails

In its Top Trails guides, Wilderness Press has paid special attention to organization so that you can find the perfect hike each and every time. Whether you're looking for a steep trail to test yourself on or a walk in the park, a romantic waterfall or a city view, Top Trails will lead you there.

Each Top Trails guide contains trails for everyone. The trails selected provide a sampling of the best that the region has to offer. These are the 'must-do' hikes, walks, runs and bike rides, with every feature of the area represented.

Every book in the Top Trails series offers:

- The Wilderness Press commitment to accuracy and reliability
- Ratings and rankings for each trail
- Distances and approximate times
- Easy-to-follow trail notes
- Maps & permit information

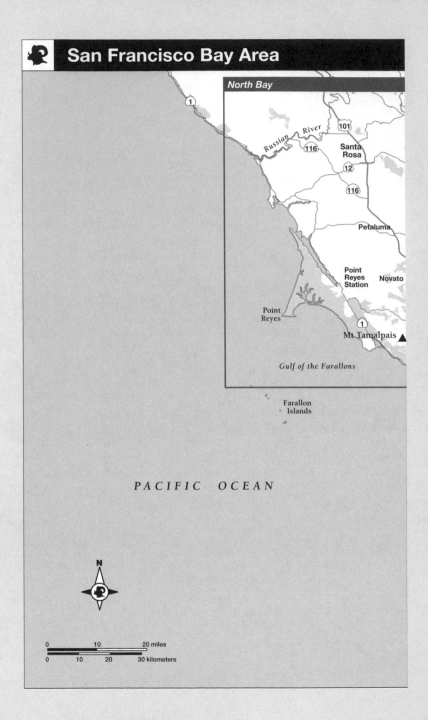

San Francisco Bay Area

North Bay

Russian River

101

116

Santa Rosa

12

116

Petaluma

Point Reyes Station

Novato

Point Reyes

1

Mt Tamalpais ▲

Gulf of the Farallons

Farallon Islands

PACIFIC OCEAN

N

0   10   20 miles
0   10   20   30 kilometers

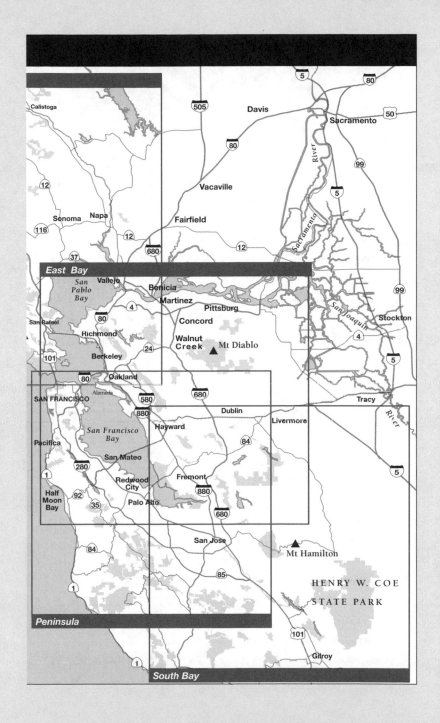

East Bay

Calistoga

505

Davis

Sacramento

80

50

12

80

Vacaville

99

Sonoma   Napa

116

12

680

Fairfield

12

37

San Pablo Bay

Vallejo

Benicia

Martinez

Pittsburg

Concord

Stockton

San Rafael

80

Richmond

4

Walnut Creek

▲ Mt Diablo

4

5

101

Berkeley

24

80   Oakland

680

Tracy

San Joaquin

99

SAN FRANCISCO

Alameda

580

880

Dublin

Livermore

River

5

Pacifica

San Francisco Bay

Hayward

84

San Mateo

Redwood City

Fremont

280

880

Half Moon Bay

92

35

Palo Alto

680

1

84

San Jose

85

Mt Hamilton ▲

HENRY W. COE

STATE PARK

Peninsula

1

101

1

South Bay

Gilroy

v

San Francisco Bay Area Trails

TRAIL NUMBER AND NAME	Page	Difficulty -12345+	Length in Miles	Type	Hiking	Running	Bicycling	Fee or Permit	Dogs Allowed	Child Friendly
1. NORTH BAY										
1 Annadel State Park	27	4	8.8	↺	🥾	🏃	🚲			👫
2 China Camp State Park	33	3	5.5	↺	🥾	🏃	🚲	P		
3 Jack London State Park	39	3	2.9	↺	🥾	🏃	🚲	P		👫
4 Marin Headlands	45	3	5.4	↺	🥾	🏃	🚲			
5 Mt. Burdell Open Space	51	4	5.6	↺	🥾	🏃	🚲[1]		🐕	👫
6 Mt. St. Helena	57	5	10.6	↗	🥾	🏃	🚲[1]			
7 Mt. Tamalpais: High Marsh	63	4	5.8	↺	🥾	🏃			🐕	👫
8 Mt. Tamalpais: Middle Peak	71	3	5.0	↺	🥾	🏃		P	🐕	👫
9 Muir Woods: Tourist Club	75	3	3.8	↺	🥾	🏃		P		👫
10 Pine Mountain	79	3	4.7	↗	🥾	🏃	🚲		🐕	👫
11 Pt. Reyes: Sky Trail	83	5	10.5	↺	🥾	🏃				
12 S.P. Taylor State Park	87	4	6.3	↺	🥾	🏃				
13 Skyline Wilderness Park	91	4	6.0	↗	🥾	🏃	🚲	P		
14 Sugarloaf Ridge State Park	97	5	6.7	↺	🥾	🏃		P		
2. EAST BAY										
15 Black Diamond Mines	111	4	7.6	↺	🥾	🏃	🚲[1]	P	🐕	
16 Briones Regional Park	117	4	6.8	↺	🥾	🏃	🚲	P	🐕	
17 Coyote Hills Regional Park	121	2	1.5	↺	🥾	🏃	🚲	P	🐕	👫
18 Dry Creek Pioneer Park	125	5	9.6	↺	🥾	🏃		P	🐕	
19 Mission Peak	131	5	6.3	↗	🥾	🏃	🚲		🐕	
20 Morgan Territory	137	5	6.3	↺	🥾	🏃	🚲		🐕	
21 Mt. Diablo: Grand Loop	141	5	6.5	↺	🥾	🏃		P		
22 Pleasanton Ridge	147	5	12.3	↺	🥾	🏃	🚲		🐕	
23 Redwood Regional Park	153	3	6.0	↺	🥾	🏃		P	🐕	
24 Sibley Volcanic Preserve	159	2	1.6	↺	🥾	🏃			🐕	👫
25 Sunol Regional Wilderness	163	3	5.9	↺	🥾	🏃	🚲[1]	☑	🐕	
26 Tilden Regional Park	169	3	3.3	↺	🥾	🏃				👫
27 Wildcat Canyon	173	4	7.0	↺	🥾	🏃	🚲		🐕	

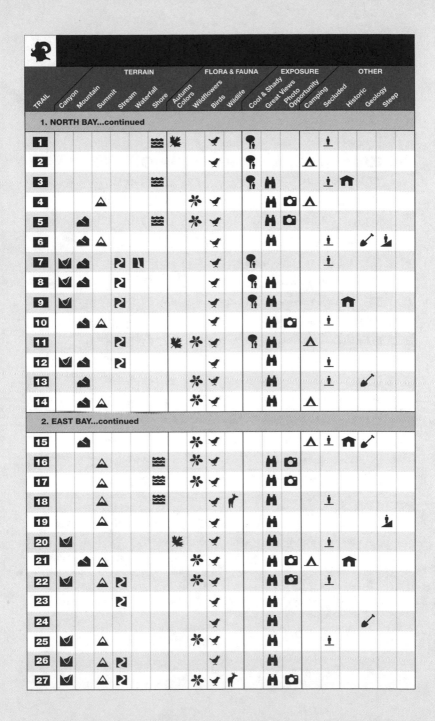

	TERRAIN						FLORA & FAUNA				EXPOSURE			OTHER				
TRAIL	Canyon	Mountain	Summit	Stream	Waterfall	Shore	Autumn Colors	Wildflowers	Birds	Wildlife	Cool & Shady	Great Views	Photo Opportunity	Camping	Secluded	Historic	Geology	Steep
1. NORTH BAY...continued																		
1						●	●		●		●				●			
2									●		●			●				
3						●					●	●			●	●		
4			●					●	●			●	●	●				
5		●				●		●	●			●	●					
6		●	●						●			●			●		●	●
7	●	●		●	●				●		●				●			
8	●	●		●					●		●	●						
9	●			●					●		●	●				●		
10		●	●						●			●	●		●			
11				●			●	●	●		●	●		●				
12	●	●		●					●			●			●			
13		●						●	●			●			●		●	
14		●	●					●	●			●		●				
2. EAST BAY...continued																		
15		●						●	●					●	●	●	●	
16			●			●		●	●			●	●					
17			●			●		●	●			●	●					
18			●			●			●	●		●			●			
19			●						●			●						●
20	●						●		●			●			●			
21		●	●					●	●			●	●	●		●		
22	●		●	●				●	●			●	●		●			
23				●					●			●						
24									●			●					●	
25	●		●					●	●			●			●			
26	●		●	●					●			●						
27	●		●	●				●	●	●		●	●					

San Francisco Bay Area Trails...continued

TRAIL NUMBER AND NAME	Page	Difficulty -12345+	Length in Miles	Type	Hiking	Running	Bicycling	Fee or Permit	Dogs Allowed	Child Friendly
3. SOUTH BAY										
28 Almaden Quicksilver	187	5	7.0	Loop	Hiking	Running			Dogs	
29 Ed R. Levin County Park	193	5	7.8	Loop	Hiking	Running		P		
30 Henry W. Coe State Park	199	4	6.3	Loop	Hiking	Running		P		
31 Joseph D. Grant Co. Park	203	5	9.8	Loop	Hiking	Running	Bicycling			
32 Sierra Azul OSP	207	3	5.2	Loop	Hiking	Running	Bicycling		Dogs	
4. PENINSULA										
33 El Corte de Madera Preserve	221	3	4.3	Loop	Hiking	Running	Bicycling			
34 Fremont Older Preserve	225	3	3.1	Loop	Hiking	Running	Bicycling		Dogs	Child Friendly
35 Long Ridge Preserve	231	3	4.6	Loop	Hiking	Running	Bicycling			
36 Montara Mountain	235	4	7.2	Out & back	Hiking	Running	Bicycling	P		
37 Monte Bello Preserve	239	4	6.0	Loop	Hiking	Running	Bicycling			
38 Kings Mountain	245	5	7.9	Loop	Hiking	Running		P		
39 Presidio of San Francisco	251	2	2.6	Loop	Hiking	Running	Bicycling		Dogs	Child Friendly
40 Purisima Creek Redwoods	257	5	10.1	Loop	Hiking	Running	Bicycling			
41 Russian Ridge Preserve	261	3	4.6	Loop	Hiking	Running	Bicycling			
42 San Bruno Mountain	267	3	3.1	Loop	Hiking	Running		P		
43 Skyline Ridge Preserve	271	3	3.4	Out & back	Hiking	Running	Bicycling			Child Friendly
44 Windy Hill Preserve	275	5	8.0	Loop	Hiking	Running				

USE & ACCESS
- Hiking
- Trail Running
- Mountain Biking
- P Parking Fee
- Permit
- Child Friendly
- Dogs Allowed
- Handicap Access
- Camping

TERRAIN
- Canyon
- Mountain
- Summit

WATER
- Stream
- Waterfall
- Beach
- Shore

FLORA & FAUNA
- Autumn Colors
- Wildflowers
- Birds
- Wildlife
- Tide Pools

OTHER
- Cool & Shady
- Great Views
- Photo Opportunity
- Secluded
- Historic
- Geologic Interest
- Moonlight Hiking
- Steep

DIFFICULTY
- 1 2 3 4 5 +
less   more

Bicyclists use alternate trails or trailheads (see text)

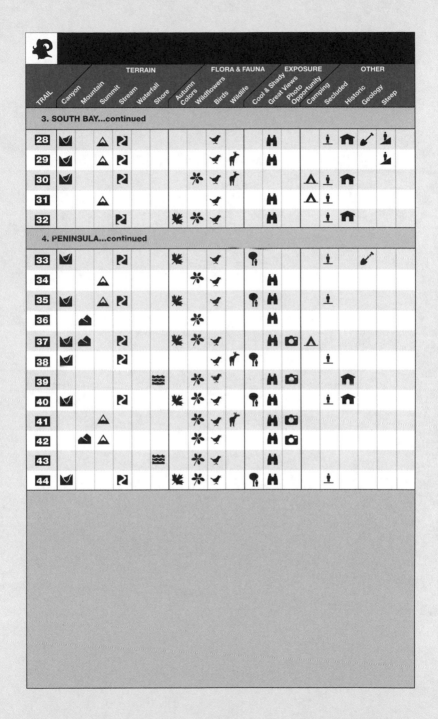

	TERRAIN						FLORA & FAUNA				EXPOSURE			OTHER				
TRAIL	Canyon	Mountain	Summit	Stream	Waterfall	Shore	Autumn Colors	Wildflowers	Birds	Wildlife	Cool & Shady	Great Views	Photo Opportunity	Camping	Secluded	Historic	Geology	Steep

3. SOUTH BAY...continued

Trail	Canyon	Mountain	Summit	Stream	Waterfall	Shore	Autumn Colors	Wildflowers	Birds	Wildlife	Cool & Shady	Great Views	Photo Opportunity	Camping	Secluded	Historic	Geology	Steep
28	●		●	●					●			●			●	●	●	●
29	●		●	●					●	●		●						●
30	●			●				●	●	●				●	●	●		
31			●						●			●		●	●			
32				●			●	●	●			●			●	●		

4. PENINSULA...continued

Trail	Canyon	Mountain	Summit	Stream	Waterfall	Shore	Autumn Colors	Wildflowers	Birds	Wildlife	Cool & Shady	Great Views	Photo Opportunity	Camping	Secluded	Historic	Geology	Steep
33	●			●			●		●		●				●		●	
34			●					●	●			●						
35	●		●	●			●		●		●	●			●			
36		●						●				●						
37	●	●		●			●	●	●			●	●	●				
38	●			●					●	●	●				●			
39					●			●	●			●	●			●		
40	●			●			●	●	●		●	●			●	●		
41			●					●	●	●		●	●					
42		●	●					●	●			●	●					
43					●			●	●			●						
44	●			●			●	●	●		●	●			●			

Contents

CHAPTER 2

East Bay

CHAPTER 3

South Bay

CHAPTER 4

Peninsula 211

Using Top Trails™

Organization of Top Trails

Top Trails is designed to make identifying the perfect trail easy and enjoyable, and to make every outing a success and a pleasure. With this book you'll find it's a snap to find the right trail, whether you're planning a major hike or just a sociable stroll with friends.

The Region

Top Trails begins with the **San Francisco Bay Area Map** (pages iv-v), displaying the entire region covered by the guide and providing a geographic overview. The map is clearly marked to show which area is covered by each chapter.

After the Regional Map comes the **San Francisco Bay Area Trails Table** (pages vi-ix), which lists every trail covered in the guide along with attributes for each trail. A quick reading of the Regional Map and the Trail Table will give a good overview of the entire region covered by the book.

Navigating the Region

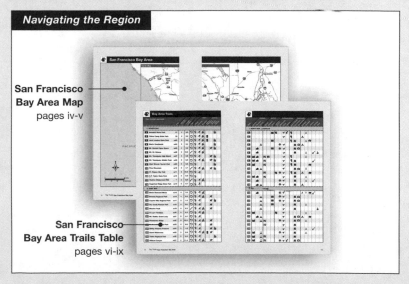

San Francisco Bay Area Map
pages iv-v

San Francisco Bay Area Trails Table
pages vi-ix

The Areas

The region covered in each book is divided into Areas, with each chapter corresponding to one area in the region.

Each Area chapter starts with information to help you choose and enjoy a trail every time out. Use the Table of Contents or the Regional Map to identify an area of interest, then turn to the Area chapter to find the following:

- An Overview of the Area, including park and permit information
- An Area Map with all trails clearly marked
- A Trail Feature Table providing trail-by-trail details
- Trail Summaries, written in a lively, accessible style

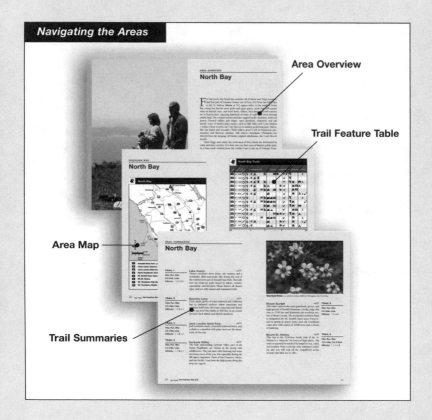

Navigating the Areas

Area Overview

Trail Feature Table

Area Map

Trail Summaries

The Trails

The basic building block of the Top Trails guide is the Trail Entry. Each one is arranged to make finding and following the trail as simple as possible, with all pertinent information presented in this easy-to-follow format:

- A Trail Map
- Trail Descriptors covering difficulty, length and other essential data
- A written Trail Description
- Trail Milestones providing easy-to follow, turn-by-turn trail directions

Some Trail Descriptions offer additional information:

- An Elevation Profile
- Trail Options
- Trail Highlights

In the margins of the Trail Entries, keep your eyes open for graphic icons that signal passages in the text.

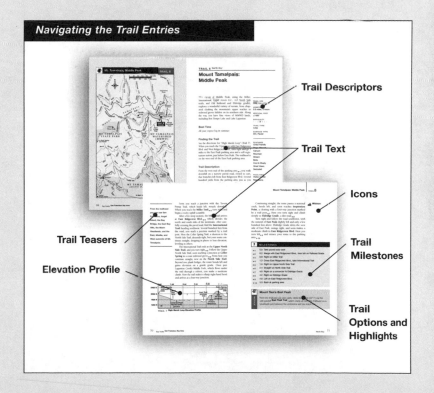

xvii

Choosing a Trail

Top Trails provides several different ways of choosing a trail, all presented in easy-to-read tables, charts, and maps.

Location

If you know in general where you want to go, Top Trails makes it easy to find the right trail in the right place. Each chapter begins with a large-scale map showing the starting point of every trail in that area.

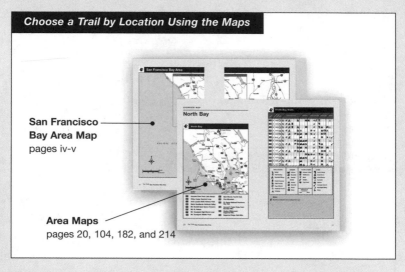

Choose a Trail by Location Using the Maps

San Francisco Bay Area Map pages iv–v

Area Maps pages 20, 104, 182, and 214

Features

This guide describes the Top Trails of the San Francisco region. Each trail is chosen because it offers one or more features that make it interesting. Using the trail descriptors, summaries, and tables, you can quickly examine all the trails for the features they offer, or seek a particular feature among the list of trails.

Season and Condition

Time of year and current conditions can be important factors in selecting the best trail. For example, an exposed grassland trail may be a riot of color in early spring, but an oven-baked taste of hell in mid-summer. Wherever relevant, Top Trails identifies the best and worst conditions for the trails you plan to hike.

Difficulty

Each trail has an overall difficulty rating on a scale of 1 to 5, which takes into consideration length, elevation change, exposure, trail quality, etc., to create one (admittedly subjective) rating.

The ratings assume you are an able-bodied adult in reasonably good shape using the trail for hiking. The ratings also assume normal weather conditions—clear and dry.

Readers should make an honest assessment of their own abilities and adjust time estimates accordingly. Also, rain, snow, heat, and poor visibility can all affect the pace on even the easiest of trails.

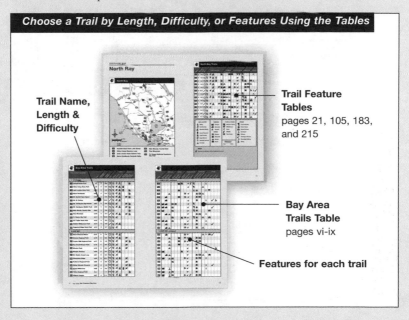

Choose a Trail by Length, Difficulty, or Features Using the Tables

Trail Name, Length & Difficulty

Trail Feature Tables
pages 21, 105, 183, and 215

Bay Area Trails Table
pages vi-ix

Features for each trail

Vertical Feet

This important measurement is often underestimated by hikers and bikers when gauging the difficulty of a trail. The Top Trails measurement accounts for all elevation change, not simply the difference between the highest and lowest points, so that rolling terrain with lots of up and down will be identifiable.

The calculation of Vertical Feet in the Top Trails series is accomplished by a combination of trail measurement and computer-aided estimation. For routes that begin and end at the same spot – i.e. Loop or Out & Back – the vertical gain exactly matches the vertical descent. With a point-to-point route the vertical gain and loss will most likely differ, and both figures will be provided in the text.

Finally, some of Trail Entries in the Top Trails series have an **Elevation Profile**, an easy means for visualizing the topography of the route. These profiles graphically depict the elevation throughout the length of the trail.

Surface Type

Each Trail Entry provides information about the surface of the trail. This is useful in determining what type of footwear or bicycle is appropriate. Surface Type should also be considered when checking the weather – on a rainy day a dirt surface can be a muddy slog; an asphalt surface might be a better choice (although asphalt can be slick when wet).

 Top Trails Difficulty Ratings

1 A short trail, generally level, that can be completed in 1 hour or less.

2 A route of 1 to 3 miles, with some up and down, that can be completed in 1 to 2 hours.

3 A longer route, up to 5 miles, with uphill and/or downhill sections.

4 A long or steep route, perhaps more than 5 miles or climbs of more than 1000 vertical feet.

5 The most severe, both long and steep, more than 5 miles long with climbs of more than 1000 vertical feet.

Map Legend

Trail	- - - - - -	River	———
Other Trail	- - - - -	Stream	———
Freeway	▬▬▬▬	Seasonal Stream	— · — · —
Major Road	▬▬▬▬	Body of Water	⬭
Minor Road	———	Dam	⬭
Tunnel	- - - - -	Marsh/Swamp	⸰⸰ ⸰⸰ ⸰⸰
Gate	•—•	Park/Forest	▭
Building	▪ ▪	Boundary	— · · — · · —
Bridge	)(		
Peak	▲	North Arrow	N ◆
Trailhead Parking	P		
Picnic	ᴨ		
Camping	▲	Start/Finish	start & finish

Pleasanton Ridge (*Trail 22*)

Introduction to the San Francisco Bay Area

The Bay Area is usually divided into four regions—North Bay, East Bay, South Bay, and Peninsula—and this book follows that scheme. The North Bay includes Marin, Napa, and Sonoma counties; the East Bay consists of Alameda and Contra Costa counties; the South Bay takes in most of Santa Clara County; and the Peninsula covers San Francisco, San Mateo, and the northwestern part of Santa Clara County. Within these regions are bustling urban areas such as San Francisco, Oakland, San Jose, and Silicon Valley, along with tranquil forests, mountains, beaches, marshes, and farmlands. The parks and open spaces here are administered by an alphabet soup of local, state, and federal agencies, including California State Parks (CSP); East Bay Regional Park District (EBRPD); the Golden Gate National Recreation Area (GGNRA); Midpeninsula Regional Open Space District (MROSD); Santa Clara County Parks and Recreation; San Mateo County Parks; Marin Municipal Water District (MMWD), and Marin County Open Space District (MCOSD).

Geography

The Bay Area lies within a geological province called the Coast Ranges, a complex system of ridges and valleys that stretches from Arcata to the north to near Santa Barbara in the south, and inland to the edge of the Central Valley. Several important sub-ranges run through our area, including the Sonoma, Mayacmas, and Vaca mountains in the North Bay; the Diablo Range in the East Bay and South Bay; and the Santa Cruz Mountains on the Peninsula and in the South Bay. The tallest peak in the North Bay is Mt. St. Helena (4339'), at the corner of Sonoma, Napa, and Lake counties. Other prominent Bay Area summits include Mt. Hamilton (4213'), Mt. Diablo (3849'), Loma Prieta (3806'), Mt. Tamalpais (2571'), and Sonoma Mountain (2295').

As everyone knows, the Bay Area is prone to earthquakes, with the last major one having occurred in 1989. The lead player in this continuing saga is the San Andreas fault, which in the Bay Area splits the Santa Cruz Mountains, crosses underwater seaward of the Golden Gate, and then slices through Point Reyes National Seashore. Movement along the fault, as the Pacific plate bumps and grinds its way northwest against the North American plate, is what rattles our teacups and collapses our freeways. Evidence of this movement can be found on the Point Reyes peninsula, where granite from the so-called Salinian Block, formed 25 million years ago near the southern end of the Sierra Nevada, has slowly shifted northward along the San Andreas fault. Sometimes the movement is not so slow—during the 1906 earthquake, the earth moved 21 feet in Olema Valley.

You can learn more about Bay Area geology and the San Andreas fault by visiting Point Reyes National Seashore, in the North Bay; Sibley Volcanic Regional Preserve and Mt. Diablo State Park, in the East Bay; and Los Trancos Open Space Preserve on the Peninsula.

Flora

There is an incredible diversity of plant life here. California has more than 5000 native plant species and an estimated 1000 introduced species. Of the native plants, about 30 per cent occur nowhere else—these are called endemics. Among the most common endemics are many types of manzanita (Arctostaphylos) and monkeyflower (Mimulus). The state also has some of the oldest species, in terms of evolution, and also some of the youngest. For example, coast redwoods date back to the dinosaurs, whereas certain species of tarweed (Madia) have evolved within the past several thousand years.

Oak woodland in Black Diamond Mines Regional Perserve

The dry interior hills of the North, East, and South bays, untouched by summer fog, are characteristic of the **oak woodland community**, which is found at elevations between 300 and 3500 feet. Common trees and shrubs found in this generally open woodland, sometimes called a **savanna**, include various oaks, California buckeye, gray pine, California bay, buckbrush, toyon, coffeeberry, snowberry, and poison oak. Especially with oaks, slope aspect and elevation determine which species occur where. Excluding hybrids, there are six common oaks in the Bay Area—valley oak, black oak, blue oak, canyon oak, interior live oak, and coast live oak. Examples of this community can be found on at Sugarloaf Ridge State Park, Black Diamond Mines Regional Preserve, and Henry W. Coe State Park.

Members of the **riparian woodland** are usually found beside rivers and creeks. Among the most common are bigleaf maple, white alder, red alder, California bay, various willows, California rose, poison oak, California wild grape, elk clover, and giant chain fern. Point Reyes National Seashore and Monte Bello Open Space Preserve give you opportunities to enjoy this community.

Coast redwoods are the world's tallest trees and are among the fastest-growing. Redwood groves once formed an extensive coastal forest that stretched from central California to southern Oregon. Commercially valuable, they were heavily logged. The remaining old-growth coast redwoods in the Bay Area are confined a few areas, most notably Muir Woods National Monument, in Marin County, and Armstrong Redwoods State Reserve, in Sonoma County. Associated with redwoods are a number of plant species, including tanbark oak, California bay, hazelnut, evergreen huckleberry, wood rose, redwood sorrel, western sword fern, and evergreen violet. You can visit second-growth redwood forests and see a few old-growth giants at Muir Woods National Monument, Redwood Regional Park, and Purisima Creek Redwoods Open Space Preserve.

In many parts of the Bay Area, **Douglas-fir** is the "default" evergreen, easily told by its distinctive cones, which have protruding, three-pointed bracts, sometimes called rat's tails. Douglas-fir and coast redwood are California's two most important commercial trees. Douglas-fir often grows in similar habitats as coast redwood but where soil conditions do not favor redwood growth. Some of the common plants associated with Douglas-fir are the same as those associated with coast redwood, namely California bay, tanbark oak, and western sword fern. Others include blue blossom, coffeeberry, and poison oak. Point Reyes National Seashore, Mt. Tamalpais State Park, and El Corte de Madera Creek Open Space Preserve have beautiful Douglas-fir forests.

A **mixed evergreen forest** contains a mixture of evergreen trees, including California bay, canyon oak, coast live oak, and madrone. The understory to this forest often contains shrubs such as toyon, blue elderberry, hazelnut, buckbrush, snowberry, thimbleberry, creambush, and poison oak. Carpeting the forest floor may be an assortment of wildflowers, including milk maids, fairy bells, mission bells, hound's tongue, and western heart's-ease. Take a stroll through a mixed evergreen forest at China Camp State Park, Dry Creek Pioneer Regional Park, and Sierra Azul Open Space Preserve.

The **chaparral community** is made up of hearty plants that thrive in poor soils under hot, dry conditions. Chaparral is very susceptible to fire,

Grassland *and coastal scrub in the Marin Headlands host a wide variety of native wildflowers.*

and some of its members, such as various species of manzanita, survive devastating blazes by sprouting new growth from ground-level burls. Despite the harsh environment, chaparral can be beautiful year-round, with certain manzanitas blooming as early as December, and other plants continuing into spring and summer. The word itself comes from a Spanish term for dwarf or scrub oak, but in the Bay Area it is chamise, various manzanitas, and various species of ceanothus that dominate the community. Other chaparral plants include mountain mahogany, yerba santa, toyon, chaparral pea, and poison oak. You can study this fascinating assembly of plants on Pine Mountain, Mt. Diablo, and in Sierra Azul Open Space Preserve.

Few if any **grasslands** in the Bay Area retain their native character. Human intervention, in the form of fire suppression, farming, and livestock grazing, along with the invasion of nonnative plants, have significantly altered the landscape. Gone from most areas are the native bunchgrasses, perennial species that once dominated our area. Remaining, thankfully, are native wildflowers, which decorate the grasslands in spring and summer. Among the most common are bluedicks, California poppy, owl's-clover, checkerbloom, lupine, and blue-eyed grass. Look for these at Skyline Wilderness Park, Sunol Wilderness, Joseph D. Grant County Park, and Russian Ridge Open Space Preserve.

Fauna

Besides deer, rabbits, and squirrels, you probably won't see many other land mammals on your hikes in the Bay Area, unless you time your visits near dawn or dusk. These are times when most mammals are active, and then you may be rewarded with a fleeting glimpse of a coyote or a bobcat. Large mammals, such as black bear and mountain lion, are seldom seen. Other more common mammals in our area include foxes, raccoons, skunks, opossums, and chipmunks. Wild pigs are present in Bay Area parks, and in some they have done extensive damage. Never approach wild pigs; they are dangerous.

It is not hyperbole to call the Bay Area one of the world's great birding areas. Its location on the western edge of the Pacific Flyway, combined with the presence of so many different habitats, from offshore islands to inland mountains, guarantees both a high species count and an enormous number—in the millions—of individual birds either resident, wintering, or passing through on migration. Point Reyes National Seashore, perhaps the area with the most variety of birds, has logged an impressive 440 different species, or just under half of all bird species found in North America north of Mexico. American Ornithologists' Union's (AOU) checklist for birds of the continental United States and Canada is the standard reference for common names of birds.

Season, location, weather, and even time of day—these together help determine which birds you are likely to see. Among the most common birds seen from the trail are acorn woodpeckers, western scrub-jays, Steller's jays, spotted towhees, dark-eyed juncos, California quail, and turkey vultures. Raptors such as hawks, falcons, golden eagles, and kites patrol the skies above many Bay Area parks. If you learn to "bird by ear," identifying species by their distinctive notes, calls, and songs, you will quickly expand your list, because many birds are frustratingly hard to spot, especially in dense foliage. Birding with a group also improves your odds of seeing and identifying a large number of species, including rarities.

A sudden scurrying in the leaves, which may take you by surprise, is probably nothing more than a western fence lizard, the Bay Area's most commonly seen reptile. When threatened, these lizards may stand their ground and begin to do "push-ups," which perhaps strike terror into their foes. Also here are the California whiptail, a lizard with a tail as long as its body, the alligator lizard, and the western skink. An animal resembling a lizard but actually an amphibian is the California newt, which spends the summer buried under the forest floor, then emerges with the first rains and migrates to breed in ponds and streams. Briones Regional Park and Monte Bello Open Space Preserve are among good places to witness these migrations. Other amphibians you might see or hear include western toad and Pacific tree frog.

Birders *are lucky in the Bay Area.*

Gopher snake, California kingsnake, rubber boa, California whipsnake, western rattlesnake, and garter snake are among the snakes present in the Bay Area. Gopher snakes are often mistaken for rattlers, and for a heart-stopping moment you may struggle to recall the differences: a gopher snake has a slim head and a fat body, whereas a rattlesnake has a relatively thin body compared with its large, triangular head. Gopher snake are common, but rattlers, although present in the Bay Area, are seldom seen.

When to Go

Where else can you find such a perfect climate for outdoor activities? Not too hot in summer, not too cold in winter, and a rain-free season that lasts generally from May through October. The moderating effect of the Pacific Ocean keeps temperatures near the coast in a narrow range year-round. The summer months are characterized by fog at the coast, but generally clear and warm conditions elsewhere. The shady canyons of Marin County and the Peninsula are perfect summer places to cool off. If you want to bake on the trail, head away from the Bay. By the time fall arrives, the hills are brown and seasonal creeks dry. These clear, cool days are perfect just about everywhere, with a modest palette of autumn colors in riparian areas. With the first rains, the change is dramatic: hillsides turn green and water returns to the creek beds.

Fall and winter storms from the Gulf of Alaska can bring copious rainfall, high winds, and even snow to the tallest Bay Area peaks. In their wakes these storms usually leave a few exceptionally cold but clear days, perfect for bundling up and visiting a vantage point with great views, such as Mt. Tamalpais or even Mt. St. Helena. As early as December, our manzanitas and currants begin to bloom, decorating chaparral areas with floral displays of white and pink. Other shrubs and the earliest wildflowers begin their show in late winter or early spring, and by the time April rolls around, especially after a wet winter, the wildflower display is usually fantastic, so this is the time to head to the grasslands of the East Bay and the Peninsula.

The farther inland you go, the less pronounced is the moderating influence of the ocean. Temperature differences—the average highs and lows for any given location—widen as you leave the coast. Here's an example: the highest average high temperature for San Francisco is 68.5 degrees, whereas the same figure for St. Helena in Napa County—only about 65 miles away—is 89.2 degrees. But San Francisco's lowest average minimum, 45.7 degrees (January), is about 10 degrees warmer than St. Helena's.

Temperatures are not the only thing to change as you move around the Bay Area. Each successive range of coastal hills blocks more and more Pacific moisture, creating a rain-shadow effect that intensifies as you move away from the coast and from San Francisco Bay. That is why coast redwoods, which depend on fog-drip to supply moisture during the dry season, grow only in a narrow band near the coast.

Time of day and weather conditions are often as important as time of year when considering a route. A pleasant hike in the cool of the morning can turn into a sweltering ordeal under the noonday sun if there is no shade. A fine hike can easily be spoiled by high winds or a sudden squall. Always check for the most current weather before heading out for the day.

Trail Selection

The San Francisco Bay Area is distinguished by its rolling hills, grassy valleys, and rugged mountain ranges, all encircling a great body of water, San Francisco and San Pablo bays, and bordering an even greater one, the Pacific Ocean. Within a single day—if you wanted—you could experience nearly every habitat the area has to offer, including beach, salt marsh, redwood forest, oak savanna, grasslands, and chaparral. If variety really is the spice of life, the fare here is tasty indeed!

The aim of this book is to steer you to the best parks and open spaces in the Bay Area. An outdoor guidebook should be a good companion on and off the trail. It should help you select a route, find the trailhead, follow the trail, and enjoy the natural and human history that enrich any outdoor experience. Above all, a guidebook reflects its author as much as it does the area described. What key features of the area? Of course this is very subjective—no one else decided what to include and what to leave out, what to emphasize and what to ignore. With so many possibilities, how were the 44 hikes in this book chosen?

Key Features

Taking the series name literally, the "top" trails are those that climb high. Many outdoor enthusiasts love vantage points with great views but also climb for sheer enjoyment. So you will find an assortment of the Bay Area's tallest **peaks**—Mt. St. Helena, Mt. Tamalpais, Mt. Diablo, and Black Mountain—represented here. If **loops** and **long-distance routes** sound like fun, check out Annadel State Park, Point Reyes National Seashore, Black Diamond Mine Regional Preserve, Pleasanton Ridge Regional Park, Almaden Quicksilver County Park, and Purisima Creek Redwoods Open Space Preserve.

If you have a passion for **water**, you'll enjoy exploring Mt. Burdell Open Space Preserve, which has a large vernal pool with rare wildflowers; Redwood Regional Park, where coast redwoods rise majestically above a rushing creek; and Monte Bello Open Space Preserve, where a self-guiding nature trail wanders through the canyon holding Stevens Creek.

Identifying **wildflowers** and **native plants** may be one of your hobbies. If you are interested in things that grow—from tiny flowers to towering redwoods—head for the Marin Headlands, Henry W. Coe State Park, and Russian Ridge Open Space Preserve. Birding, too, is a popular pastime , and you can see birds just about anywhere in the Bay Area.

Finally, the Bay Area's fascinating **human history**, from the earliest Native Americans to today's Silicon Valley entrepreneurs, has touched even our remotest parks and preserves. Many of the trails in the Bay Area take you through terrain once trod by Ohlone Indians, Spanish missionaries, Mexican ranchers, Italian winemakers, Portuguese dairymen, Chinese fishermen, a host of famous and infamous personalities, and a generation of environmental activists who expressed their love of the land through a commitment to save it from encroaching development. Without this human history, the Bay Areas peaks and valleys, its forests and fields, would certainly look the same, but our experience here would be much less rich.

Multiple Uses

Many of the trails in the Bay Area are multi-use trails, which means they are shared by hikers, bicyclists, runners, and equestrians. Most of these are actually dirt roads, fire roads, or wide dirt paths. In general, bicycles are not permitted on single-track trails, but there are exceptions—the most notable being Annadel and China Camp state parks in the North Bay—and these are noted in the text. Whenever possible, if a route described has a segment closed to bikes, the text provides alternate trails that are open. A few trails, designated "hiking only," are closed to both bikes and horses.

Some agencies, such as MROSD, close their trails to bikes and horses during wet weather with special gates that allow hikers to pass through. Where this is the case, it is noted in the text. Call ahead to the agency in charge of the park or open space you are planning to visit, and have an alternate route selected. Agency phone numbers and their Web site addresses, if any, are listed in the Appendix.

Please note that dogs (and other pets) are not allowed on the trails in any Bay Area state park, and there are restrictions at other parks and open spaces as well. In areas where dogs are allowed, they generally must be on a leash no longer than 6 feet. Some agencies allow dogs off-leash, but the dogs must be under immediate voice command of the person they are with, and must never be allowed to threaten or harm people or wildlife. People with dogs must clean up after their pets. When planning a hike with your dog, check to make sure pets are allowed, and obey all posted rules and regulations.

Poison Oak *Learn to recognize the stems and lobed leaves in all seasons.*

Trail Safety

Poison oak produces an itchy rash in people allergic to its oil. Learn to identify poison oak's shiny green foliage—"leaves of three, let it be"—and avoid it. In fall the shrub's leaves turn yellow and red, adding a wonderful touch of color to the woods. In winter, you can identify the plant by its upward-reaching clusters of bare branches. Staying on the trail is the best way to avoid contact with poison oak, and wearing long pants and a long-sleeved shirt helps too. Anything that touches poison oak—clothing, pets—should be washed in soap and water.

The **tick**, a tiny, almost invisible insect, has been the cause of much woe among hikers and others who spend time outdoors. Western black-legged ticks carry a bacteria that causes **Lyme disease**, which can produce serious symptoms in people who have been bitten. These include flu-like aches and pains which, if left untreated, may progress to severe cardiac and neurological disorders. Often the tick bite produces a rash that over time clears from the center, producing a bull's-eye pattern.

You can take several steps to protect against Lyme disease. Wear light-colored clothing, so ticks are easier to spot. Use long-sleeved pants with the legs tucked into your socks, and a long-sleeved shirt tucked into your pants. Spray your clothing with an insect repellent containing DEET before hiking. When you return home, shake out and brush all clothing, boots, and packs outdoors. If you find an attached tick, use tweezers to remove it by grasping the tick as close to your skin as possible and gently pulling straight out. Do not squeeze the tick while it is attached, as this may inject the bacterium into your skin. Wash the area and apply antiseptic, then call your doctor.

Although present in the Bay Area, **western rattlesnakes** are shy and seldom seen. Most snake bites are the result of a defensive reaction: a foot or hand has suddenly landed in the snake's territory. A rattlesnake often, but not always, gives a warning when it feels threatened. Stand still until you have located the snake, and then back slowly away. If you are bitten, seek medical attention as quickly and effortlessly as possible, to avoid spreading the venom.

Mountain lions, also called **cougars** or **pumas**, are rarely seen in our area. They hunt at night and feed mostly on deer. If you do encounter a mountain lion, experts advise standing your ground, making loud noises, waving your arms to appear larger, and fighting back if attacked. Above all, never run.

Note from the Author

During the course of several years, I walked every trail included in this book at least once. In many cases, I returned to favorite areas in different seasons. I tried to be accurate and thorough in both my observations and my writing. The natural world, however, is always in a state of flux, and although this is a fine thing in general, it plays havoc with outdoor guidebooks. Your experience on the trail—affected as it is by season, weather, time of day, and acts of God and various federal, state, and local agencies—will very likely be different from mine. I acknowledge this variability by the use of the word "may" in the text, as in "The upper slopes of the mountain host dramatic displays of wildflowers in spring, and this area may be full of wild irises." I certainly hope you get to see the irises, but like so many other things, the blooming of wildflowers is beyond my control.

On the Trail

Every outing should begin with proper preparation, which usually takes just minutes. Even the easiest trail can turn up unexpected surprises. People seldom think about getting lost or suffering an injury, but unexpected things can and do happen. Simple precautions can make the difference between a miserable outcome – or merely a good story to tell afterwards.

Use the Top Trails ratings and descriptions to determine if a particular trail is a good match with your fitness and energy level, given current conditions and time of year.

Have a Plan

Prepare and Plan

- Know your abilities and your limitations
- Leave word about your plans
- Know the area and the route

Choose Wisely The first step to enjoying any trail is to match the trail to your abilities. It's no use overestimating your experience or fitness – know your abilities and limitations, and use the Top Trails Difficulty Rating that accompanies each trail.

Leave Word About your Plans The most basic of precautions is leaving word of your intentions with family or friends. Many people will hike the backcountry their entire lives without ever relying on this safety net, but establishing this simple habit is free insurance.

It's best to leave specific information – location, trail name, intended time of travel – with a responsible person. However, if this is not possible or if plans change at the last minute, you should still leave word. If there is a registration process available, make use of it. If there is a ranger station or park office, check in.

Review the Route Before embarking on any trail, be sure to read the entire description and study the map. It isn't necessary to memorize every detail, but it is worthwhile to have a clear mental picture of the trail and the general area.

If the trail and terrain are complex, augment the trail guide with a topographic map; Top Trails will point out when this could be useful. Maps as well as current weather and trail condition information are often available from local ranger and park stations.

Trail Essentials

- **Dress to keep cool but be ready for cold**
- **Plenty of water**
- **Adequate food**

Carry the Essentials

Proper preparation for any type of trail use includes gathering the essential items to carry. The checklist will vary tremendously by trail and conditions.

Clothing When the weather is good, light, comfortable clothing is the obvious choice. It's easy to believe that very little spare clothing is needed, but a prepared hiker has something tucked away for any emergency from a surprise shower to an unexpected overnight in a remote area.

Clothing includes proper footwear, essential for hiking and running trails. As a trail becomes more demanding, you will need footwear that performs. Running shoes are fine for many trails. If you will be carrying substantial weight or encountering sustained rugged terrain, step up to hiking boots.

In hot, sunny weather, proper clothing includes a hat, sunglasses, long-sleeved shirt and sunscreen. In cooler weather, particularly when it's wet, carry waterproof outer garments and quick-drying undergarments (avoid cotton). As general rule, whatever the conditions, bring layers that can be combined or removed to provide comfort and protection from the elements in a wide variety of conditions.

Water Never embark on a trail without carrying water. At all times, particularly in warm weather, adequate water is of key importance. Experts recommend at least 2 quarts of water per day, and when hiking in heat a gallon or more may be more appropriate. At the extreme, dehydration can be life threatening. More commonly, inadequate water brings on fatigue and muscle aches.

For most outings, unless the day is very hot or the trail very long, you should plan to carry sufficient water to last you and your party for the entire trail. Unfortunately, in North America natural water sources are too often questionable, generally loaded with various risks: bacteria, viruses and fertilizers.

Water Treatment If it's necessary to make use of trailside water, you should filter or treat it. There are three methods for treating water: boiling, chemical treatment, and filtering. Boiling is best, but often impractical – it requires a heat source, a pot, and time. Chemical treatments, available in sporting goods stores, handle some problems, including the troublesome Giardia parasite, but will not combat many man-made chemical pollutants. The preferred method is filtration, which removes Giardia and other contaminants and doesn't leave any unpleasant aftertaste.

If this hasn't convinced you to carry all the water you need, one final admonishment: be prepared for surprises. Water sources described in the text or on maps can change course or dry up completely. Never run your water bottle dry in expectation of the next source; fill up when water is available and always keep a little in reserve.

Food

While not as critical as water, food is energy and its importance shouldn't be underestimated. Avoid foods that are hard to digest, such as candy bars and potato chips. Carry high energy, fast-digesting foods: nutrition bars, dehydrated fruit, gorp, jerky. Bring a little extra food--it's good protection against an outing that turns unexpectedly long, perhaps due to weather or losing your way.

Less than Essential, But Useful Items

Map and Compass (*and the know-how to use them*) Many trails don't require much navigation, meaning a map and compass aren't always as essential as water or food – but it can be a close call. If the trail is remote or infrequently visited, a map and compass should be considered necessities.

A hand-held GPS (Global Positioning Satellite) receiver is also a useful trail companion, but is really no substitute for a map and compass; knowing your longitude and latitude is not much help without a map.

Cell Phone Most parts of the country, even remote destinations, have some level of cellular coverage. In extreme circumstances, a cell phone can be a lifesaver. But don't depend on it; coverage is unpredictable and batteries fail. And be sure that the occasion warrants the phone call – a blister doesn't justify a call to search and rescue.

Gear Depending on the remoteness and rigor of the trail, there are many additional useful items to consider; pocket knife, flashlight, fire source (water-proof matches, light, or flint), and a first-aid kit.

Every member of your party should carry the appropriate essential items described above; groups often split up or get separated along the trail. Solo hikers should be even more disciplined about preparation, and carry more gear. Traveling solo is inherently more risky. This isn't meant to discourage solo travel, simply to emphasize the need for extra preparation. Solo hikers should make a habit of carrying a little more gear than absolutely necessary.

Trail Etiquette

> ### Trail Checklist
>
> - Leave no trace
> - Stay on the trail
> - Share the trail
> - Leave it there

The overriding rule on the trail is "**Leave No Trace**." Interest in visiting natural areas continues to increase in North America, even as the quantity of unspoiled natural areas continues to shrink. These pressures make it ever more critical that we leave no trace of our visit.

Never Litter If you carried it in, it's easy enough to carry it out. Leave the trail in the same, if not better condition than you find it. Try picking up any litter you encounter and packing it out – it's a great feeling! Just one piece of garbage and you've made a difference.

Stay on the Trail Paths have been created, sometimes over many years, for many purposes: to protect the surrounding natural areas, to avoid dangers, and to provide the best route. Leaving the trail can cause damage that takes years to undo. Never cut switchbacks. Shortcutting rarely saves energy or time, and it takes a terrible toll on the land, trampling plant life and hastening erosion. Moreover, safety and consideration intersect on the trail. It's hard to get truly lost if you stay on the trail.

Share the Trail The best trails attract many visitors and you should be prepared to share the trail with others. Do your part to minimize impact. Commonly accepted trail etiquette dictates that **bike riders yield to both hikers and equestrians**, **hikers yield to horseback riders**, **downhill hikers yield to uphill hikers**, and **everyone stays to the right**. Not everyone knows these rules of the road, so let common sense and good humor be the final guide.

Leave it There Destruction or removal of plants and animals, or historical, prehistoric or geological items, is certainly unethical and almost always illegal.

Getting Lost If you become lost on the trail, stay on the trail. Stop and take stock of the situation. In many cases, a few minutes of calm reflection will yield a solution. Consider all the clues available; use the sun to identify directions if you don't have a compass. If you determine that you are indeed lost, stay on the main trail and stay put. You are more likely to encounter other people if you stay in one place.

North Bay

North Bay

For this book, the North Bay includes all of Marin and Napa counties, and that part of Sonoma County east of Hwy. 101 from San Pablo Bay to Mt. St. Helena. **Marin**, at 521 square miles, is the smallest North Bay county but has the most parks and open spaces, more than 200 square miles in federal, state, and local lands. Hikers, bicyclists, and trail runners are in heaven here, enjoying hundreds of miles of trails that wind through public land. The county's terrain includes rugged Pacific shoreline, redwood groves, forested valleys and ridges, open grassland, chaparral, and salt marsh.

Some of Marin's place names, such as Mill Valley and Corte Madera ("a place where wood is cut") are clues to its lumber-producing past. Others, like San Rafael and Sausalito ("little willow grove") tell of Franciscan missionaries and Mexican ranchos. Still others—Tamalpais, Olompali—are derived from the language of Marin's original inhabitants, the Coast Miwok people.

Often foggy and windy, the rural areas of West Marin are dominated by cattle and dairy ranches. It is here that you find most of Marin's public land, in a long swath running from the Golden Gate to the tip of Tomales Point. The jewel in the crown is Mt. Tamalpais, at 2571 feet the highest North Bay peak near the coast. Low on its southern slope lies Muir Woods National Monument, one of the last remaining groves of old-growth coast redwoods.

Fronting San Francisco and San Pablo bays, you find a more suburban, residential Marin, where open space, including wooded areas, grasslands, and salt marsh, is tucked between towns and housing developments. This part of Marin, usually sheltered from the fog, is often 10°F to 20°F warmer than coastal areas, including San Francisco.

Napa needs no introduction. Thanks to its world-class wines, Napa's reputation is well known and well deserved. At 758 square miles, it ranks between Marin and Sonoma in size, but offers the least amount of public land for hiking. The land here is devoted to growing grapes, and nearly every tillable acre is taken up with that pursuit. The City of Napa has about 40 parks, some of which have hiking trails, and a volunteer group operates Skyline Wilderness Park, a paradise for hikers, bicyclists, and trail runners. In the days before wine became queen, Napa had, at various times, large ranchos, fruit and nut orchards, and mines that produced gold, silver, and cinnabar. Today, especially on weekends, the valley is inhabited by tourists, whose cars move at a snail's pace up and down Hwy. 29.

Sonoma is the largest of the three North Bay counties, about 1600 square miles. It is also the most varied, stretching from the volcanic highlands of the Mayacmas Mountains to the wave-washed Pacific shore. Along its northern coast and in the Russian River area are found some of the North Bay's most beautiful and remote parks. The area's tallest peak, Mt. St. Helena (4339'), is just inside the county line at the edge of Napa and Lake counties. Sonoma has some of the finest hiking, bicycling, and horseback riding in the North Bay, in state parks such as Annadel, Jack London, and Sugarloaf Ridge. The county maintains its own system of regional parks, which offer hiking and riding, camping, swimming, picnicking, fishing, and sports.

For thousands of years, Sonoma's natural resources supported three Indian tribes—Coast Miwok, Pomo, and Wappo. Prized by early European and American settlers, Sonoma has seen six flags raised over its soil, those of England, Spain, Russia, Mexico, the U.S., and the Bear Flag Republic. Rich in history, Sonoma has been home to some of California's most colorful personalities, including General Mariano G. Vallejo and author Jack London. Today, the county supports dairy farming, cattle and sheep ranching, fishing, timber harvesting, and tourism. Sonoma has several wine-growing regions, including the Sonoma Valley, the Valley of the Moon, the Alexander and Dry Creek valleys, and the Russian River area. The Sonoma Valley and its northward extension, the Valley of the Moon, are divided from Napa County on the east by the Mayacmas Mountains, and are bordered on the west by the Sonoma Mountains.

Governing Agencies

The parks and open spaces described in this chapter are managed by four government agencies and one volunteer organization, all listed in the Appendix. The best map for Mt. Tamalpais, the Marin Headlands, and Muir Woods is the Olmsted trail map, available at REI stores or through the Web site www.rei.com. A Point Reyes National Seashore trail map is available at the visitor center, and a Point Reyes and surrounding area recreation map is available from Wilderness Press. Maps for California state parks are problematic—sometimes they are available only at entrance kiosks or visitor centers, and these may be closed during the week. Marin County Open Space District has maps available by mail and from its Web site. Lands of the Marin Municipal Water District are covered by Olmsted's Mt. Tamalpais map. The Skyline Wilderness Park map is available at the entrance kiosk and from the Skyline Park Citizens Association Web site.

For contact information, see Appendix (p. 280).

North Bay

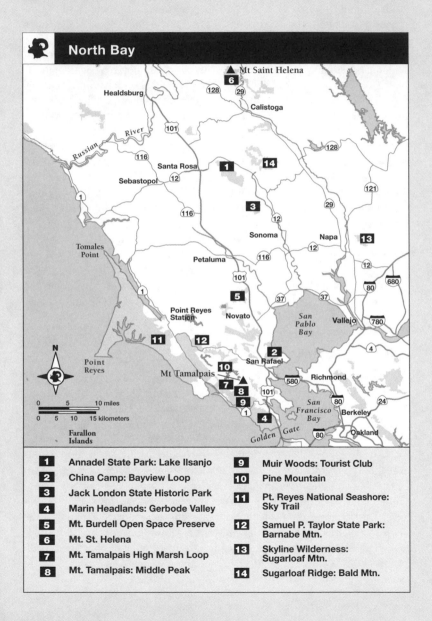

North Bay

Mt Saint Helena
6
128 29
Healdsburg
Calistoga
River
101
River
Russian
116
Santa Rosa
Sebastopol 12
1 **14**
128
3
116
12
Sonoma Napa **13**
12
121
29
1
Tomales Point
Petaluma
116
12
12
101
80 680
5
37 37
Point Reyes Station Novato
San Pablo Bay
Vallejo 780
11 **12**
2
San Rafael
4
N
Point Reyes
Mt Tamalpais
10
7
8
580 Richmond
0 5 10 miles
0 5 10 15 kilometers
9
101
4
San Francisco Bay
80 24
Berkeley
Golden Gate
Farallon Islands
80 Oakland

1	Annadel State Park: Lake Ilsanjo		**9**	Muir Woods: Tourist Club
2	China Camp: Bayview Loop		**10**	Pine Mountain
3	Jack London State Historic Park		**11**	Pt. Reyes National Seashore: Sky Trail
4	Marin Headlands: Gerbode Valley		**12**	Samuel P. Taylor State Park: Barnabe Mtn.
5	Mt. Burdell Open Space Preserve			
6	Mt. St. Helena		**13**	Skyline Wilderness: Sugarloaf Mtn.
7	Mt. Tamalpais High Marsh Loop			
8	Mt. Tamalpais: Middle Peak		**14**	Sugarloaf Ridge: Bald Mtn.

North Bay Trails

TRAIL	Difficulty	Length	Type
1	4	8.8	
2	3	5.5	
3	3	2.9	
4	3	5.4	
5	4	5.6	
6	5	10.6	
7	4	5.8	
8	3	5.0	
9	3	3.8	
10	3	4.7	
11	5	10.5	
12	4	6.3	
13	4	6.0	
14	5	6.7	

USE & ACCESS
- Hiking
- Trail Running
- Mountain Biking
- P Parking Fee
- Permit
- Child Friendly
- Dogs Allowed
- Handicap Access
- Camping

TERRAIN
- Canyon
- Mountain
- Summit

WATER
- Stream
- Waterfall
- Beach
- Shore

FLORA & FAUNA
- Autumn Colors
- Wildflowers
- Birds
- Wildlife
- Tide Pools

DIFFICULTY
- 1 2 3 4 5 +
less   more

OTHER
- Cool & Shady
- Great Views
- Photo Opportunity
- Secluded
- Historic
- Geologic Interest
- Moonlight Hiking
- Steep

Notes:

Bicyclists use alternate trails or trailheads (see text)

North Bay

Visitors encounter dense forest, oak savanna, and a wonderful, albeit man-made, lake during this tour of the northwestern part of Annadel State Park. The trails here are multi-use paths shared by hikers, runners, equestrians, and bicyclists. Please observe all closure signs, and use only named and maintained trails.

From shady groves of coast redwood and California bay to sheltered enclaves where manzanita and madrone hold sway, this route starts and ends barely above sea level but climbs to 600 feet on its course between Back Ranch and Miwok meadows.

Jack London's ranch, a beautiful redwood forest, and a climb to a meadow with great views are the attractions of this trip.

The hills surrounding Gerbode Valley, part of the Marin Headlands, are vibrant in the spring with wildflowers. They are alive with birdsong and avian acrobatics most of the year, but especially during the fall raptor migration. Views of San Francisco, Marin, and the Pacific Coast from the high points along this loop are superb.

Blue Eyed Grass *is a common spring wildflower in grasslands throughout the North Bay.*

Mt. Burdell 51

This route explores the open grasslands, groves, and high ground of Burdell Mountain, a bulky ridge that rises to 1558 feet and dominates the northeast corner of Marin County. The mountain's southern flank is designated the Mt. Burdell Open Space Preserve, and in spring its grassy slopes and oak woodlands come alive with carpets of wildflowers and a chorus of birdsong.

TRAIL 5

Hike, Run, Bike
5.6 miles, Loop
Difficulty: 1 2 3 **4** 5

Mt. St. Helena 57

This trip to the 4339-foot North Peak of Mt. St. Helena is a "must-do" for lovers of high places. The route is exposed for much of its length to sun, wind, and weather. Pick a cool day with unlimited visibility, and you will reap all the magnificent scenic rewards this hike has to offer.

TRAIL 6

Hike, Run, Bike
10.6 miles, Out & Back
Difficulty: 1 2 3 4 **5**

Point Reyes: Sky Trail

This is one of the premier hikes in the Point Reyes area, offering a grand tour of Inverness Ridge and Bear Valley, with the Pacific shoreline thrown in for good measure. The route has something for everyone, including a wonderful array of plant and bird life, and fine views.

Samuel P. Taylor: Barnabe Mtn.

This loop climbs gently through mixed forest, alive with birdsong and brightened by wildflowers, struggles steeply to high ground just below the summit of Barnabe Mountain (1466'), and then descends through open country with wonderful views of west Marin, Point Reyes and the Tomales Bay area.

Skyline Wilderness Park: Sugarloaf Mtn.

This route ascends the 1630-foot west peak of Sugarloaf Mountain, the highest point in Skyline Wilderness Park. In season, wildflowers decorate the grasslands. Park maintenance is a volunteer effort, so some trails may be in better shape than others—long pants are advised. The park welcomes equestrians and bicyclists as well as hikers.

Sugarloaf Ridge: Bald Mtn.

This route is a challenge, but well worth the effort. A superb array of trees, shrubs, and wildflowers, along with some of the best views in the North Bay, are the rewards for tackling the 1500-foot climb to the summit of Bald Mountain.

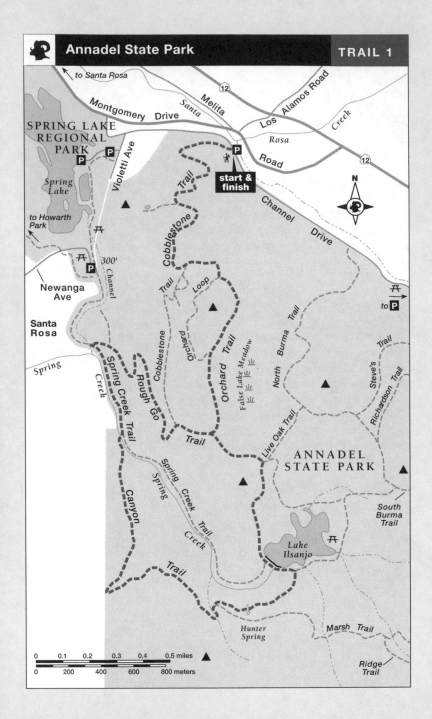

to Santa Rosa

12

Montgomery Drive

Melita

Santa

Los Alamos Road

Creek

12

SPRING LAKE
REGIONAL
PARK

P

P

Spring
Lake

Violetti Ave

P

start &
finish

Rosa

Road

Channel Drive

N

to Howarth
Park

300'

Channel

Cobblestone Trail

Trail

to P

Newanga
Ave

Cobblestone

Trail

Loop

Orchard

Orchard Trail

False Lake Meadow

North Burma Trail

Steve's

Trail

Santa
Rosa

Spring

Creek

Rough Go

Spring Creek Trail

Cobblestone

Trail

Live Oak Trail

ANNADEL
STATE PARK

Richardson Trail

Canyon

Spring Creek Trail

Creek

Lake
Ilsanjo

South
Burma
Trail

Trail

Hunter
Spring

Marsh Trail

Ridge
Trail

0   0.1   0.2   0.3   0.4   0.5 miles

0   200   400   600   800 meters

Annadel State Park: Lake Ilsanjo

This semi-loop route encounters dense forest, oak savanna, and a wonderful, albeit man-made, lake during its tour of the northwestern part of Annadel State Park. A massive and ongoing restoration effort, begun in 1998, has completely transformed many of the park's eroded dirt roads into winding multi-use paths shared by hikers, runners, equestrians, and bicyclists. Many of the trails are subject to seasonal closure during wet weather. Please observe all closure signs, and use only named and maintained trails. Length, not terrain, earns this trip its difficulty rating.

Finding the Trail

From Hwy. 101 in Santa Rosa, take the Sebastopol/Sonoma/Hwy. 12 exit and follow Hwy. 12 east toward Sonoma. At 1.4 miles, turn left onto Farmers Ln., go 0.8 mile, and turn right onto Montgomery Dr. Go 2.7 miles and turn right onto Channel Dr., signed for Annadel State Park and Spring Lake. Go 0.6 mile to a large dirt-and-gravel parking area, left.

From Hwy. 12 going northwest from Kenwood to Santa Rosa, turn left on Los Alamos Rd. and go 0.2 mile to Melita Rd. Turn right on Melita Rd. and then immediately left onto Montgomery Dr. Go 0.5 mile to Channel Dr., turn left, and go 0.6 mile to a large, dirt-and-gravel parking area, left.

The trailhead is opposite the east end of the parking area, across Channel Dr. on its south side.▶1

TRAIL USE
Hike, Run, Bike
LENGTH
8.8 miles/5-6 hours
VERTICAL FEET
±1600'
DIFFICULTY
− 1 2 3 **4** 5 +
TRAIL TYPE
Loop
SURFACE TYPE
Dirt

FEATURES
Child Friendly
Lake
Autumn Colors
Birds
Wildlife
Cool & Shady
Secluded

FACILITIES
Ranger Station
Restrooms
Picnic Tables
Water

Trail Description

Look for wild turkeys near Hunter's Spring, in a dense, fern-floored forest of Douglas-fir, coast live oak, bay, and bigleaf maple.

Your route, the **Cobblestone Trail**, alternates between moderate uphill and level sections as it wanders generally south through rocky terrain, which may become muddy during wet weather. Due east, across Hwy. 12, rises the forested summit of Mt. Hood (2730'), a destination for another day. After traversing an open, grassy field, where you may see the remains of a dirt road, the route bends sharply left and is crossed by a trail that has been closed for restoration. At a junction where the Frog Pond Trail goes straight, you stay on the Cobblestone Trail as it curves left.

Gently gaining elevation, you enjoy a pleasant stroll through oak groves and across open fields, one holding the remains of an old orchard. At a junction with a dirt road, right,▶2 you go straight, now on the **Orchard Trail**. After passing an unsigned trail, right, you make a long traverse, then climb to an open area where manzanita thrives in company with oaks, whose outstretched limbs arch over the trail.

 Great Views

Passing the remains of a several cobblestone quarries, right, you soon reach a fork marked by a trail post, where you stay left, still on the Orchard Trail. Ahead rises Bennett Mountain, at 1887 feet the highest point in Annadel State Park, its slopes dappled in fall with colorful foliage. Now crossing a beautiful oak savanna, you come to a T-junction with the Rough Go Trail,▶3 where you turn left.

Climbing on a gentle grade, the **Rough Go Trail** soon meets the Live Oak Trail, left, and then bends right, finding a level course. At last nearing

---

More Annadel Trails

OPTIONS

You can explore the south and east parts of Annadel State Park via the **Marsh** and **Ridge trails** to **Ledson Marsh**, an added excursion of about 8 miles.

Lake Ilsanjo

Picnickers enjoy lunch *at Lake Ilsanjo*

📷 Photo Opportunity

Lake Ilsanjo, you bear right at a fork, and then pass a trail, left. About 25 feet ahead, your route becomes paved, and 100 feet or so farther it arrives at a T-junction with a dirt road. Turning left, you walk about 200 feet to the lake.

On the far side of the dam, the route, a dirt road, swings left and begins a gentle climb. Topping a low rise, the road descends to a junction,►4 where your route, the **Canyon Trail**, also a dirt road, turns right and heads for Hunter's Spring.

Now you reach a junction with a picnic table, left, and a rest bench, right.►5 The dirt road heading left is the Marsh Trail, part of the Bay Area Ridge Trail. You continue straight on the Canyon Trail, now also part of the Bay Area Ridge Trail. Soon you turn sharply right to cross a bridge over Spring Creek.

Just across the creek, the Canyon Trail ends at a T-junction with the **Spring Creek Trail**.►6 Turning left, you walk along Spring Creek and soon pass a junction where a gravel road heads left to a flood-control dam and levee. Just before the road veers left to cross a wooden bridge, you turn sharply right onto the **Rough Go Trail**.►7

Veering left at the maze, a bit more climbing brings you to a junction with the Cobblestone Trail, left. Continuing straight, you wind uphill past stands of oak and manzanita to the junction with the **Orchard Trail**►8 you arrived at earlier. Now turn left and retrace your steps on the Orchard and Cobblestone trails to the parking area.►9

> Along the Rough Go Trail, look for a large circular maze built of small rocks, perched on the edge of a steep hillside near the crest of a ridge.

🚶	MILESTONES
►1	0.0 From parking area, start up Cobblestone Trail
►2	0.8 Left on Orchard Trail at junction with Cobblestone Trail
►3	2.0 Left on Rough Go Trail
►4	3.0 Right on Canyon Trail
►5	3.6 Straight on Canyon Trail at junction with Marsh Trail
►6	5.2 Left on Spring Creek Trail
►7	5.7 Right on Rough Go Trail
►8	6.9 Left on Orchard Trail
►9	8.1 Right on Cobblestone Trail
►9	8.8 Back at parking area

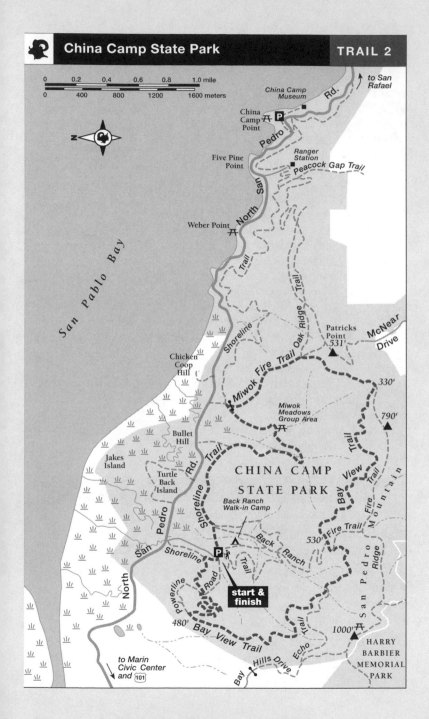

0   0.2   0.4   0.6   0.8   1.0 mile
0   400   800   1200   1600 meters

N

to San
Rafael

China Camp
Museum

China
Camp
Point

P

Pedro

Five Pine
Point

Ranger
Station

Peacock Gap Trail

San

North

Weber Point

Trail

San Pablo Bay

Shoreline

Oak Ridge Trail

Miwok Fire Trail

Patricks
Point
531'

McNear
Drive

330'

Chicken
Coop
Hill

790'

Bullet
Hill

Miwok
Meadows
Group Area

Trail

Jakes
Island

Turtle
Back
Island

CHINA CAMP

STATE PARK

Bay View Trail

Pedro

Rd.

Shoreline

Back Ranch
Walk-in Camp

Back Ranch

530' Fire Trail

San Pedro Ridge

Fire Trail

Mountain

San

North

Shoreline

Road

P

Trail

start &
finish

1000'

Powerline

480' Bay View Trail

Echo

Trail

HARRY
BARBIER
MEMORIAL
PARK

to Marin
Civic Center
and 101

Bay Hills Drive

China Camp State Park: Bayview Loop

This loop samples China Camp's wide variety of habitats, from shady groves of coast redwood and California bay to sheltered enclaves where manzanita and madrone hold sway. This route starts and ends barely above sea level but climbs to 600 feet on its course between Back Ranch and Miwok meadows. The multi-use trails and fire trails of this park are enjoyed by bicyclists and equestrians as well as by hikers and runners.

Best Time

All year; in summer this may be one of the few fog-free places close to the Golden Gate.

Finding the Trail

From Hwy. 101 northbound in San Rafael, take the N. San Pedro Rd. exit, which is also signed for the Marin County Civic Center and China Camp State Park. After exiting, bear right, following the lane marked "east." After 0.3 mile you join N. San Pedro Rd. Once on it, go 2.9 miles to the Back Ranch Meadows walk-in campground entrance road, right.

From Hwy. 101 southbound in San Rafael, take the N. San Pedro Rd. exit, which is also signed for the Marin County Civic Center and China Camp State Park. After 0.2 mile, you come to a stop sign. Turn left, go 0.1 mile to a stop light, and turn left again, onto N. San Pedro Rd. At 0.3 mile, the exit ramp from Hwy. 101 northbound joins on your right. From here, follow the directions above.

There is a parking fee.

TRAIL USE
Hike, Run, Bike
LENGTH
5.5 miles, 3-4 hours
VERTICAL FEET
±1450'
DIFFICULTY
- 1 2 **3** 4 5 +
TRAIL TYPE
Loop
SURFACE TYPE
Dirt, paved

FEATURES
Birds
Cool & Shady
Camping

FACILITIES
Restrooms
Picnic Tables
Water
Phone

Hikers enjoy a quiet moment *along China Camp State Park's Shoreline Trail.*

Facilities

There are restrooms, water, phone, and a campground host at the campground parking area, about 0.1 mile ahead on the entrance road. Maps are sold at the ranger station, 1.8 miles ahead on N. San Pedro Rd. opposite the Bullhead Flat picnic area, or at the China Camp museum.

Trail Description

From the west end of the parking area, just past the self-registration station and an information board, you pass through a gap in a split-rail fence and come to a four-way junction▶1 marked with a trail post. Here the Powerline Fire Trail goes straight, and the multi-use **Shoreline Trail** goes both left and right. You turn right and, after about 100 feet, pass a dirt-and-gravel road, left. Soon you turn left and cross a wood bridge near a seasonal wetland. After a few hundred yards, you come to a T-junction.▶2 Here the Shoreline Trail turns right and reaches the park's entrance kiosk in 0.2 mile. Your route, the multi-use **Bay View Trail**, turns left and makes a gentle ascent that alternates between open areas and stands of blue oak.

Soon you reach another T-junction,▶3 this one with the **Powerline Fire Trail**, a dirt road. You go right and uphill, and in 100 feet come to a continuation of the **Bay View Trail**, sharply left.

Following a split-rail fence, left, you soon pass a junction with a closed trail, right. Leaving the fence behind, you traverse just below the top of a north–south ridge, with a steep drop on your left. Just past a picnic table, right, you get the first unobstructed view across San Pablo Bay to the East Bay shoreline and Point Pinole. Using wooden bridges to cross several watercourses, the route wanders in deep shade through stands of redwoods. Now on a gentle but rocky uphill grade, you soon reach a junction with a trail merging sharply from the right, signed TO BAY HILLS DRIVE. A few feet past this junction, you turn sharply left, cross a bridge over a watercourse, and enjoy a level walk that follows the folds of a hillside falling away left.

Under a set of power lines, the route descends, then levels and reaches a junction with the **Back Ranch Fire Trail**,▶4 which goes straight and also right. You continue straight, now on an eroded dirt road, descending past a power-line tower in a clearing,

China Camp State Park takes its name from a Chinese fishing village that flourished here during the 1880s and 1890s, one of 26 on San Francisco Bay.

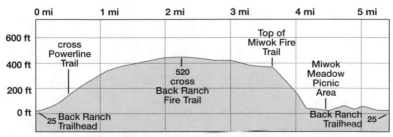

TRAIL 2 China Camp State Park Elevation Profile

Three hills — Turtle
Back, Bullet Hill, and
Chicken Coop Hill —
rise from the salt
marsh just north of
North San Pedro
Road and the
Shoreline Trail.

left, and then bending right and heading back into
the trees. At a T-junction, you turn right onto the
continuation of the **Bay View Trail**.

After slightly more than a mile of mostly level
walking on a multi-use trail, you reach a junction in
a clearing ringed with eucalyptus trees.▶5 There is a
confusing welter of trails converging here, some of
them unofficial. The Bay View Trail ends at a T-junction with the **Ridge Fire Trail**, a dirt road heading
left and right. Your route is the Ridge Fire Trail, the
dirt road climbing left on a gentle grade.

Once over a little rise, you begin to descend,
only to climb again on a moderate grade to a T-junction with the **Miwok Fire Trail**, a dirt road.▶6 Here
you turn left and begin a moderate descent, passing
a junction with the Oak Ridge Trail, right.

With a view of the marshlands bordering North
San Pedro Road, you make a final steep descent over
eroded ground and reach a gate, which you can pass
around on either side. After about 75 feet you come
to a four-way junction.▶7 Here you turn left onto a
dirt road that provides access from North San Pedro
Road to the group picnic area near Miwok Meadows.
This is now the **Shoreline Trail**, which also heads
right from this junction as a multi-use path towards
China Camp. Soon the road divides. One branch
goes straight, into the group day-use area, which has
picnic tables and toilets. The other branch, your

China Camp Variations

For a shorter loop, you can descend the Back Ranch Fire Trail▶4
from its junction with the Bay View Trail. At a four-way junction with
the Shoreline Trail, turn left and follow the Shoreline Trail back to the
day-use parking area.

For a longer loop or one-way hike using a car shuttle, turn right
from the Ridge Fire Trail▶8 onto the Oak Ridge and Shoreline trails.
Right on the Shoreline Trail takes you to China Camp.

Back Ranch Meadows Campground

Overnight camping is available in the Back Ranch Meadows walk-in campground. There are 30 walk-in family campsites, each with picnic table, food locker, and fire ring. Camping reservations: (800) 444-7275. Picnic site reservations: (415) 456-0766

route, marked by a trail post for the Shoreline Trail, turns right into a large dirt parking area.▶8

After about 150 feet, you reach the end of the parking area, where you turn left and find the continuation of the Shoreline Trail, marked by a trail post. Soon level, the route crosses a wood bridge, swings right, and comes into the open. At a junction, right, with the Bullet Hill Trail, you continue straight.

Great Views

Now the route gains elevation and bends left, running parallel to North San Pedro Road. Just south of Turtle Back, you veer away from the road and continue a level trek over mostly open ground, with woodland left and marshland right. Soon the route forks, and you bear right, toward the campground parking area.▶9 Once on pavement, go west across the parking area to the park entrance road, and follow it 100 yards to the day-use parking area.▶10

🚶 MILESTONES

▶1 0.0 Take the Shoreline Trail north

▶2 0.1 Left on Bay View Trail

▶3 0.4 Right on Powerline Fire Trail, then left on Bay View Trail

▶4 2.3 Back Ranch Fire Trail, alternate descent, goes left

▶5 3.4 Angle left on Ridge Fire Trail

▶6 3.7 Left on Miwok Fire Trail

▶7 4.2 Left on Shoreline Trail

▶8 4.5 Miwok Meadows group day-use area

▶9 5.4 Parking area for Back Ranch Meadows walk-in campground

▶10 5.5 Back at trailhead

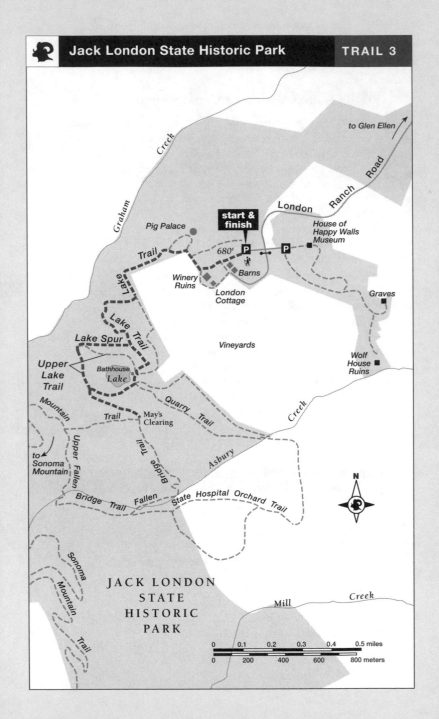

to Glen Ellen

Graham   Creek

London   Ranch   Road

Pig Palace

start & finish

Trail

680'

House of
Happy Walls
Museum

Lake

Winery
Ruins

Barns

London
Cottage

Graves

Lake   Trail

Lake Spur

Vineyards

Upper
Lake
Trail

Bathhouse
Lake

Wolf
House
Ruins

Mountain

Trail   May's
Clearing

Quarry   Trail

Creek

Upper Fallen

Bridge Trail

Asbury

to
Sonoma
Mountain

Bridge   Trail   Fallen   State Hospital Orchard Trail

N

JACK LONDON
STATE
HISTORIC
PARK

Sonoma

Mountain

Trail

Mill   Creek

0	0.1	0.2	0.3	0.4	0.5 miles
0	200	400	600	800 meters

Jack London State Historic Park

Jack London's ranch, a beautiful redwood forest, and a vista point with superb views are the attractions of this semi-loop trip that uses the Lake, Upper Lake, and Mountain trails. After your hike, be sure to visit the park's fine visitor center and museum, open daily 10 A.M. to 5 P.M., devoted to the work of its namesake author.

Best Time

All year, but trails may be muddy in wet weather.

Finding the Trail

From Hwy. 12 just north of Sonoma Valley Regional Park, take Arnold Dr. southwest to Glen Ellen. At 0.9 mile, Arnold Dr. crosses a bridge over Calabazas Creek and begins to turn left. Here you bear right onto London Ranch Rd., which is heavily used by bicyclists. Go 1.3 miles to the park's entrance kiosk; turn right just past the kiosk into a large paved parking area.

The trailhead is on the parking area's southwest side, just behind the self-registration station. Equestrians must use a trailhead located a few hundred feet to the right.

Trail Description

Your route begins on a paved path that changes to a dirt-and-gravel road leading through a shady picnic area.▶1 Passing the three stone barns, left, you come to a T-junction with another dirt-and-gravel road,

TRAIL USE
Hike, Run, Bike

LENGTH
2.9 miles, 2-3 hours

VERTICAL FEET
±450'

DIFFICULTY
− 1 2 **3** 4 5 +

TRAIL TYPE
Loop

SURFACE TYPE
Dirt, Paved

FEATURES
Child Friendly
Lake
Birds
Cool & Shady
Great Views
Historic
Secluded

FACILITIES
Visitor Center
Restrooms
Picnic Tables
Water

Jack London's adventure books, such as *The Call of the Wild*, *The Sea Wolf*, and *White Fang*, made him world famous and one of the highest-paid authors of his time.

part of the Bay Area Ridge Trail. Turning right at the T-junction, you soon pass a trail, left, to **London's cottage**, which the author purchased in 1911 and where he died in 1916.

Rising dramatically behind London's vineyard is **Sonoma Mountain**, a long ridge capped by a 2463-foot summit, which is on private land just west of the park boundary.

About 75 feet from the T-junction, you bear right at a fork onto a dirt road, signed LAKE and PIG PALACE. Several hundred feet ahead, the trail from the equestrian trailhead, labeled LAKE TRAIL on the park map, joins from the right.▶2 You continue straight, now on the **Lake Trail**. Follow the road as it curves left, with a beautiful view of the vineyard beyond. When you approach a gate across the road, look for the **hikers-only** Lake Trail heading downhill and right.▶3 Bikes and horses must stay on the road, passing to the side of the gate.

Veering right onto the Lake Trail, you soon begin climbing. Reaching a closed trail, right, your route turns left and continues to climb. Now you come to a rest bench and a junction with a trail taking off sharply right, signed here as the UPPER LAKE TRAIL, but listed on the park map as LAKE SPUR.▶4Here you turn right, gaining elevation on a moderate and then steep grade. Soon you come to a T-junction where you turn right, now without doubt on the **Upper Lake Trail**.▶5

After a couple of hundred feet, your route turns

Wolf House

HISTORY

From the museum, located next to a parking area just east of the entrance kiosk, you can walk to **London's grave site** and the remains of his elaborate mansion, called Wolf House, which was destroyed by fire in 1913, a month before the Londons were scheduled to move in.

The Lake Trail *starts along a working vineyard, with Sonoma Mountain in the distance.*

sharply left, and now you enjoy a level walk among towering redwoods. Just after an abandoned road joins your trail sharply from the right, you reach a junction with the **Mountain Trail**, a wide dirt road.▶6

Turning right, you leave the forest and reach a big meadow called **Mays Clearing**.▶7 A rest bench just ahead beckons you to pause and enjoy the stunning view, which extends southeast all the way to Mt. Diablo.

 Great Views

When you are thoroughly satiated with scenery, retrace your steps to the junction of the Upper Lake and Mountain trails.▶8 At this junction, the Mountain Trail makes an almost-180° bend to the right, and you follow it downhill on a gentle and then moderate grade. As you approach the lake, you pass a path leading left to the stone dam, and then the Quarry Trail, right. Just ahead is a T-junction with a dirt road.▶9 On the map the road heading right is labeled VINEYARD ROAD, and here you turn left and walk down the road toward the **lake**, with the stone dam in front of you.

Once on the far side of the lake, you can see London's **bathhouse** and a picnic area with tables, left. Now you are on **Lake Service Road**, but only briefly. Where the road begins to descend, you leave it and bear left, coming in about 50 feet to a trail post signed with the Bay Area Ridge Trail emblem and the words PARKING LOT, 1 MILE.▶10 This is the **Lake Trail**; continue straight and retrace your route to the parking area.▶11

Sonoma Mountain

From Mays Clearing,▶7 ascend the Mountain Trail and then the short Mountain Spur to just below the 2463-foot summit of Sonoma Mountain. This adds 5.1 miles to the described route.

OPTIONS

Jack London's Cottage *was the author's residence until his death in 1916.*

🚶 MILESTONES

▶1   0.0 Take paved path to dirt-and-gravel road southwest
through picnic area

▶2   0.3 Join Lake Trail from equestrian staging area

▶3   0.6 Right on Lake Trail at junction with Lake Service Rd.

▶4   0.9 Right on Upper Lake Trail (Lake Spur on park map)

▶5   1.1 Right on Upper Lake Trail

▶6   1.3 Right on Mountain Trail

▶7   1.5 Mays Clearing

▶8   1.7 Left to stay on Mountain Trail at junction with Upper Lake Trail

▶9   1.9 Left at junction with Vineyard Rd.,
then left on Lake Trail at junction with Lake Service Rd.

▶10 2.0 Straight on Lake Trail

▶11 2.9 Back at parking area

Marin Headlands: Gerbode Valley

TRAIL 4

Tennessee Valley Road

Marincello

Tennessee Valley Trailhead

Oakwood Valley Trail

Sausalito

Miwok

Trail

101

1

200'

Old

Miwok

Trail

1041'

Bobcat

Trail

Alta

Trail

to Golden Gate Bridge

Springs

Hawk Camp

800'

Trail

Miwok

Alta

Trail

Coast Trail

Trail

600'

GOLDEN GATE
NATIONAL
RECREATION
AREA

Rodeo Valley Cutoff

Trail

Wolf

Ridge

Trail

Miwok

Gerbode Valley

Bobcat

Valley

Wolf Ridge

960'

Trail

Bobcat

Rodeo

Road

McCullogh Road

start & finish

Marine Mammal Center

Fort Cronkhite

Bunker

Trail

Rodeo Lagoon

Road

Coastal

Rodeo Beach

Fort Barry
Marin Headlands Visitor Center

NIKE Missile Site

Conzelman

Road

Hawk Hill

one way

Field

Road

Bonita Cove

Point Diablo

Pt. Bonita Lighthouse

Point Bonita

| 0 | 0.2 | 0.4 | 0.6 | 0.8 | 1.0 mile |

| 0 | 400 | 800 | 1200 | 1600 meters |

Golden   Gate

Marin Headlands: Gerbode Valley

This scenic loop uses the Miwok and Bobcat trails to circle Gerbode Valley, an area slated in the 1960s for urban development but later protected as part of the **Golden Gate National Recreation Area**. In spring, the surrounding hills of the Marin Headlands are vibrant with wildflowers. They are alive with bird-song and avian acrobatics most of the year, but especially during the fall raptor migration. Views of San Francisco, Marin, and the Pacific Coast from the high points along this loop are superb.

Best Time

Spring wildflowers are the prime attraction here, but the hiking is good all year; expect fog in summer.

Finding the Trail

From Hwy. 101 northbound, just north of the Golden Gate Bridge, take the Alexander Ave. exit, go north 0.2 mile, and turn left onto Bunker Rd. After 0.1 mile you reach a one-direction-only tunnel where traffic is controlled by a stop light. After emerging from the 0.5-mile tunnel, go a total of 2.5 miles from Alexander Ave. Just past a horse stable, left, there is a parking turn-out on the right shoulder of Bunker Rd.

From Hwy. 101 southbound, just south of the Waldo Tunnel, take the Sausalito Exit, which is also signed for the GGNRA. Bear right (despite the left-pointing GGNRA sign) and go 0.25 mile to Bunker Rd. Turn left, and follow the directions above.

TRAIL USE
Hike, Run, Bike
LENGTH
5.4 miles, 3-4 hours
VERTICAL FEET
±1100'
DIFFICULTY
− 1 2 **3** 4 5 +
TRAIL TYPE
Loop
SURFACE TYPE
Dirt

FEATURES
Summit
Wildflowers
Birds
Great Views
Photo Opportunity
Camping

FACILITIES
Visitor Center
Restrooms
Water

The Gerbode Valley
loop takes you into
some of the best
wildflower terrain in
the North Bay.

The trailhead is on the north side of the parking area, at its midpoint.▶1

Facilities

Just west of the parking area, the **Marin Headlands visitor center** has interpretive displays, books and maps for sale, helpful rangers, restrooms, and water. Reach it by going 0.2 mile past the first parking area on Bunker Rd.; turn left onto Field Rd. and go 0.1 mile to the parking lot on the right.

Trail Description

Walk north on a dirt-and-gravel path to a wood-plank bridge that crosses a creek. In another 75 feet or so you come to a T-junction▶2 with a dirt road. Just before the junction is a trail post, left, telling you the trail ahead is open to hikers, equestrians, and bicyclists. You turn right onto the dirt-and-gravel road, the **Miwok Trail**. Bicyclists may use the Miwok and Bobcat trails to connect with the Bay Area Ridge Trail, which is farther east. The route here is level, and soon you reach a junction.▶3 Here the Bobcat Trail goes right, and your route, the Miwok Trail, continues straight. Now the Miwok Trail begins a

🚶 MILESTONES

▶1 0.0 Take dirt-and-gravel path north from trailhead
▶2 0.1 Right at T-junction on Miwok Trail
▶3 0.2 Straight on Miwok Trail at junction with Bobcat Trail
▶4 2.5 Miwok Trail ends; straight on Bobcat Trail
▶5 3.2 Straight on Bobcat Trail at junction with Bay Area Ridge Trail
hiker/horse route
▶6 5.2 Left on Miwok trail
▶7 5.4 Back at parking area

Mt. Tamalpais, *viewed from the Miwok Trail, stretches across the northern horizon.*

relentless and unshaded climb toward the east end of Wolf Ridge. The hillside, right, falls steeply to Gerbode Valley.

This loop takes you into some of the best wildflower terrain in the Bay Area. In spring, especially after a wet winter, the hills are decorated with a dazzling display of California poppies, mule ears, paintbrush, Ithuriel's spear, yarrow, blow wives, and blue-eyed grass.

 Wildflowers

Soon you reach a notch at the east end of **Wolf Ridge**. From this vantage point, you can look northwest to Mt. Tamalpais and west to the Pacific Ocean. A few paces ahead is a junction with the Wolf Ridge Trail,▶4 left. This trail is for hiking only, and dogs must be leashed. Your route, the Miwok Trail, which from here on is closed to dogs, continues straight and uphill.

With Mt. Tamalpais and the north end of San Pablo Bay in view, you pass a faint trail through the grass to a viewpoint, left. You route bends right, and in a few hundred feet reaches a junction with a single-track trail, right, that climbs to a vantage point beside a fenced-in communication facility, used by the FAA to direct commercial aircraft. Just left of this junction are a few large rocks, a convenient place to sit and rest.

After enjoying the scenery, you continue uphill on a gentle grade. The high point on the ridge dividing Tennessee and Gerbode valleys, a 1041-foot summit

Hawk Camp

OPTIONS

Hawk Camp has three sites that can each hold up to four people. There are picnic tables and a toilet, but no water. No fires are allowed, so if you want to cook, you need a camp stove. For reservations, call (415) 331-1540 between 9:30 a.m. and 4:30 p.m. You must pick up your permit at the visitor center during the above hours. Reservations may be made up to 90 days in advance.

and home of the FAA facility, is uphill and right.

Now you come to a four-way junction. You turn left and begin walking downhill. There is a sign here, partially obliterated, that reads Miwok Trail North, which is open to hikers and horses but closed to bikes. You continue downhill through an unattractive area that resembles a gravel pit.

Soon you reach a trail post signed for the Bobcat Trail, and about 30 feet farther, a junction, left, with the Marincello Trail, part of the Bay Area Ridge Trail.▶5 This trail is open to hikers, horses, and bikes.

 Mountain Biking

You continue following the **Bobcat Trail**, a dirt road that descends and then levels. After passing a steep dirt road that joins from the left, and an eroded dirt road, right, you come to a junction with the road to **Hawk Camp**, also right, one of three walk-in campgrounds in the Headlands.

Past the road to Hawk Camp, a trail post, right, with the Bay Area Ridge Trail emblem, marks a junction.▶6 Here, hikers and equestrians on the Bay Area Ridge Trail turn left onto a route which is closed to bikes. Your route continues straight on the Bobcat Trail, which is multi-use.

After passing through a eucalyptus grove, you enjoy a level walk parallel to the creek. Soon you pass the Rodeo Valley Trail, a dirt road heading uphill and left. Now you cross the creek draining Gerbode Valley, which passes under the road through a culvert, and in about 50 feet, you come to a T-junction with the Miwok Trail you passed at the start of your trip. Here you turn left and retrace your route to the parking area.▶7

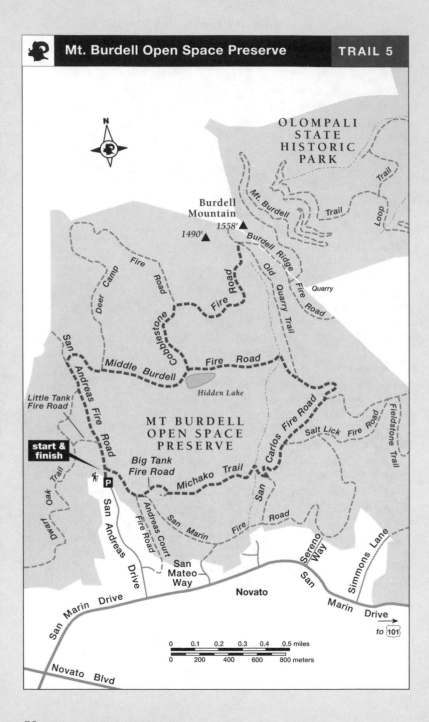

OLOMPALI
STATE
HISTORIC
PARK

N

Trail

Loop

Mt. Burdell   Trail

Burdell
Mountain

1558'
1490'

Burdell Ridge Fire Road

Old Quarry Trail

Quarry

Deer Camp Fire Road

Cobblestone Fire Road

Fire Road

San Andreas Fire Road

Middle Burdell   Fire   Road

Little Tank
Fire Road

Hidden Lake

MT BURDELL
OPEN SPACE
PRESERVE

Carlos Fire Road

Salt Lick Fire Road

Fieldstone Trail

start &
finish

Dwarf Oak Trail

Big Tank
Fire Road

P

Michako   Trail

San

Andreas Court Fire Road

San   Marin   Fire   Road

Sereno Way

Simmons Lane

San
Mateo
Way

Novato

San

Marin   Drive

San Andreas Drive

to 101

San Marin Drive

0   0.1   0.2   0.3   0.4   0.5 miles
0   200   400   600   800 meters

Novato Blvd

Mt. Burdell Open Space Preserve

This loop explores the open grasslands, groves, and high ground of Burdell Mountain, a bulky ridge that rises to 1558 feet and dominates the northeast corner of Marin County.

Best Time

Spring wildflowers are a prime attraction; avoid the heat of summer.

Finding the Trail

From Hwy. 101 in Novato, take the Atherton Ave./San Marin Dr. exit. Go west 2.2 miles on San Marin Dr., turn right onto San Andreas Dr., and go 0.6 mile to where the road makes a sweeping bend to the left. Park on the shoulder and observe the NO PARKING signs.

The trailhead is at the foot of the San Andreas Fire Road, by the gate just northeast of the parking area.

Trail Description

From the trailhead, ▶1 you head east on a dirt path, and, in about 50 feet pass through a gate and then make a sharp left-hand bend. After 100 feet or so, you merge with the **San Andreas Fire Road**, which climbs on a gentle grade.

The road reaches a low point, then bends left and begins to climb. In a shady grove of valley oak, a single-track trail departs uphill and right, but you continue straight. In about 50 feet, you come to a junction marked by a trail post. Here, the San

TRAIL USE
Hike, Run, Bike

LENGTH
5.6 miles, 3-4 hours

VERTICAL FEET
±1200'

DIFFICULTY
– 1 2 3 **4** 5 +

TRAIL TYPE
Loop

SURFACE TYPE
Dirt

FEATURES
Dogs Allowed
Child Friendly
Mountain
Lake
Wildflowers
Birds
Great Views
Photo Opportunity

FACILITIES
None

Summit

Andreas Fire Road heads left, and your route, the **Middle Burdell Fire Road** (also part of the Bay Area Ridge Trail) goes straight.▶2

At an unsigned fork you bear left, and soon pass another dirt road, the other branch of the fork. Now your route wanders back and forth as it gains elevation. At a junction, the Deer Camp Fire Road (Bay Area Ridge Trail) goes left, but you continue straight, still on Middle Burdell Fire Road.

Your route climbs moderately over rocky ground, bends north, and follows a barbed-wire fence and a streambed, both right. Passing a single-track trail that goes through a gate in the fence, you reach level ground and a T-junction.▶3 Here, the Middle Burdell Fire Road turns right, and the **Cobblestone Fire Road**, the way to the top of Burdell Mountain, heads left.

Turning left, you begin climbing on a moderate grade. The route gets steeper and rockier, but you are rewarded by terrific views west toward Bolinas Ridge, and southeast to San Pablo Bay and the peninsula that holds China Camp State Park. At a fork, the Deer Camp Fire Road comes in on the left, and your route, the Cobblestone Fire Road, veers right.

Now the road turns north, trying to find the easiest way up Burdell Mountain. The climbing is moderate, with a few level areas to ease your efforts, and some groves of bay and coast live oak for shade. There is higher ground ahead, but the true summit of **Burdell Mountain** (1558') is just beyond the preserve boundary, unreachable on private land.

Nearing the end of the climb, you come to a junction with the Old Quarry Trail, right, and, almost immediately, a T-junction with the **Burdell Mountain Ridge Fire Road**, a paved road.▶4 The preserve's high point lies just ahead, across the road and at the end of a faint single-track trail that heads north and uphill.

Lunch stop *along the trail in Mt. Burdell Open Space Preserve*

Olompali State Historic Park

From near the summit of Burdell Mountain, the **Mount Burdell Trail** descends into **Olompali State Historic Park**, making a long car-shuttle trip possible. Auto access to the park is only from southbound U.S. 101.

Great Views

After exploring Burdell Mountain's high ground, retrace your route to the **Middle Burdell Fire Road**.►5 Turning right, you pass **Hidden Lake**, a large vernal pool on your right, and head east over level ground.

Dipping into and then out of a small wooded ravine, you soon come to a junction, left, with the Old Quarry Trail, which climbs steeply to join the Cobblestone Fire Road just a few feet from the Burdell Mountain Ridge Fire Road. Continue straight, and in about 25 feet you pass a rough trail heading left and straight up the side of a high grassy ridge. Several hundred feet past these trails, the continuation of the Old Quarry Trail descends right, but you continue straight.

Soon you reach a junction and a watering trough for animals.►6 Here the Middle Burdell Fire Road continues straight, but your route, the **San Carlos Fire Road**, turns right. Descending gently for about 75 feet, you come to a gated fence. After passing through the gate, you enjoy a level, shady walk but soon resume a gentle descent in the open. You pass the Old Quarry Trail, right, and, about 350 feet ahead, the Salt Lick Fire Road, left. Continuing straight and downhill, the San Carlos Fire Road soon veers right, and then makes a sharp left-hand bend, putting you on a southeast course.

At a four-way junction,►7 where the San Carlos Fire Road continues straight and a faint trace heads left, you turn right onto the **Michako Trail**, a single track that is closed to bikes. Still descending, you pass through an opening in a fence, cross a seasonal creek on rocks, and then find level ground. Just past the creek, a faint trail heads left, but the Michako Trail continues straight and soon begins a gentle climb.

After about 100 feet, the route forks and you bear left. Soon you come to a four-way junction. Continue straight across a grassy field to the next junction, where you reach a junction with the **Big Tank Fire Road**, right.▶8 From here, you continue straight now on the Big Tank Fire Road, heading west.

About 150 feet ahead, you bear left at a fork, passing a few private homes and the Andreas Court Fire Road, left. Your route now swings right, climbs, and is soon joined by the single-track trail coming from the previous fork. Now on an easy descent, you soon reach the junction with the San Andreas Fire Road you passed at the start of this loop.▶9 Turn left here and retrace your route to the parking area.

Bikes are not allowed on the Michako Trail and instead must use the San Carlos, San Marin, and Big Tank fire roads to complete the loop.

🚶 MILESTONES

▶1 0.0 Take San Andreas Fire Road north

▶2 0.8 Right on Middle Burdell Fire Road

▶3 1.5 Left on Cobblestone Fire Road

▶4 2.5 Burdell Mountain Ridge Fire Road and top of mountain, return to junction with Middle Burdell Fire Road

▶5 3.5 Left on Middle Burdell Fire Road

▶6 4.3 Right on San Carlos Fire Road

▶7 4.8 Right on Michako Trail

▶8 5.4 Straight on Big Tank Fire Road

▶9 5.6 Left on San Andreas Fire Road, back at parking area

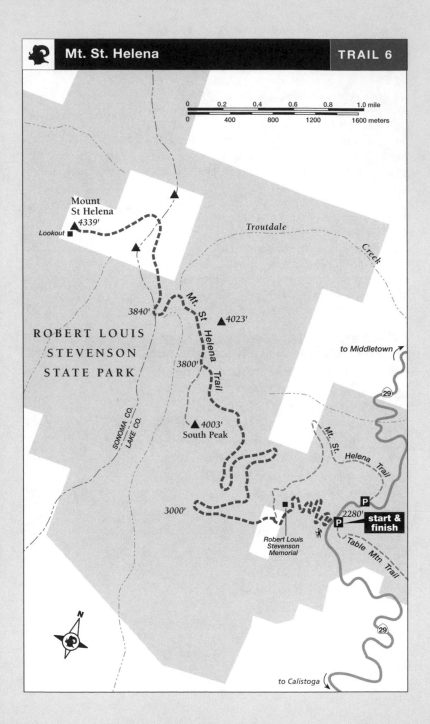

0   0.2   0.4   0.6   0.8   1.0 mile

0   400   800   1200   1600 meters

Mount
St Helena
▲4339'
Lookout ■

Troutdale

Creek

3840'

Mt. St. Helena Trail

▲4023'

ROBERT LOUIS
STEVENSON
STATE PARK

3800'

to Middletown ↗

29

SONOMA CO.
LAKE CO.

▲4003'
South Peak

Mt. St. Helena Trail

P
3000'

2280'
P start &
finish

Robert Louis
Stevenson
Memorial

Table Mtn Trail

N

29

to Calistoga

Mt. St. Helena

A "must-do" for lovers of high places, this route takes you to the 4339-foot North Peak of Mt. St. Helena, the tallest summit in the North Bay. Using an 0.8-mile single-track trail and a 4.5-mile section of the Mt. St. Helena Trail, a dirt road, the route is exposed for much of its length to sun, wind, and weather. Mt. St. Helena is in Robert Louis Stevenson State Park, which is named for the author of *The Silverado Squatters, Treasure Island,* and other books. In 1880 Stevenson, who was recuperating from tuberculosis, brought his new bride to live in a cabin here.

TRAIL USE
Hike, Run, Bike
LENGTH
10.6 miles, 4-6 hours
VERTICAL FEET
±2100'
DIFFICULTY
– 1 2 3 4 **5** +
TRAIL TYPE
Out & Back
SURFACE TYPE
Dirt

Best Time

Spring and fall; winter may provide best visibility, but also very cold conditions and even snow.

FEATURES
Mountain
Summit
Birds
Great Views
Secluded
Geologic Interest
Steep

Finding the Trail

From the junction of Hwys. 128 and 29 in Calistoga (at Lincoln Ave.), go northwest 8.7 miles on Hwy. 29 to a small parking area on the left side of the road at the highway's summit. If this area is full, park in the large area just across the highway, right. The trailhead is on the west side of Hwy. 29, adjacent to the small parking area. If you need to cross Hwy. 29, do so carefully!

FACILITIES
Picnic Tables

OPTIONS

Nearby Trails

The **Table Rock** and **Palisades trails**, closed to bikes and horses, lead southeast from the parking area to Table Rock, the Palisades, and Oat Hill Mine Rd.

Volcanic rock outcrops *overlook parts of the Mt. St. Helena Trail.*

The trailhead for **bicyclists** is about 0.2 mile ahead on the left side of Hwy. 29, at the foot of Mount Saint Helena Trail. Parking is on the right side of the highway, just past this gated fire road.

Trail Description

From the small parking area on the west side of Highway 29, ▶1 you ascend a set of wooden steps to the trail, here a wide dirt track, and pass a signboard with information about the park's namesake. The trail rises through terrain that alternates between forest and open areas. Soon you pass a **stone marker** indicating the site of the Stevensons' honeymoon cabin, nothing of which remains. ▶2 Just past the marker, the route makes a sharp right-hand switchback, and you climb a gently angled slab of rock, aided by footholds carved in its surface.

🏠 **Historic**

At a junction with the **Mt. St. Helena Trail**, a dirt road, ▶3 you turn left and climb gently, now with good views of the rocky abutments and ramparts on the mountain's southeast flank.

From this point on, you follow this well-graded road upward on a steepness that alternates between easy and moderate. At a wide clearing, crossed by power lines, you make a 180° turn to the left. Another sharp turn, this one right, aims you almost due north and soon brings you to very eroded ground. Now on a moderate grade, you have sweeping views east and

🚶 **MILESTONES**

▶1 0.0 Take steps and then trail northwest
▶2 0.6 Stevenson monument
▶3 0.8 Left on Mount St. Helena Trail
▶4 3.6 Junction with road to South Peak, left
▶5 5.3 Summit of North Peak (4339'), retrace to parking area
▶6 10.6 Back at parking area

Mt. St. Helena Trail *ascends via long, exposed switchbacks.*

HISTORY

Mt. St. Helena

How did Mt. St. Helena get its name? *California Place Names* gives no definitive answer but suggests several possibilities. A Russian party climbed the mountain in 1841, and legend has it that one of its members, Princess Helena de Gagarin, a niece of the Czar, bestowed the name in honor of Saint Helena, her patron saint.

northeast toward the series of ridges and summits that form the border between Napa and Yolo counties; beyond lies the Central Valley.

After a long, steady climb, you come to a junction, ▶4 left, with the road to **South Peak** (4003'). Reaching a clearing, you pass a road, left, that heads toward several communication towers. Your route swings left and finds a level course, with North Peak in view at last. Soon a turnaround marks the spot where the well-graded road ends and a short, steep, rocky track to North Peak begins.

Passing several communication facilities, you arrive at last on the summit of **North Peak** ▶5—in the Bay Area, only Copernicus Peak on Mt. Hamilton is higher, by a mere 34 feet. The 360° views, on a clear day, are stunning, taking in all the familiar North Bay summits, plus Mt. Lassen and even Mt. Shasta, 192 miles away.

 Summit

After enjoying the scenery, retrace your route to the parking area. ▶6

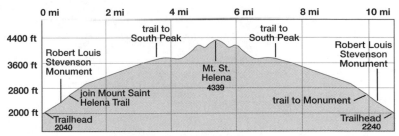

TRAIL 6 Mt. St. Helena Elevation Profile

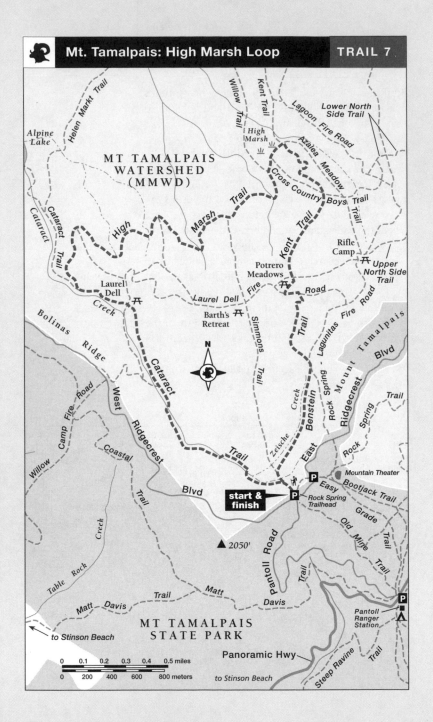

Alpine
Lake

Helen Markt Trail

Willow Trail

Kent Trail

Lagoon Fire Road

Lower North
Side Trail

High
Marsh

Azalea Meadow

MT TAMALPAIS
WATERSHED
(MMWD)

Cross Country Boys Trail

Cataract
Cataract
Trail

High

Marsh

Trail

Kent Trail

Rifle
Camp

Upper
North Side
Trail

Potrero
Meadows

Laurel
Dell

Fire

Road

Laurel Dell

Bolinas

Ridge

Creek

Barth's
Retreat

Simmons Trail

N

Camp Fire Road

West

Cataract

Ridgecrest

Coastal

Trail

Zetische Creek

East Benstein Trail

Rock Spring - Lagunitas Fire Road

Mount

Tamalpais

Blvd

Ridgecrest

Rock Spring

Trail

Trail

Blvd

start &
finish

P

P

P

Rock Spring
Trailhead

Mountain Theater

Easy

Bootjack Trail

Grade

Willow Creek

Table Rock

▲ 2050'

Pantoll Road

Trail

Old Mine

Trail

P

Pantoll
Ranger
Station

Matt   Davis   Trail

Matt

Davis

MT TAMALPAIS
STATE PARK

→ to Stinson Beach

Panoramic Hwy

Steep Ravine

Trail

to Stinson Beach

| 0 | 0.1 | 0.2 | 0.3 | 0.4 | 0.5 miles |
| 0 | 200 | 400 | 600 | 800 meters |

Mt. Tamalpais: High Marsh Loop

This beautiful and strenuous loop takes you past a scenic waterfall, beside a freshwater marsh, through areas of chaparral, and into groves of Sargent cypress and forests of Douglas-fir and oak as it explores the rugged canyons and ridges of MMWD lands above Alpine Lake on the north side of Mt. Tamalpais.

TRAIL USE
Hike, Run
LENGTH
5.8 miles, 4-5 hours
VERTICAL FEET
±1400'
DIFFICULTY
– 1 2 3 **4** 5 +
TRAIL TYPE
Loop
SURFACE TYPE
Dirt

Best Time

All year; Cataract Falls is best in the winter and early spring.

FEATURES
Child Friendly
Dogs Allowed
Canyon
Mountain
Stream
Waterfall
Birds
Cool & Shady
Secluded

Finding the Trail

From Hwy. 101 northbound in Mill Valley, take the Hwy 1/Mill Valley/Stinson Beach exit (which is also signed for Muir Woods and Mt. Tamalpais). After exiting, stay in the right lane as you go under Hwy. 101. At about 1 mile from Hwy. 101, get in the left lane, and, at a stoplight, follow Shoreline Highway as it turns left.

Continue 2.7 miles to Panoramic Highway and turn right. At 5.4 miles from Hwy. 1, you reach the Pantoll Campground and Ranger Station, left, and Pantoll Rd., right. Turn right, and go 1.4 miles to a T-junction with East Ridgecrest Blvd. and West Ridgecrest Blvd. Across the junction is a large paved parking area, shown on the map as the Rock Spring picnic area. Park here.

From Hwy. 101 southbound in Mill Valley, take the Hwy. 1 North/Stinson Beach exit (which is also signed for Muir Woods and Mt. Tamalpais). After exiting, bear right, go 0.1 mile to a stop sign, and

FACILITIES
Restrooms
Picnic Tables

Leaving Laurel Dell,
visit Cataract Falls by
staying left on the
Cataract Trail at its
junction with the High
Marsh Trail, and
walking several
hundred feet.

Stream

bear left on Highway 1. Go 0.5 mile, get in the left lane, and, at a stoplight, follow Shoreline Highway as it turns left. Then follow the directions in the second paragraph above.

Trail Description

From the north side of the parking area, ▶1 you head north on the **Cataract Trail**, a wide dirt-and-gravel path. The trail descends gently, and in about 100 yards you reach a fork. Your route, the Cataract Trail, bends left. The route takes you gently downhill and across a wood bridge over **Cataract Creek**, which drains Serpentine Swale and flows into Alpine Lake. Several hundred feet downstream from the bridge, you come to a jumble of big, moss-covered boulders. Although you may see a trail across the creek, left, stay on the creek's right side and follow the Cataract Trail through the boulders. Soon you reach a clearing and another wood bridge, this one over Ziesche Creek.

Where the route once continued straight, it now turns left, descends a few wooden steps, and then crosses a bridge over Cataract Creek. The trail leads you back into forest. Soon you pass a trail, left, that crosses Cataract Creek via a large wood bridge and then joins Laurel Dell Road. You continue straight, keeping the creek on your left. Just as you emerge from forest, at the edge of a clearing, you reach a junction with the Mickey O'Brien Trail heading sharply right.

Continue on the Cataract Trail as it branches left and crosses a bridge over a stream. Skirting a large meadow, left, you soon reach Laurel Dell Road and the **Laurel Dell picnic area**. ▶2 Here are restrooms, a watering trough, and a place to hitch horses.

The Cataract Trail leaves the picnic area from its west side, with the creek on your left. During winter and spring, you will soon see a waterfall cascading down over the ledge of a rocky cliff, downhill and left.

Cataract Creek

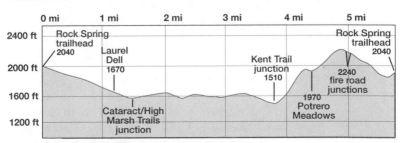

TRAIL 7 High Marsh Loop Elevation Profile

At a T-junction,▶3 the Cataract Trail turns left; turn right on the **High Marsh Trail**, a narrow single track. Soon you reach a fork where the trail splits temporarily; follow the right-hand, uphill branch. A steep climb brings you to a junction with a short side trail to Laurel Dell Road, uphill and right.

The route now alternates between wooded and open areas. Back in forest, the trail pursues a rolling course. Soon you pass a creek bed, which may be dry, and begin a steep climb, passing an unsigned trail heading uphill and right. Descending over rough ground, you drop steeply into a ravine that holds a seasonal creek.

The trail soon plunges steeply to **Swede George Creek**. If the creek is flowing, look uphill for a series of beautiful miniature waterfalls.

Ahead, you reach an unsigned fork. Here, the Willow Trail descends left, but your route, the High Marsh Trail, climbs right on a moderate grade. After topping a ridge, the trail descends and then reaches level ground and a T-junction. Your route turns left. The route passes around High Marsh's southeast edge and soon reaches a four-way junction▶4 marked by a trail post. Here, the High Marsh Trail ends, the **Kent Trail** runs left-to-right, and the Azalea Meadow Trail continues straight. You turn right onto the Kent Trail.

Now the trail ascends parallel to a streambed. Out of the trees, you cross a manzanita barren, giving you a chance to enjoy a fine view north of Big Rock Ridge, topped by two communication towers, and, beyond it, Burdell Mountain.

You now begin a moderate descent, soon finding a lovely stream, the headwaters of Swede George Creek, on your right. Reaching a trail post and a T-junction,▶5 you have **Potrero Meadows** in front of you, toilets to your left, and the **Potrero Camp picnic area**, with tables and fire grates, to your right. Turning right, you follow the trail as it crosses a

Benstein Trail *crosses Serpentine Swale.*

bridge over the stream and leads, in about 75 feet, to the picnic area. Here you turn left and follow a dirt-and-gravel road steeply uphill and south about 100 yards to a T-junction with **Laurel Dell Road**.▶6

Now you turn left onto a dirt road and descend gently for about 150 feet to a junction, right, with the **Benstein Trail**.▶6 Turn right and climb steeply on the Benstein Trail, a single track which is closed to bikes and horses.

At a fork in the route, you turn sharply right and continue to climb. Once across the ridge, the trail descends gently to a junction with **Rock Spring–Lagunitas Road**.▶7 Bear right and follow it downhill to a junction marked by a trail post. Here your route, the single track **Benstein Trail**,▶8 veers right, away from the road, and follows the creek.

Soon the Benstein Trail turns right and descends. The trail stays in a wooded area along the edge of the swale, and after a few switchbacks reaches a T-junction with the **Simmons Trail**.▶9 A left turn here puts you on track for the **Rock Spring picnic area** and the trailhead you left hours ago.▶10

🚶 MILESTONES

▶1   0.0 Take Cataract Trail north

▶2   1.2 Laurel Dell picnic area

▶3   1.6 T-junction: Cataract Trail and falls viewpoint are left; turn right on High Marsh Trail

▶4   3.8 Right on Kent Trail

▶5   4.4 Right at T-junction to Potrero Camp picnic area, then left to Laurel Dell Rd.

▶6   4.5 Left on Laurel Dell Rd., then right on Benstein Trail

▶7   5.0 Right on Rock Spring–Lagunitas Rd., then right to stay on Benstein Trail

▶8   5.4 Left at fork to stay on Benstein Trail

▶9   5.7 Left on Simmons Trail

▶10 5.8 Left on Cataract Trail, back at parking area

Coast redwoods *flourish in sheltered, inland canyons, such as at Muir Woods (Trail 10) and Samuel P. Taylor State Park (Trail 12).*

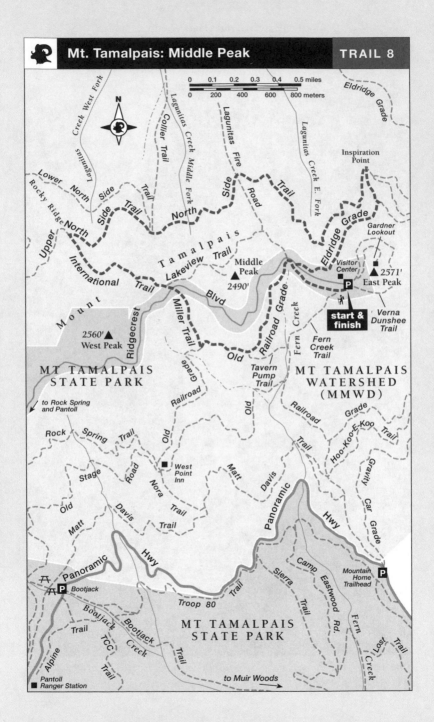

Mt. Tamalpais: Middle Peak

This circuit of Middle Peak explores a wonderful variety of terrain, from chaparral cloaking the mountain's upper reaches to redwood groves hidden on its northern side. Along the way, you have fine views of MMWD lands, including Bon Tempe Lake and Lake Lagunitas.

Best Time

All year; expect fog in summer

Finding the Trail

See the directions for "High Marsh Loop" (Trail 7). When you reach the T-junction with East Ridgecrest Blvd. and West Ridgecrest Blvd., turn right and go 3 miles to the East Peak parking area and a self-registration station, just below East Peak. The trailhead is on the west end of the East Peak parking area.

Trail Description

From the west end of the parking area, ►1 you walk downhill on a narrow paved road, closed to cars, that branches left from East Ridgecrest Blvd. Several hundred yards from the parking area, just as you join East Ridgecrest Blvd., you pass Eldridge Grade, a dirt road on your right. About 100 feet farther, you turn left onto **Old Railroad Grade**, a dirt road favored by mountain bikers. ►2

Soon you reach a junction with the Tavern Pump Trail, which heads left, steeply downhill.

TRAIL USE
Hike, Run

LENGTH
5.0 miles, 3 hours

VERTICAL FEET
±1450'

DIFFICULTY
− 1 2 **3** 4 5 +

TRAIL TYPE
Loop

SURFACE TYPE
Dirt, Paved

FEATURES
Child Friendly
Dogs Allowed
Canyon
Mountain
Stream
Birds
Cool & Shady
Great Views

FACILITIES
Visitor Center
Restrooms
Picnic tables
Water
Phone

From the trailhead you can see San Francisco, Angel Island, the Bay Bridge, the East Bay Hills, the Marin Headlands, and the East, Middle, and West summits of Mt. Tamalpais.

When you reach the **Miller Trail,**▶3 turn right and begin a rocky uphill scramble.

After a few steep sections, the Miller Trail arrives at **East Ridgecrest Blvd.,**▶4 which divides the north and south sides of the mountain. After carefully crossing the paved road, find the **International Trail** heading northwest. Several hundred feet from the road, you reach a junction marked by a trail post. Here the Colier Spring Trail, a shortcut to the North Side Trail, descends right, but your route continues straight, dropping in places to lose elevation, leveling in others.

The International Trail ends at the **Upper North Side Trail**, and you turn right.▶5 Follow the Upper North Side Trail, soon reaching a junction at **Colier Spring** in a coast redwood grove.▶6 From here you continue straight, now on the **North Side Trail**. Beyond two plank bridges, the route bends left and gains elevation on a gentle grade. Once past Lagunitas Creek's Middle Fork, which flows under the trail through a culvert, you make a moderate

Mt. Tam's East Peak

NOTICE

From the trailhead you can easily climb East Peak (2571') via the well-graded **East Peak Trail**, which starts off from the trailhead on a boardwalk just between the restrooms and the snack bar.

climb. Now the trail makes a sharp right-hand bend and arrives at a four-way junction.

 Mountain

Continuing straight, the route passes a seasonal creek, bends left, and soon reaches **Inspiration Point**, a clearing with a four-way junction marked by a trail post.▶7 Here you turn right and climb steeply to **Eldridge Grade**, a dirt road.▶8

Turn right and follow the road southwest, with the summit of **East Peak** slightly left and only a few hundred feet above. Eldridge Grade skirts the west side of East Peak, swings right, and soon makes a moderate climb to **East Ridgecrest Blvd**. Here you turn left▶9 and retrace your route to the parking area.▶10

MILESTONES

▶1 0.0 Take paved road west

▶2 0.2 Merge with East Ridgecrest Blvd., then left on Railroad Grade

▶3 0.9 Right on Miller Trail

▶4 1.3 Cross East Ridgecrest Blvd., take International Trail

▶5 1.9 Right on Upper North Side Trail

▶6 2.4 Straight on North Side Trail

▶7 4.0 Right on a connector to Eldridge Grade

▶8 4.2 Right on Eldridge Grade

▶9 4.8 Left on East Ridgecrest Blvd.

▶10 5.0 Back at parking area

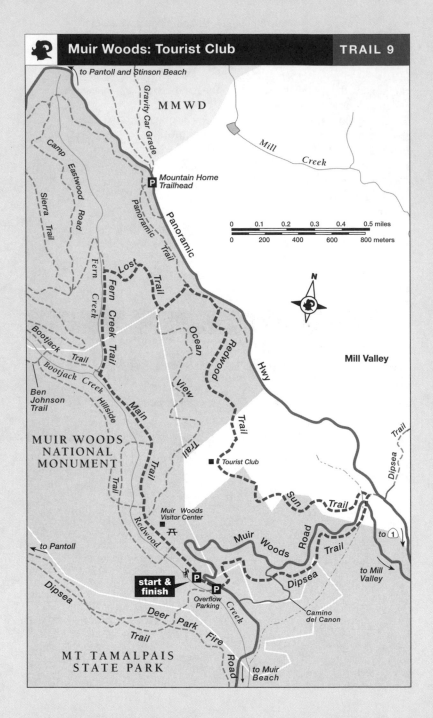

to Pantoll and Stinson Beach

MMWD

Gravity Car Grade

Camp Eastwood Road

Sierra Trail

Fern Creek

P Mountain Home Trailhead

Panoramic Trail

Panoramic Trail

Lost Trail

Fern Creek Trail

Bootjack Trail

Bootjack Creek

Ben Johnson Trail

MUIR WOODS NATIONAL MONUMENT

Hillside Trail

Main Trail

Trail

Ocean View

Redwood Trail

Mill Creek

0   0.1   0.2   0.3   0.4   0.5 miles
0   200   400   600   800 meters

N

Mill Valley

Tourist Club

Hwy

Sun Trail

Dipsea Trail

Muir Woods Visitor Center

Redwood Creek

to Pantoll

Dipsea

start & finish

P

P Overflow Parking

Deer Park Trail

Muir Woods Road

Trail

Dipsea

to 1

to Mill Valley

Camino del Canon

MT TAMALPAIS STATE PARK

Fire Road

to Muir Beach

Muir Woods: Tourist Club

This loop climbs high above Redwood Creek, visiting Mt. Tamalpais State Park and also the grounds of the Bavarian-style Tourist Club before plunging back to the redwood groves named for John Muir. Along the way you will walk beside giant redwoods, enjoy views of the Pacific Ocean—or the fog bank that shrouds it—and test your mettle on a stretch of the famous Dipsea footrace route from Mill Valley to Stinson Beach.

TRAIL USE
Hike, Run
LENGTH
3.8 miles, 2-3 hours
VERTICAL FEET
±1250'
DIFFICULTY
− 1 2 **3** 4 5 +
TRAIL TYPE
Loop
SURFACE TYPE
Dirt, Paved

Best Time

All year; expect fog in summer.

Finding the Trail

See the directions for "High Marsh Loop" (Trail 7). At 0.8 mile on Panoramic Hwy., where the road splits in three directions, turn left onto Muir Woods Rd. After 1.6 miles, turn right, into main parking area for Muir Woods National Monument. If this area is full, there is another about 100 yards southeast on Muir Woods Rd.

The trailhead is on the northwest end of main parking area, just left of entrance station and visitor center.▶1

Trail Description

You head northwest into **Muir Woods** on a level, paved path, passing an information board with history of the national monument. At Bridge 1, stay on the east side of **Redwood Creek**. When you reach

FEATURES
Child Friendly
Canyon
Stream
Birds
Cool & Shady
Great Views
Historic

FACILITIES
Visitor Center
Restrooms
Water
Phone

Bridge 2, where a vending machine has maps for sale, look across the creek. There stand two notable coast redwoods: the monument's tallest tree—253 feet—and its most stout—13 feet in diameter. Passing Bridge 3, left, you enter **Cathedral Grove**, where the path divides around this fantastic stand of trees.

At a junction with the **Fern Creek Trail,▶2** you turn right, leaving the paved path. With Fern Creek on your left, you enter **Mt. Tamalpais State Park**. After a short climb, the trail returns to the level of the creek, which runs along the bottom of a narrow canyon. Two bridges take you back and forth across Fern Creek, and a third, parallel to the creek, crosses a gully which holds a seasonal stream. Soon the trail makes a sharp right-hand switchback and begins to climb.

At a junction,▶3 you turn right on the **Lost Trail**, a single track cut into a steep hillside that falls dramatically left. A bridge takes you over a tributary of Fern Creek, and, after more climbing, you meet the **Ocean View Trail.▶4** Here you turn left. A rising traverse across a steep, open hillside brings you to a four-way junction.▶5 You turn right onto the **Panoramic Trail** and go straight through several junctions to a fork, where your route, the **Redwood Trail,▶6** veers right and descends.

The Tourist Club

The Tourist Club is part of an international conservation organization, founded in 1895 in Vienna, which has approximately 600,000 members in the U.S. and Europe. The club's collection of colorful Bavarian-style buildings, with a bandstand, a dance floor, and a few palm trees thrown in for good measure, is remarkable. Hikers are welcome.

Soon you cross several creeks via wooden bridges and enter land owned by the **Tourist Club**, which is just ahead.►7 The Redwood Trail skirts the upper edge of the club's grounds and joins their dirt access road from Panoramic Highway. Bearing left onto the dirt road, you reach a junction with the **Sun Trail**, where you turn right. True to its name, this trail brings you out of the shade and into a clearing.

At the end of the Sun Trail, turn right on the **Dipsea Trail**►8 and descend over rocky ground, finally reaching Muir Woods Road via several sets of wooden steps.►9 Carefully cross the road. The winding trail soon leaves the forest and traverses an open hillside. After crossing Camino del Canyon, a sign points you to the Dipsea Trail, which drops steeply via wooden steps, and then finds a moderate downhill grade.

When you arrive again at Muir Woods Road, cross it, turn right, and follow a dirt trail for about 100 yards to the main parking area.►10

Stretching from Mill Valley to Stinson Beach, the Dipsea Trail is the route of a rugged footrace, held nearly every year since 1905.

MILESTONES

►1	0.0	Take paved path north
►2	0.6	Right on Fern Creek Trail
►3	1.0	Right on Lost Trail
►4	1.3	Left on Ocean View Trail
►5	1.4	Right on Panoramic Trail
►6	1.6	Right on Redwood Trail
►7	2.1	Tourist Club, take Sun Trail
►8	2.8	Right on Dipsea Trail, cross Muir Woods Rd., continue on trail
►9	3.6	Cross Muir Woods Rd., right on dirt path
►10	3.8	Back at parking area

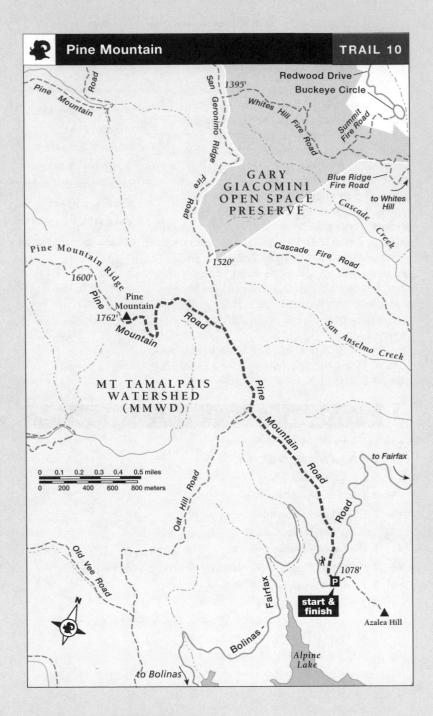

Redwood Drive
Buckeye Circle

1395'

Whites Hill Fire Road

Summit Fire Road

Pine Mountain Road

San Geronimo Ridge Fire Road

Blue Ridge Fire Road

to Whites Hill

GARY GIACOMINI OPEN SPACE PRESERVE

Cascade Creek

Cascade Fire Road

1520'

Pine Mountain Ridge

1600'

Pine Mountain

Pine Mountain

1762'

San Anselmo Creek

Road

Pine Mountain

MT TAMALPAIS WATERSHED (MMWD)

| 0 | 0.1 | 0.2 | 0.3 | 0.4 | 0.5 miles |

| 0 | 200 | 400 | 600 | 800 meters |

Oat Hill Road

to Fairfax

Old Vee Road

Pine Mountain Road

1078'

P

start & finish

Azalea Hill

N

Fairfax - Bolinas

Alpine Lake

to Bolinas

Pine Mountain

This out-and-back route takes you to one of the best vantage points in the Bay Area, where on a clear day your efforts will be rewarded by fantastic views. Along the way, plant lovers will stay busy identifying a variety of trees and shrubs, some found only on the locally prevalent serpentine soil. This area is also a favorite with mountain bikers.

Best Time

This hike is enjoyable all year.

Finding the Trail

From Hwy. 101 northbound, take the San Anselmo exit, also signed for San Quentin, Sir Francis Drake Blvd., and the Richmond Bridge. Stay in the left lane as you exit, toward San Anselmo. Follow Sir Francis Drake Blvd. 5.5 miles a stop light at Claus Dr. in Fairfax. Jog left onto Broadway and right onto Bolinas Rd., which is heavily used by bicyclists. (Bolinas Rd. soon becomes Fairfax–Bolinas Rd.) Go 3.9 miles to gravel Azalea Hill parking area, left.

From Hwy. 101 southbound, take the Sir Francis Drake/Kentfield exit and follow the directions above.

The trailhead is on the west side of Fairfax-Bolinas Rd., about 50 feet north of the parking area.

Trail Description

After carefully crossing Fairfax–Bolinas Rd.,▶1 you walk north about 50 feet from the parking area to a

TRAIL USE
Hike, Run, Bike
LENGTH
4.7 miles, 2-3 hours
VERTICAL FEET
±1000'
DIFFICULTY
– 1 2 **3** 4 5 +
TRAIL TYPE
Out & Back
SURFACE TYPE
Dirt

FEATURES
Child Friendly
Dogs Allowed
Mountain
Summit
Birds
Great Views
Photo Opportunity
Secluded

FACILITIES
None

Look northwest from
The Saddle to find
Barnabe Mountain, a
1466-foot peak on the
edge of Samuel P.
Taylor State Park. A
route to Barnabe
Mountain's summit is
described in Trail 12.

▲ Summit

gated dirt road. This is **Pine Mountain Road**, which
brings you to within a hundred yards or so of the
mountain's summit; a short, narrow trail covers the
remaining ground. You climb on a gentle and then
moderate grade to a high point, from where you can
see The Saddle, a windy gap between Pine Mountain
and an unnamed peak to its northeast.

Dropping slightly, you soon pass Oat Hill Road,
signed OATHILL, on your left. Gaining elevation once
again, you reach a junction with San Geronimo Ridge
Fire Road. You turn left on Pine Mountain Road▶2
and begin a moderate ascent, with a deep valley on
your left and a grassy hillside rising right. As you near
The Saddle, flattened grasses downhill and left attest
to the wind's power as it rushes unhindered from the
Pacific Ocean through the gap.

From The Saddle, the road swings left and rises
on a moderate grade, soon changing to steep. The
rough and rocky road eventually levels, and now
you find a single-track trail, right, signed pine
mountain summit.▶3 Turning right, you begin the
final push to the summit.

Atop Pine Mountain,▶4 the 360° panorama may
keep you busy for a while identifying such landmarks as Mt. Tamalpais, Mt. Diablo, the East Bay
hills, San Pablo Bay, Big Rock Ridge, Bolinas Ridge,
Tomales Bay, and Kent Lake. Without a doubt, this
is one of the best vantage points in the Bay Area.

After you've had your fill of the scenery, retrace
your route to the parking area.▶5

🚶 MILESTONES

▶1	0.0	Take Pine Mountain Rd. northwest
▶2	1.4	Left to stay on Pine Mountain Rd.
▶3	2.4	Right on single-track trail
▶4	2.5	Summit of Pine Mountain (1762')
▶5	4.7	Back at parking area

Sky Trail *(Trail 11) offers dramatic views of Drakes Bay and Point Reyes.*

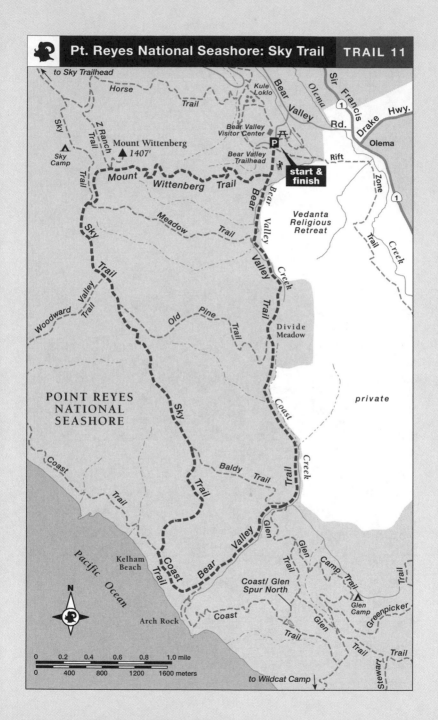

to Sky Trailhead

Horse

Trail

Kule Loklo

Bear Valley

Olema

Sir Francis

1

Drake

Hwy.

Olema

Bear Valley
Visitor Center

Bear Valley
Trailhead

start &
finish

Rift

Zone

Creek

1

Vedanta
Religious
Retreat

Sky

Z Ranch Trail

Sky Camp

Mount Wittenberg
▲ 1407'

Mount

Wittenberg

Trail

Trail

Meadow

Trail

Sky

Trail

Bear

Valley

Creek

Trail

Woodward Valley Trail

Old

Pine

Trail

Divide
Meadow

POINT REYES
NATIONAL
SEASHORE

Sky

Trail

Coast

Trail

Creek

private

Coast

Trail

Baldy

Trail

Pacific Ocean

Kelham
Beach

Coast

Trail

Bear

Valley

Glen

Glen

Glen
Camp
Trail

Trail

N

Coast/
Glen
Spur North

Glen Camp

Greenpicker

Trail

Arch Rock

Coast

Trail

Glen

Trail

Stewart

Trail

to Wildcat Camp

| 0 | 0.2 | 0.4 | 0.6 | 0.8 | 1.0 mile |

| 0 | 400 | 800 | 1200 | 1600 meters |

Point Reyes National Seashore: Sky Trail

This is one of the premier hikes in the Point Reyes area, offering a grand tour of Inverness Ridge and Bear Valley, with the Pacific shoreline thrown in for good measure. The route has something for everyone, including a wonderful array of plant and bird life, and fine views.

Best Time

This hike is enjoyable all year.

Finding the Trail

From Hwy. 1 northbound in Olema, just north of the junction with Sir Francis Drake Blvd., turn left onto Bear Valley Rd. and go 0.5 mile to the visitor-center entrance road. Turn left and go 0.2 mile to a large paved parking area in front of the visitor center. If this lot is full, there is a dirt parking area ahead and left.

From Hwy. 1 southbound in Point Reyes Station, go 0.2 mile from the end of the town's main street to Sir Francis Drake Blvd. and turn right. Go 0.7 mile and turn left onto Bear Valley Rd. At 1.7 miles you reach the visitor-center entrance road; turn right and follow the directions above.

The Bear Valley trailhead is at the end of the paved visitor-center entrance road, about 150 feet south of the paved parking area.▶1

Trail Description

After walking through a gap in a wooden fence that marks the trailhead, you pass the Rift Zone Trail,

TRAIL USE
Hike, Run

LENGTH
10.5 miles, 5-7 hours

VERTICAL FEET
±1650'

DIFFICULTY
– 1 2 3 4 **5** +

TRAIL TYPE
Loop

SURFACE TYPE
Dirt

FEATURES
Stream
Autumn Colors
Wildflowers
Birds
Cool & Shady
Great Views
Camping

FACILITIES
Visitor Center
Restrooms
Picnic Tables
Water
Phone

Sky Camp

Sky Camp, a hike-in campground, is on the Sky Trail, northwest of its junction with the Mt. Wittenberg Trail. For reservations, call (415) 663-8054 weekdays from 9 A.M. to 2 P.M.

Mount Wittenberg is named for a rancher who once lived nearby, not for Hamlet's alma mater.

 Photo Opportunity

left, and the Woodpecker Trail, right. When you reach the **Mt. Wittenberg Trail,**▶2 a single track, you turn right and begin to climb. Short level stretches relieve the otherwise constant climbing.

You reach a marked junction▶3 where your route, the Mt. Wittenberg Trail veers left. After a pleasant downhill ramble, the Mt. Wittenberg Trail ends, and you merge at a junction with the **Sky Trail,**▶4. You stay on the Sky Trail, enjoying a rolling course through a wonderful Douglas-fir forest.

You pass the Old Pine Trail, left.▶5 Emerging from forest, you negotiate a steep descent over rough ground. Passing the Baldy Trail,▶6 and after a 180° bend to the right, the route continues its descent. Soon the Sky Trail merges with the **Coast Trail**, a dirt road. Here you continue nearly straight on the Coast Trail. An easy 0.5-mile walk brings you to the turn-off for **Arch Rock.**▶7 Visit Arch Rock during the spring wildflower bloom for great photos!

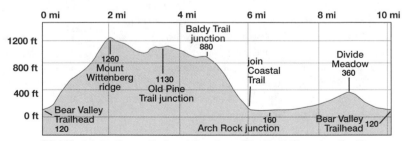

TRAIL 11 Pt. Reyes National Seashore: Sky Trail Elevation Profile

Now the Coast Trail turns left, away from the coast. Soon you reach a junction where the Coast Trail bends sharply right and the **Bear Valley Trail**, your route, goes straight.▶8

Continuing straight, you ascend gradually to **Divide Meadow,**▶9 where there are restrooms and a junction with the Old Pine Trail, both left. The route makes a sweeping bend to the right and begins to descend. A rest bench signals a junction with the Meadow Trail. You emerge from the wooded canyon at the junction with the Mt. Wittenberg Trail; continue straight and retrace your route to the parking area.▶10

𝕩 MILESTONES

▶1   0.0 Take Bear Valley Trail south

▶2   0.2 Right on Mt. Wittenberg Trail

▶3   2.0 Junction with trail to Mt. Wittenberg summit; veer left

▶4   2.4 Merge with Sky Trail; Meadow Trail on left

▶5   3.4 Old Pine Trail on left; go straight on Sky Trail

▶6   4.8 Baldy Trail on left; go straight on Sky Trail

▶7   6.0 Left on Coast Trail

▶8   6.5 Coastal Trail and side trail to Arch Rock on right; continue straight on Bear Valley Trail

▶9   8.9 Divide Meadow; Old Pine Trail on left; go straight

▶10 10.5 Back at parking area

Shorter Loops

NOTE

To shorten the route, turn left from the Sky Trail onto either the Meadow, Old Pine, or Baldy trail and then left on the Bear Valley Trail.

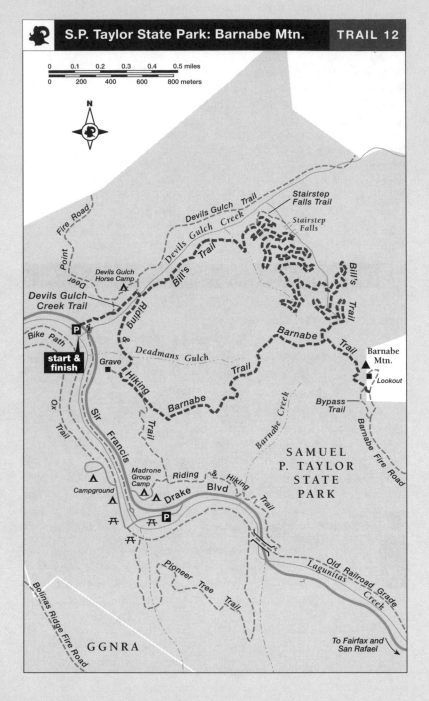

0　　0.1　　0.2　　0.3　　0.4　　0.5 miles

0　　200　　400　　600　　800 meters

N

Devils Gulch Trail

Stairstep Falls Trail

Devils Gulch Creek

Stairstep Falls

Bill's Trail

Fire Road

Deer Point

Devils Gulch Horse Camp

Devils Gulch Creek Trail

Riding & Hiking Trail

Bill's Trail

Barnabe Trail

Barnabe Mtn.

Lookout

Bike Path

start & finish

P

Grave

Deadmans Gulch

Barnabe Trail

Bypass Trail

Ox Trail

Sir Francis

Hiking Trail

Barnabe Creek

Barnabe Fire Road

SAMUEL P. TAYLOR STATE PARK

Campground

Madrone Group Camp

Riding & Hiking Trail

Drake Blvd

P

Old Railroad Grade

Lagunitas Creek

Pioneer Tree Trail

Bolinas Ridge Fire Road

GGNRA

To Fairfax and San Rafael

Samuel P. Taylor State Park: Barnabe Mountain

This loop climbs gently through mixed forest, alive with birdsong and brightened by wildflowers, struggles steeply to high ground just below the summit of Barnabe Mountain (1466'), and then descends through open country with wonderful views of west Marin, Point Reyes and the Tomales Bay area.

Best Time

All year, but trails may be muddy in wet weather.

Finding the Trail

From Hwy. 101 northbound, take the San Anselmo exit (also signed for San Quentin, Sir Francis Drake Blvd., and the Richmond Bridge). Stay in the left lane as you exit, toward San Anselmo, crossing over Hwy. 101. After 0.4 mile you join Sir Francis Drake Blvd., with traffic from Hwy. 101 southbound merging on your right. From here, it is 3.6 miles to a stop light at the intersection with Red Hill Ave. Stay on Sir Francis Drake Blvd. as it first goes straight and then immediately bends left.

At 15.5 miles on Sir Francis Drake Blvd., you pass the main entrance to Samuel P. Taylor State Park. At 16.5 miles you reach a wide turn-out, left, at Devil's Gulch. Park here.

From Hwy. 101 southbound, take the Sir Francis Drake/Kentfield exit and follow the directions above.

The Devils Gulch trailhead is across Sir Francis Drake Blvd. from the parking area. ▶1

TRAIL USE
Hike, Run
LENGTH
6.3 miles, 4 hours
VERTICAL FEET
±1900'
DIFFICULTY
− 1 2 3 **4** 5 +
TRAIL TYPE
Loop
SURFACE TYPE
Dirt, Paved

FEATURES
Canyon
Mountain
Stream
Birds
Great Views
Secluded

FACILITIES
None

Trail Description

Enjoy the view from the park boundary atop Barnabe Mountain: Mt. Diablo (east), Mt. Tamalpais (southeast), Kent Lake (south), and Big Rock Ridge (northeast).

After carefully crossing Sir Francis Drake Blvd., you follow a paved road that heads northeast beside Devil's Gulch Creek. Turn right onto unsigned **Devil's Gulch Creek Trail,**▶2 a single-track that descends toward the creek, and follow it to a four-way junction.▶3

Turn right and cross a long wooden bridge spanning the creek. Once across, you arrive at a T-junction. Your route, **Bill's Trail**, heads left and begins a long, gentle climb. Soon you reach a junction with the **Stairstep Falls Trail,**▶4 left, a short side trail to a vantage point where you can view the falls.

Bearing right from this junction, you climb across a steep hillside that falls away left, and then begin a long series of switchbacks. Finally leaving most of the trees behind, you reach a superb vantage point, where the view extends west to the lands of Point Reyes National Seashore and northwest to Tomales Bay. Now you meet the **Barnabe Fire Road.**▶5 From here, you can turn left to continue your ascent of Barnabe Mountain.

After struggling uphill, and passing the Barnabe Fire Road Connector, right, you reach a T-junction at the state park boundary.▶6 From here, a dirt road goes left and uphill to a **fire lookout**, and also right. (Please respect all private property postings.)

Retrace your route downhill to the junction with Bill's Trail.▶7 From here, continue descending on the dirt Barnabe Fire Road. Far down the hill you continue straight at a junction with the Riding and Hiking Trail, left, and reach a four-way junction.▶8

Waterfall

Summit

Here a short trail to **Taylor's grave site** goes straight, and your route, the **Riding and Hiking Trail**, turns right towards Devil's Gulch.

Heading into forest, you follow a rough, eroded road steeply downhill into **Deadman's Gulch**. Your route narrows, veers left, and skirts a hillside. Now with Devil's Gulch Creek downhill and left, you make a steep descent and soon reach the junction with Bill's Trail and the **wooden bridge** you crossed at the start of this loop.▶9 Here you turn left, cross the bridge, turn left again, and retrace your route to the parking area. Look both ways crossing the highway!▶10

Samuel P. Taylor (1827–1896) established the West Coast's first paper mill nearby on the banks of Lagunitas Creek.

🚶 MILESTONES

▶1	0.0	Take paved road northeast
▶2	0.1	Right on Devil's Gulch Creek Trail
▶3	0.2	Right across bridge, then left on Bill's Trail
▶4	0.9	Trail to Stairstep Falls, left
▶5	4.0	Left on Barnabe Fire Road
▶6	4.3	Park boundary, retrace to previous junction
▶7	4.6	Bill's Trail on right; go straight to stay on Barnabe Fire Road
▶8	5.6	Trail to Taylor's grave site straight; go right on Riding and Hiking Trail
▶9	6.1	Left across bridge, then retrace steps on Devil's Gulch Trail
▶10	6.3	Back at parking area

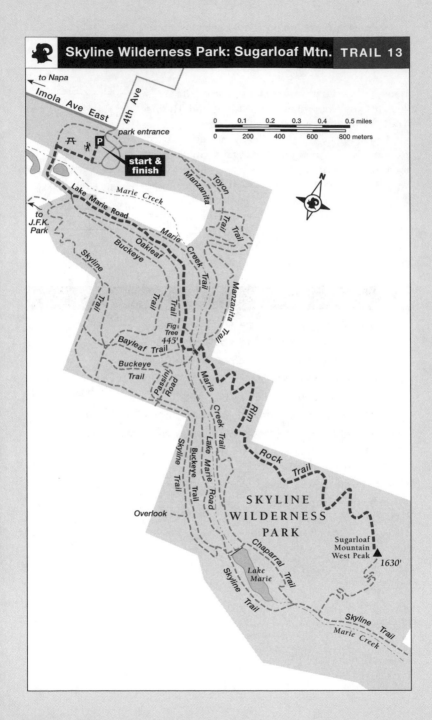

Skyline Wilderness Park: Sugarloaf Mtn. TRAIL 13

to Napa

Imola Ave East

4th Ave

park entrance

0   0.1   0.2   0.3   0.4   0.5 miles
0   200   400   600   800 meters

N

start & finish

Marie Creek

Lake Marie Road

to J.F.K. Park

Manzanita Trail

Toyon Trail

Marie Creek Trail

Skyline Trail

Buckeye Trail

Oakleaf Trail

Manzanita Trail

Fig Tree 445'

Bayleaf Trail

Buckeye Trail

Passini Road

Marie Creek Trail

Skyline Trail

Buckeye Trail

Lake Marie Road

Rim Rock Trail

Overlook

SKYLINE WILDERNESS PARK

Chaparral Trail

Lake Marie

Skyline Trail

Sugarloaf Mountain West Peak 1630'

Skyline Trail

Marie Creek

Skyline Wilderness Park: Sugarloaf Mountain

Lake Marie Road and the Rim Rock Trail ascend the 1630-foot west peak of Sugarloaf Mountain, the highest point in the park. Park maintenance is a volunteer effort, so some trails may be in better shape than others—long pants are advised. The park welcomes equestrians and bicyclists as well as hikers and runners.

TRAIL USE
Hike, Run, Bike
LENGTH
6.0 miles, 4 hours
VERTICAL FEET
±1700'
DIFFICULTY
– 1 2 3 **4** 5 +
TRAIL TYPE
Out & Back
SURFACE TYPE
Dirt, Paved

Best Time

Spring and fall, especially when spring wildflowers are at their peak; park is closed on Thanksgiving and Christmas.

Finding the Trail

From Hwy. 29 in Napa, take the Imola Ave./Lake Berryessa/Hwy. 121 North exit and go east 2.9 miles on Imola Ave. to the Skyline Wilderness Park entrance, right. After paying a fee at the entrance kiosk, bear right and go about 200 feet to a paved parking area. The trailhead is on the southwest corner of parking area.

FEATURES
Mountain
Wildflowers
Birds
Great Views
Secluded
Geologic Interest

FACILITIES
Restrooms
Picnic Tables
Water

Facilities

A campground adjacent to the parking area hosts RVs year-round, and tent camping during spring and summer. Also in the park are picnic and barbecue areas, an activity center, a cookhouse, a social center for meetings and indoor parties, and an equestrian arena.

Trail Description

Martha Walker Native Habitat Garden is a volunteer effort established in 1986 to honor its namesake, a local botanist.

You walk downhill from the parking area on a dirt path, and in about 25 feet reach a junction.▶1 Continue straight beside the **Martha Walker Native Habitat Garden**.

Passing the garden's entrance, you continue about 400 feet, and at the next T-junction▶2 turn left onto a dirt road. The road crosses a bridge over **Marie Creek** and merges with a paved road, where you veer left. Ahead is a locked gate, signed CAMP COOMBS, NAPA STATE HOSPITAL PROPERTY. Before reaching the gate, you turn right onto a dirt road, fenced on both sides, that passes between two man-made lakes—**Lake Louise**, left, and **Lake Camille**, right. After approximately 200 feet, the road bends left and soon reaches a junction.▶3 Here, the Skyline Trail, a dirt-and-gravel road that is part of the Bay Area Ridge Trail, turns right, but you continue straight on **Lake Marie Road**.

Lake Marie Road is a rough and rocky dirt track shared by hikers, bicyclists, and equestrians. A rest bench, right, and a watering trough for horses, left, mark a junction. Here, a closed trail heads steeply right, and the Marie Creek Trail, which may be overgrown and not maintained, veers left. You continue straight. Just past the junction is a cave—a number of which can be found in the park—gouged from the rocky hillside, right. These may have been dug to find sources of water for the hospital, or perhaps they were the beginnings of mine shafts.

Geologic Interest

Now descending on a moderate grade, the road reaches one of the park's most remarkable features, a giant **fig tree** whose branches droop to the ground, forming a living tree house.▶4

Just past the fig tree, you leave Lake Marie Road and turn left onto a single-track trail, heading toward **Marie Creek**. A bridge provides an easy way across the creek, and about 60 feet farther you come

Hikers ascending Sugarloaf *enjoy views of Napa Valley and surrounding mountains.*

to a junction with the Marie Creek Trail, right. Continue straight, passing two signs, one for the MANZANITA AND TOYON TRAILS, the other for your route, the RIM ROCK TRAIL.

In about 15 feet, where the trail starts to bend

Loop Option

OPTIONS

From the fig tree junction,▶4 take the Bayleaf Trail to the Skyline Trail, part of the Bay Area Ridge Trail; then turn right on the Skyline Trail to return to Lake Marie Road.

left, you come to another junction, this one unsigned.▶5 Here you turn right, onto the **Rim Rock Trail**, which passes through a gap in a rock wall and then reaches a fork, where you bear right. The route eventually curves east, following a tributary of Marie Creek, far below and right. The grade eases as you reach the head of a canyon, but then rises steeply via a series of switchbacks.

⚠ **Summit**

The route zigzags up a grassy hillside, then passes through a grove of bay and coast live oak. The neighboring summit, Sugarloaf Mountain, East Peak (1686'), topped with several communication towers, is due east. In the midst of another wooded grove, you reach a clearing centered around a low rock. This undistinguished spot, ringed by trees, marks the 1630-foot summit of **Sugarloaf Mountain, West Peak.**▶6

After you have enjoyed relaxing on the summit, retrace your route to the parking area.▶7

🚶 MILESTONES

▶1 0.0 Take dirt path south to T-junction, right on paved road

▶2 0.2 Left onto dirt road, across bridge, then left on paved road

▶3 0.4 Straight on Lake Marie Rd. at junction with Skyline Trail

▶4 1.2 Left past fig tree, across bridge, straight at junction with Marie Creek Trail

▶5 1.3 Right on Rim Rock Trail, right again at fork

▶6 3.0 Sugarloaf Mountain, West Peak; retrace steps to parking area

▶7 6.0 Back at parking area

The Rim Rock Trail *ascends through oak woodlands to the top of Sugarloaf Mountain.*

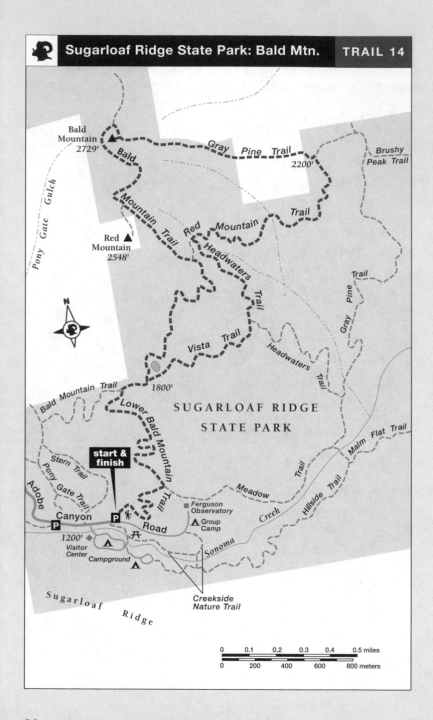

Sugarloaf Ridge State Park: Bald Mtn. TRAIL 14

Bald
Mountain
2729'

Gray Pine Trail

2200'

Brushy
Peak Trail

Bald

Mountain Trail

Red Mountain Trail

Headwaters

Red
Mountain
2548'

N

Gray Pine Trail

Vista Trail

Trail

Headwaters

Trail

Bald Mountain Trail

1800'

SUGARLOAF RIDGE
STATE PARK

Lower Bald Mountain Trail

Stern Trail

**start &
finish**

Pony Gate Trail

Malm Flat Trail

Meadow

Creek

Trail

Hillside Trail

Adobe

Canyon

P

P

Road

Ferguson
Observatory

Group
Camp

Sonoma

1200'

Visitor
Center

Campground

Creekside
Nature Trail

Sugarloaf Ridge

0	0.1	0.2	0.3	0.4	0.5 miles
0	200	400	600	800 meters

Sugarloaf Ridge State Park: Bald Mountain

This semi-loop route is a challenge, but well worth the effort. A superb array of trees, shrubs, and wild-flowers, along with some of the best views in the North Bay, are the rewards for tackling the 1500-foot climb to the summit of Bald Mountain.

Best Time

This hikes is best done in spring and fall.

Finding the Trail

From Hwy. 12 just north of Kenwood, take Adobe Canyon Rd. and go northeast 3.4 miles to the Sugarloaf Ridge State Park entrance kiosk. If the entrance kiosk is not staffed, pay fee at the self-registration station here. Continue 0.1 mile to a dirt parking area, left. The trailhead is on the northeast corner of the parking area.▶1

Trail Description

The **Lower Bald Mountain Trail**, a single track, heads east from the parking area through a wet area into open grassland and finds a gentle uphill course. At a junction with the Meadow Trail, you veer left and soon begin a moderate uphill climb via a series of switchbacks in a densely wooded area. Your trail now merges with the **Bald Mountain Trail**, part of the Bay Area Ridge Trail.▶2 Bearing right on this paved road, you follow it steadily uphill on a moderate grade. Where the road angles sharply left, you turn right onto the single track **Vista Trail**▶3

TRAIL USE
Hike, Run
LENGTH
6.7 miles, 5 hours
VERTICAL FEET
±1900'
DIFFICULTY
– 1 2 3 4 **5** +
TRAIL TYPE
Loop
SURFACE TYPE
Dirt, Paved

FEATURES
Mountain
Summit
Wildflowers
Birds
Great Views
Camping

FACILITIES
Restrooms
Picnic Tables
Water
Phone

(closed to bikes year-round and closed in winter to horses.)

The Vista Trail turns left and then descends steeply over loose, rocky ground to a junction with the **Headwaters Trail**, left.▶4 Bearing left, you walk in the shade of Douglas-fir and coast live oak. Reaching Sonoma Creek but staying on its west side, the trail bends left and rises on a moderate grade. After struggling uphill over rough ground, the trail at last reaches a T-junction with the **Red Mountain Trail**,▶5 a single track. Here you turn right and descend to a crossing of Sonoma Creek near its upper reaches.

On a rolling course, the trail swings north, and now you descend steeply to a creek and cross it on a wooden bridge. Suddenly you are atop a manzanita barren—the sandy, rocky soil is perfect for these hearty, pioneering plants. From here you have a won-

Atop Bald Mountain, *two display panels help you identify landmarks to the north and south.*

derful 360° view that, at last, reveals your goal, the summit of Bald Mountain, slightly north of west.

You join the **Gray Pine Trail**, a dirt road, at a T-junction.▶6 Now turning left, you continue uphill on a moderate grade. After several steep pitches, you leave the Gray Pine Trail where it bends right, and continue west over windswept open ground a few hundred feet to the top of **Bald Mountain** (2729').▶7

When it is time to head down, retrace your steps to the Gray Pine Trail turn left onto it, and follow it steeply downhill to a T-junction with the **Bald Mountain Trail**, a dirt road.▶8 Here you turn left, climb briefly, and then circle the west side of Bald Mountain to a T-junction with a paved road.▶9 Turning left, you head downhill on a gentle and then moderate grade into forest.

After passing the junction with the Vista Trail, continue downhill on the Bald Mountain and **Lower Bald Mountain**▶10 trails, retracing your route to the parking area.▶11

According to *California Place Names*, more than 100 peaks in California are named Bald; only Black and Red are more popular mountain names.

 Summit

🚶	MILESTONES	
▶1	0.0	Take Lower Bald Mountain Trail east, then north
▶2	0.9	Right on Bald Mountain Trail (paved)
▶3	1.2	Right on Vista Trail
▶4	1.8	Left on Headwaters Trail
▶5	2.3	Right on Red Mountain Trail
▶6	3.2	Left on Gray Pine Trail
▶7	3.9	Summit of Bald Mountain (2729')
▶8	4.0	Left at T-junction with Bald Mountain Trail (dirt)
▶9	4.4	Left at T-junction with Bald Mountain Trail (paved)
▶10	5.8	Left at junction with Lower Bald Mountain Trail
▶11	6.7	Back at parking area

CHAPTER 2

East Bay

East Bay

Imagine a landscape of oak-studded hills, grassy ridges, rocky peaks, forested valleys, and salt-marsh shoreline. Picture this landscape in a region once devoted to farms, orchards, dairies, and cattle ranches, where echoes of the past can be heard above the din of development. Reserve a sizable chunk of land for public enjoyment in parks and preserves, and thread through them more than 1000 miles of trails for hiking, bicycling, walking, jogging, and horseback riding. Often this kind of outdoor recreation paradise is only found tucked away in remote corners of national parks or set aside in wilderness areas, inaccessible to many of us. But all of these things can be found in the East Bay, within easy reach of millions of people.

The East Bay, which extends eastward from San Francisco Bay to the edge of the Central Valley, and southeast from the Carquinez Strait and Suisun Bay to the foothills of Mt. Hamilton, is made up of two counties, Alameda and Contra Costa, a 1745-square-mile area that is home to some 2.5 million people. The East Bay today is an exciting and vibrant place, where many cultures and communities contribute their history and heritage, where industry and commerce thrive, and where open space has been preserved and protected for all to enjoy. Agricultural land for crops and cattle grazing is steadily being lost to residential and industrial development, much of it densely packed along freeway and highway corridors. The area is an important transportation hub, with major air, rail, and port facilities. It is a world-renowned mecca for learning and research, and a lively center of culture and the arts.

During the Depression, East Bay residents concerned about preserving open space lobbied to create the Bay Area's first regional park district, and then voted to tax themselves five cents per $100, not an inconsiderable sum at the time, to pay for land acquisition. The resounding success of the East Bay Regional Park District led to the creation of other, similar agencies in the Bay Area, including Marin County Open Space District and Midpeninsula Regional Open Space District.

Governing Agencies

This chapter describes trails in parks administered by the East Bay Regional Park District (EBRPD) and Mt. Diablo State Park. They, along with two other agencies—East Bay Municipal Utility District and Don Edwards San Francisco Bay National Wildlife Refuge—oversee more than 164,000 acres, or about 260 square miles.

A trail map of **Mt. Diablo State Park** is available at the park's visitor centers and from the Mount Diablo Interpretive Association. The **East Bay Regional Park District** offers maps at its trailheads, by mail, and from its Web site. For agency contact information, see Appendix (p. 280)

Equestrians *ride on Mount Diablo.*

East Bay

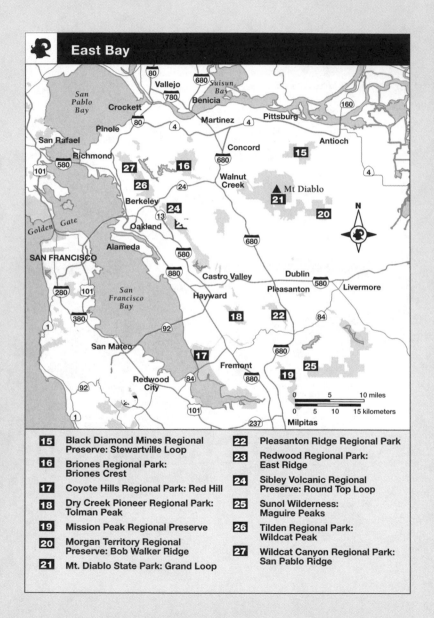

15	Black Diamond Mines Regional Preserve: Stewartville Loop
16	Briones Regional Park: Briones Crest
17	Coyote Hills Regional Park: Red Hill
18	Dry Creek Pioneer Regional Park: Tolman Peak
19	Mission Peak Regional Preserve
20	Morgan Territory Regional Preserve: Bob Walker Ridge
21	Mt. Diablo State Park: Grand Loop
22	Pleasanton Ridge Regional Park
23	Redwood Regional Park: East Ridge
24	Sibley Volcanic Regional Preserve: Round Top Loop
25	Sunol Wilderness: Maguire Peaks
26	Tilden Regional Park: Wildcat Peak
27	Wildcat Canyon Regional Park: San Pablo Ridge

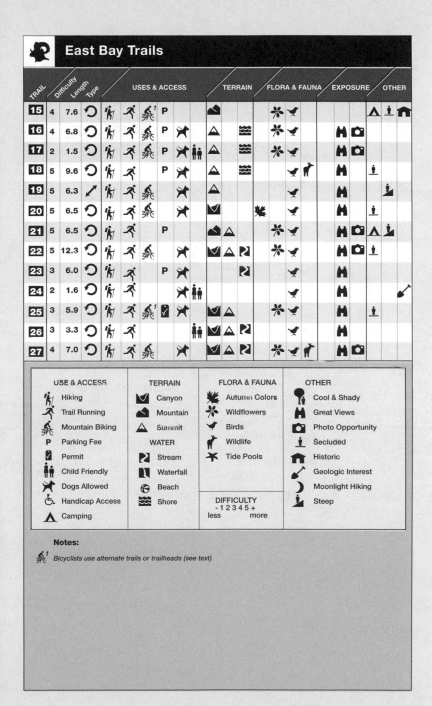

TRAIL	Difficulty	Length	Type	USES & ACCESS	TERRAIN	FLORA & FAUNA	EXPOSURE	OTHER
15	4	7.6		Hiking, Trail Running, Mountain Biking[1], Parking Fee	Canyon	Wildflowers, Birds		Camping, Secluded, Historic
16	4	6.8		Hiking, Trail Running, Mountain Biking, Parking Fee, Dogs Allowed	Summit, Shore	Wildflowers, Birds	Great Views, Photo Opportunity	
17	2	1.5		Hiking, Trail Running, Mountain Biking, Parking Fee, Dogs Allowed, Child Friendly	Summit, Shore	Wildflowers, Birds	Great Views, Photo Opportunity	
18	5	9.6		Hiking, Trail Running, Parking Fee, Dogs Allowed	Summit, Shore	Birds, Wildlife	Great Views	Secluded
19	5	6.3		Hiking, Trail Running, Mountain Biking, Dogs Allowed	Summit	Birds	Great Views	Steep
20	5	6.5		Hiking, Trail Running, Mountain Biking, Dogs Allowed	Canyon, Autumn Colors	Birds	Great Views	Secluded
21	5	6.5		Hiking, Trail Running, Mountain Biking, Parking Fee	Canyon, Summit	Wildflowers, Birds	Great Views, Photo Opportunity	Camping, Secluded, Steep
22	5	12.3		Hiking, Trail Running, Mountain Biking, Dogs Allowed	Canyon, Summit, Stream	Wildflowers, Birds	Great Views, Photo Opportunity	Secluded
23	3	6.0		Hiking, Trail Running, Parking Fee	Stream	Birds	Great Views	
24	2	1.6		Hiking, Trail Running, Dogs Allowed, Child Friendly		Birds	Great Views	Geologic Interest
25	3	5.9		Hiking, Trail Running, Mountain Biking[1], Permit, Dogs Allowed	Canyon, Summit	Wildflowers, Birds	Great Views	Secluded
26	3	3.3		Hiking, Trail Running, Child Friendly	Canyon, Summit, Stream	Birds	Great Views	
27	4	7.0		Hiking, Trail Running, Mountain Biking, Dogs Allowed	Canyon, Summit, Stream	Wildflowers, Birds, Wildlife	Great Views, Photo Opportunity	

Legend

USE & ACCESS
- Hiking
- Trail Running
- Mountain Biking
- P Parking Fee
- Permit
- Child Friendly
- Dogs Allowed
- Handicap Access
- Camping

TERRAIN
- Canyon
- Mountain
- Summit

WATER
- Stream
- Waterfall
- Beach
- Shore

FLORA & FAUNA
- Autumn Colors
- Wildflowers
- Birds
- Wildlife
- Tide Pools

DIFFICULTY
- 1 2 3 4 5 +
- less   more

OTHER
- Cool & Shady
- Great Views
- Photo Opportunity
- Secluded
- Historic
- Geologic Interest
- Moonlight Hiking
- Steep

Notes:

[1] Bicyclists use alternate trails or trailheads (see text)

East Bay

Dry Creek Pioneer: Tolman Peak 125

This route explores a regional park gem, an oasis in the middle of one of the East Bay's most heavily industrial and residential areas. Scenery, views, and variety of habitat combine to make hiking to Tolman Peak more than just a challenging workout.

Mission Peak 131

A steady climb of more than 2000 feet in just over 3 miles brings you to the top of Mission Peak, one of the East Bay's most dramatic summits, offering views of the entire Bay Area.

Morgan Territory: Bob Walker Ridge ...137

Morgan Territory is one of the most remote and scenic parks in the East Bay, perched on the southeastern edge of Mt. Diablo State Park, within sight of Livermore, Altamont Pass, and the Central Valley. Seclusion and wilderness make hiking here a special experience, as you drop into a deep canyon, then climb lofty Bob Walker Ridge.

Mt. Diablo: Grand Loop 141

A complete circle around Mt. Diablo, the East Bay's tallest peak, plus a trip to its 3849-foot summit, makes this one of the Bay Area's premier hikes, and a great way to learn more about the trees, shrubs, and wildflowers that struggle for survival on the rugged mountain's upper reaches.

Mules ear (right) is a large, showy yellow flower found in East and South Bay grasslands.

Sunol: Maguire Peaks 163

This circuit of Maguire Peaks explores a hidden corner of Sunol Wilderness, divided by Welch Creek Road from the main part of the park. The scenery is beautiful and serene, and the vistas from several vantage points are superb. Literally to top it off, you can make an ascent of Maguire Peaks west summit (1688'), a mountain climb in miniature.

TRAIL 25

Hike, Run, Bike
5.9 miles, Loop
Difficulty: 1 2 **3** 4 5

Tilden: Wildcat Peak 169

This scenic loop takes you from the Tilden Park Environmental Education Center to the summit of Wildcat Peak, with terrific views of the Bay Area and a variety of plants and birds keep to keep things interesting throughout.

TRAIL 26

Hike, Run, Bike
3.3 miles, Loop
Difficulty: 1 2 **3** 4 5

Wildcat Canyon: San Pablo Ridge 173

This loop takes you from the lowlands of Wildcat Creek to the high, open slopes of San Pablo Ridge, rewarding you with some of the best views in the Bay Area, including a 360° panorama from an old Nike missile site.

TRAIL 27

Hike, Run, Bike
7.0 miles, Loop
Difficulty: 1 2 3 **4** 5

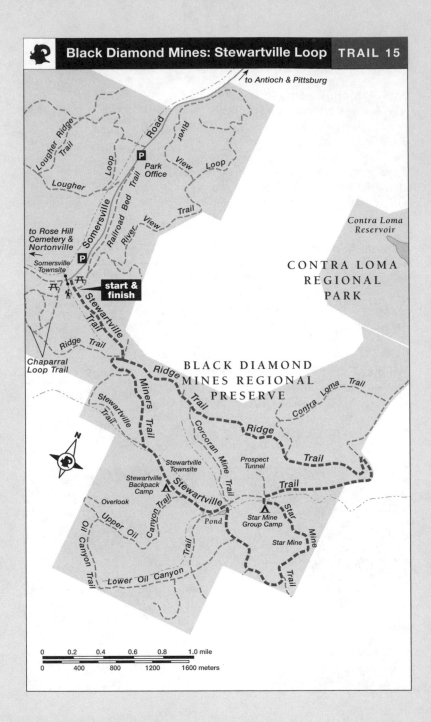

Black Diamond Mines: Stewartville Loop   **TRAIL 15**

to Antioch & Pittsburg

Lougher Ridge Trail

Lougher

Somersville Loop

Road

Railroad Bed Trail

River View Loop

P
Park Office

to Rose Hill
Cemetery &
Nortonville

Somersville

River View

River View Trail

P
Somersville
Townsite

**start &
finish**

Stewartville Trail

*Contra Loma
Reservoir*

CONTRA LOMA
REGIONAL
PARK

Ridge Trail

Chaparral
Loop Trail

Ridge Trail

Miners Trail

Stewartville Trail

BLACK DIAMOND
MINES REGIONAL
PRESERVE

Corcoran Mine Trail

Contra Loma Trail

Ridge Trail

N

Stewartville
Townsite

Prospect
Tunnel

Stewartville
Backpack Camp

Overlook

Canyon Trail

Stewartville Trail

Trail

Pond

Star Mine
Group Camp

Star Mine Trail

Star Mine

Upper Oil Canyon Trail

Oil Canyon Trail

Lower Oil Canyon

0	0.2	0.4	0.6	0.8	1.0 mile
0	400	800	1200	1600 meters	

Black Diamond Mines Regional Preserve: Stewartville Loop

Following the Stewartville and Ridge trails past Star Mine and the Stewartville town site is like stepping back in time, when this area echoed with the clang of pick and shovel as eager miners tried to pry coal loose from the surrounding rocks. The Old West is evident here in other ways too, as you walk through grassy valleys dotted with grazing cows or contemplate sweeping vistas from high ridgetops. Parts of the route may be extremely muddy in wet weather.

Best Time

Fall through spring, but trails may be muddy in wet weather.

Finding the Trail

From Hwy. 4 in Antioch, take the Somersville Rd. exit and go south, staying in the left lane as you approach and pass Buchanan Rd. At 1.5 miles, follow Somersville Rd. as it continues straight, while the main road, here called James Donlon Blvd., bends sharply left. At 2.6 miles from Hwy. 4, you reach the entrance kiosk, park office, and emergency telephone; continue another 0.9 mile to a large parking area, right, with an overflow area, left.

Trail Description

From the south end of the parking area, ▶1 you pass a gate and continue uphill on the **Nortonville Trail**, a paved road, for about 200 feet to a level area and then a junction, left, with the **Stewartville Trail**, a

TRAIL USE
Hike, Run, Bike
LENGTH
7.6 miles, 4-6 hours
VERTICAL FEET
±1900'
DIFFICULTY
– 1 2 3 **4** 5 +
TRAIL TYPE
Loop
SURFACE TYPE
Dirt, Paved

FEATURES
Dogs Allowed
Mountain
Wildflowers
Birds
Camping
Secluded
Historic
Geologic Interest

FACILITIES
Restrooms
Picnic Tables
Water

Rose Hill Cemetery is the last resting place for some of the miners, their wives, and children, who came here in the 1860s hoping to strike it rich on coal—"black diamonds." The cemetery, well worth a visit, is a short climb from the parking area on the Nortonville Trail.

 **Geologic Interest**

dirt road. Turn left and begin walking uphill on a moderate grade that soon levels. Once through a cattle gate, you pass the Railroad Bed Trail, left.

Continue straight on the Stewartville Trail, climbing southeast to an obvious notch in the skyline. As you crest a ridge, you come to a junction with the Ridge Trail, right, just before you reach a barbed-wire fence with a cattle gate. From here your route, the Stewartville Trail, joined for a short distance by the Ridge Trail, continues straight through the gate. About 75 feet beyond the gate, you reach a T-junction.▶2 Here you turn left and head uphill on the moderate and then steep **Ridge Trail**, a dirt road, soon arriving at another ridgetop.

You turn east and follow the narrow ridgetop. Just past a pond you come to a junction, right, with the Corcoran Mine Trail. Here you stay on the Ridge Trail by bearing left. The route alternates between the north and south sides of a ridge.

You continue straight on the Ridge Trail and make a moderate and then steep descent to the **Stewartville Trail**▶3, a level, dirt-and-gravel road with sections of broken pavement. You turn right and follow this road as it swings right, turning the end of the ridge you just descended.

After walking almost a mile from the last junction, you pass a creek flowing under the road through a culvert, and come to a four-way junction, marked by a trail post, left.▶4 You turn left onto the **Star Mine Trail**, a dirt-and-gravel road with paved sections, and follow it through a cattle gate, across another culvert, and past **Star Mine group camp** (picnic tables, toilet), where the trail begins to climb on a gentle and then moderate grade.

Once past the campground, the road turns to dirt and soon descends. To the right of the road, look for the gated tunnel of **Star Mine**,▶5 one of the last coal mines in the area to shut down.

Hikers don hard hats *for a guided tour of one of the restored coal mine tunnels.*

Prospect Tunnel *entrance provides a cool contrast to the surrounding sun-baked hills.*

The route turns southwest, climbs through a rocky canyon, and levels out in a pine forest. You bear right at a fork, staying on the Star Mine Trail. Soon you reach one of the star attractions of this route, in addition to the mines—a manzanita forest.

The climbing is steep, but soon your route leaves the road, turns right, and descends on a single track, closed to bicycles and horses. Losing elevation via switchbacks, you reach a valley located east of the Stewartville town site. Here you pass through a wooden gate in a barbed-wire fence, and in about 75 feet reach a fork in the route. The left fork, a path through the grass, connects to the Lower Oil Canyon Trail. The right fork, your route, leads to a junction with the **Stewartville Trail**.

The route circles a wet area, climbs an embankment, and meets the Stewartville Trail, a dirt road.▶6 Turn left and go past a windmill, a cattle pen, and junctions with the Lower and Upper Oil Canyon

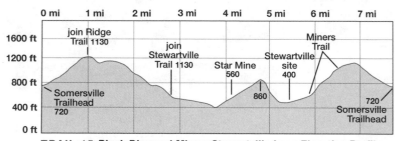

TRAIL 15 Black Diamond Mines: Stewartville Loop Elevation Profile

trails. You pass the **Stewartville backpack camp**, where a toilet is available. **Camping here is by reservation**; (510) 636-1684.

▲ Camping

Then walk through a grazing area, which may be flooded, to a junction marked by a trail post, right.▶7 This is the site of **Stewartville**, one of five mining towns that thrived in this area between the 1860s and the turn of the century. Here you turn sharply right on the **Miners Trail,**▶8 a single track closed to bicycles and horses, and begin a gentle climb. An old dirt road runs east–west here, across your route, but you continue uphill, steeply now, past mine tailings and the remnants of a wooden structure.

After crossing a small wooden bridge, you join the **Stewartville Trail** at the elbow of a sharp switchback.▶9 Bear right and continue to climb on a moderate grade. After making a switchback right, you pass a rest bench and reach a flat area where the Stewartville and Ridge trails meet. Turn left, go through the gate, and retrace your route to the parking area.▶10

🚶 **MILESTONES**

▶1 0.0 Take Nortonville Trail south, the left on Stewartville Trail

▶2 0.7 Left at T-junction on Ridge Trail

▶3 2.8 Right on Stewartville Trail

▶4 3.7 Trail to Prospect Tunnel on right; left on Star Mine Trail

▶5 4.2 Star Mine

▶6 5.3 Left on Stewartville Trail

▶7 5.5 Stewartville townsite and backpack camp

▶8 6.0 Right on Miners Trail

▶9 6.5 Right on Stewartville Trail

▶10 7.6 Back at parking area

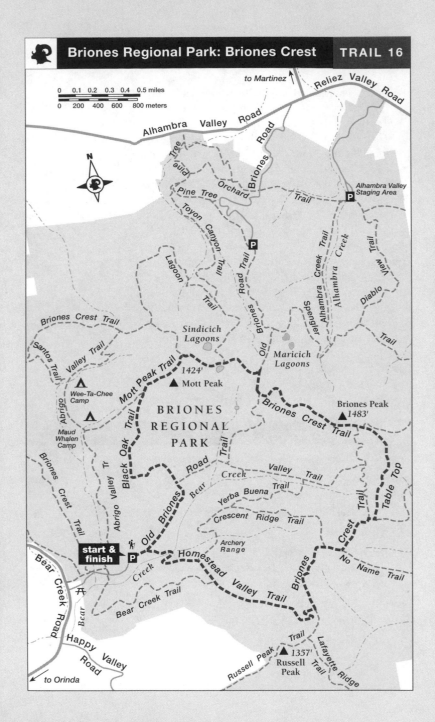

to Martinez

Reliez Valley Road

Alhambra Valley Road

0 0.1 0.2 0.3 0.4 0.5 miles

0 200 400 600 800 meters

N

Pine Tree Trail

Orchard Trail

Briones Road

Alhambra Valley Staging Area

P

Pine Tree Trail

Toyon Canyon Trail

P

Road Trail

Old Briones Road

Alhambra Creek Trail

Alhambra Creek

Diablo View Trail

Lagoon Trail

Briones Crest Trail

Valley Trail

Santos Trail

Sindicich Lagoons

Spengler

Maricich Lagoons

Trail

1424'
▲ Mott Peak

Mott Peak Trail

Wee-Ta-Chee Camp

Abrigo Valley Trail

Briones Crest Trail

Briones Peak
▲ 1483'

BRIONES
REGIONAL
PARK

Maud Whalen Camp

Black Oak Trail

Briones Crest Trail

Abrigo Valley Tr

Old Briones Road

Bear Creek

Valley Trail

Trail

Briones Crest Trail

Table Top

Yerba Buena Trail

Crescent Ridge Trail

Archery Range

start & finish
P

Homestead Valley Trail

Briones Crest Trail

No Name Trail

Bear Creek

Bear Creek Trail

Bear Creek Road

Happy Valley Road

to Orinda

Russell Peak Trail

1357'
▲ Russell Peak

Lafayette Ridge Trail

Briones Regional Park: Briones Crest

This rambling loop offers a great introduction to the southwest half of this expansive park, an area of rolling hills, high ridges, and forested canyons. The rewards for climbing along the Briones Crest include spring wildflowers and 360° views.

Best Time

Spring and fall; trails may be muddy in wet weather.

Finding the Trail

From Hwy. 24 in Orinda, take the Orinda Exit and go northwest 2.2 miles on Camino Pablo to Bear Creek Rd. Turn right and go 4.5 miles to the park's Bear Creek Valley entrance. Turn right, and after 0.3 mile reach the entrance kiosk; continue 0.1 mile to the last parking area. Fees for parking and dogs. The trailhead is at the end of the park entrance road, just past the last parking area. ▶1

Trail Description

Passing a trail post bearing the emblem of the **Ivan Dickson Memorial Loop**, you go through a gate and follow a paved road—the continuation of the park entrance road—east through a brushy area, soon reaching a fork and the end of pavement. ▶2 Here Old Briones Road, once the main route between Orinda and Martinez, heads left, and the **Homestead Valley Trail**, your route, goes right. You cross Bear Creek, then climb past a cattle gate and into the open. Reaching a junction with the Crescent

TRAIL USE
Hike, Run, Bike
LENGTH
6.8 miles, 4-6 hours
VERTICAL FEET
±1300'
DIFFICULTY
– 1 2 3 **4** 5 +
TRAIL TYPE
Loop
SURFACE TYPE
Dirt, Paved

FEATURES
Dogs Allowed
Summit
Lake
Wildflowers
Birds
Great Views
Photo Opportunity

FACILITIES
None

117

Ridge Trail, which goes straight, you turn right and continue on the Homestead Valley Trail.

The route re-enters forest and climbs moderately. Breaking into the open again and sweeping uphill on several sharp bends, you pass through a gate and reach the **Briones Crest Trail**.▶3 Turning left, you follow the rolling ridgecrest through a wooded area. The view east is of Walnut Creek and Mt. Diablo, beautifully set off by a foreground of rolling hills.

Now you meet a junction, left, with the Crescent Ridge Trail. Continuing straight, the trail stays in the open, on top of the world. When you reach a fork with the No Name Trail, right, bear left and descend past several cattle gates through a lush wildflower meadow. At the next junction, where the Briones Crest Trail veers left,▶4 go straight on the **Ivan Dickson Memorial Loop** to the **Table Top** and **Spengler trails**.

Where the Spengler Trail makes a hard right, you continue straight on the **Table Top Trail**, heading for the high ground around Briones Peak. A short, steep climb rewards you with great views, marred only by the large cable-television facility ahead.

When you come to a cattle gate and the next junction, continue straight and merge with the **Briones Crest Trail**,▶5 joining from the left. Beyond a small grove of oaks, just before the route begins to descend, you come upon two unsigned paths, one left, the other right. The right-hand path leads up to the summit of Briones Peak (1483'), where a rest bench and terrific views await you. Martinez, Benicia, the Carquinez Strait, and Suisun Bay, home to the mothball fleet of World War II ships are all in view.

After a well-deserved break, return to the main route, turn right, and continue northwest over rolling terrain to a T-junction with **Old Briones**

▲ **Summit**

Part of this scenic loop follows a route named for Ivan Dickson, a dedicated member of the Berkeley Hiking Club and park enthusiast who, upon his death in 1993 at age 95, left a surprise bequest of $500,000 to EBRPD.

Road.►6 Here you turn right. For the next 0.1 mile, the Briones Crest Trail and Old Briones Road are the same. At a junction,►7 you follow the Briones Crest Trail as it splits left.

Continue straight and uphill to a junction with the **Mott Peak Trail,**►8 a wide dirt road, where you turn left and climb toward a saddle just north of Mott Peak (1424'). At the next junction,►9 leave the Mott Peak Trail, right, and continue straight on the **Black Oak Trail**, following a roller-coaster ride past a connector to the Mott Peak Trail and then to the valley floor.

At a T-junction with **Old Briones Road,**►10 you turn right, crossing a tributary of Bear Creek. After passing through a cattle gate, you arrive at the junction with the Homestead Valley Trail. Bear right, now on pavement, and retrace your route to the parking area.►11

Sindicich lagoons are a breeding ground for thousands of California newts, which migrate here in early spring from hiding places in nearby forests.

🚶 MILESTONES

►1	0.0	Take paved road east
►2	0.2	Right on Homestead Valley Trail
►3	1.7	Left on Briones Crest Trail
►4	2.7	Left on Table Top Trail
►5	3.4	Merge with Briones Crest Trail; trail to Briones Peak on right
►6	4.2	Right at T-junction with Old Briones Rd.
►7	4.3	Left to stay on Briones Crest Trail
►8	4.8	Left on Mott Peak Trail
►9	5.2	Straight on Black Oak Trail
►10	6.1	Right at T-junction with Old Briones Rd.
►11	6.8	Back at parking area

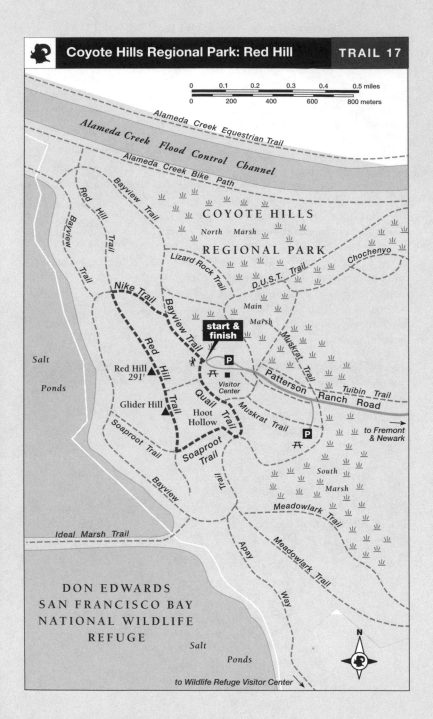

0   0.1   0.2   0.3   0.4   0.5 miles
0   200   400   600   800 meters

Alameda Creek Equestrian Trail

Alameda Creek Flood Control Channel

Alameda Creek Bike Path

Bayview Trail

Red Hill Trail

Bayview Trail

COYOTE HILLS

North Marsh

REGIONAL PARK

Lizard Rock Trail

D.U.S.T. Trail

Chochenyo

Nike Trail

Main Marsh

Muskrat Trail

start & finish

P

Salt

Ponds

Red Hill 291'

Red Hill Trail

Patterson Ranch Road

Tuibin Trail

Visitor Center

to Fremont & Newark

Glider Hill

Quail Trail

Hoot Hollow

Muskrat Trail

P

Soaproot Trail

Soaproot Trail

Bayview

Trail

South Marsh

Meadowlark Trail

Ideal Marsh Trail

Apay

Meadowlark Trail

DON EDWARDS
SAN FRANCISCO BAY
NATIONAL WILDLIFE
REFUGE

Way

Salt

Ponds

to Wildlife Refuge Visitor Center

N

Coyote Hills Regional Park: Red Hill

This short loop over the summits of Red and Glider hills offers more scenery per calorie expended than any other hike in the East Bay. Besides open summits, which provide 360° views that extend from San Francisco to the Santa Cruz Mountains, this park contains an extensive brackish marsh, habitat for waterfowl and shorebirds.

Best Time

This hike is enjoyable all year.

Finding the Trail

From Hwy. 84 at the east end of the Dumbarton Bridge in Fremont, take the Thornton Ave./Paseo Padre Pkwy. exit, and go north 1.1 miles on Paseo Padre Pkwy. to Patterson Ranch Rd. Turn left and go 0.5 mile to the entrance kiosk. Another 1.0 mile brings you to the parking area for the visitor center. Fees for parking and dogs.The trailhead is on the west end of parking area, at its entrance.

Trail Description

From the west end of the parking area►1 head northwest on the paved **Bayview Trail**, passing the Quail Trail, a dirt road, left. The Bayview Trail is gated just beyond the parking area. When you reach the **Nike Trail**, about 0.1 mile from the trailhead, you climb left, leaving the Bayview Trail. (The Nike Trail is named for the missiles perched atop these hills during the Cold War not for the running shoe.)

TRAIL USE
Hike, Run, Bike

LENGTH
1.5 miles, 1 hour

VERTICAL FEET
±350'

DIFFICULTY
− 1 **2** 3 4 5 +

TRAIL TYPE
Loop

SURFACE TYPE
Dirt

FEATURES
Dogs Allowed
Child Friendly
Summit
Lake
Wildflowers
Birds
Great Views
Photo Opportunity

FACILITIES
Visitor Center
Restrooms
Picnic Tables
Water

Hikers on Red Hill *overlook the Main Marsh, with the East Bay hills and Fremont on the distant horizon.*

Turning left at a four-way junction onto the **Red Hill Trail**,▶2 a dirt road, continue your ascent over open terrain. After a short, steep pitch just below the summit of **Red Hill**, you gain the summit itself.▶3 To the northwest is the faint outline of San Francisco, with the dark hulk of Mt. Tamalpais looming behind. Oakland is also in view, beyond Hayward, San Leandro, and Alameda. To the south, the vista extends past the Dumbarton Bridge and the Don Edwards San Francisco Bay National Wildlife Refuge, all the way to the Santa Cruz Mountains.

After crossing the level summit, you descend steeply to a saddle, then reach the top of **Glider Hill**, where the views equal those from Red Hill. The open, grassy summit even has a convenient picnic table.

Now a short, steep descent brings you to another saddle and a four-way junction. At this point, the Red Hill Trail, which continues straight, is crossed by the **Soaproot Trail**, a dirt road.▶4 Turn left and begin a gentle descent. Continue descending to a junction with the Bayview and Quail trails.▶5 Turn left onto the **Quail Trail**, a wide dirt-and-gravel road that climbs north. Just after the road crosses a rise, a single-track trail, right, offers you an easy side trip to Castle Rock, a jumble of pinnacles made from the same red chert as Red Hill.

Following the Quail Trail downhill, you pass the Hoot Hollow Trail, left, and the **Hoot Hollow picnic area**. Beyond the picnic area, you pass an unsigned path heading left up some wooden steps, and a paved path, right, that leads to the visitor center. About 200 feet downhill from these paths you reach a gate and the entrance to the parking area.▶6

The brackish Main Marsh is a haven for birds. Along the Bayview Trail you may see herons, egrets, ducks, and shore-birds.

🚶 MILESTONES

▶1   0.0   Take paved Bay View Trail east; left on Nike Trail
▶2   0.4   Left on Red Hill Trail
▶3   0.7   Red Hill summit
▶4   1.0   Left on Soaproot Trail
▶5   1.2   Left on Quail Trail
▶6   1.5   Back at parking area

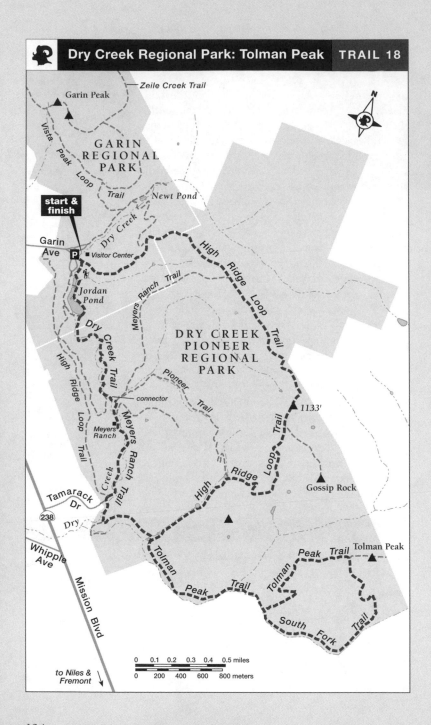

Zeile Creek Trail

Garin Peak

Vista Peak Loop Trail

GARIN REGIONAL PARK

Newt Pond

start & finish

Dry Creek

Garin Ave

P

Visitor Center

High Ridge Loop Trail

Jordan Pond

Dry Creek Trail

Meyers Ranch Trail

DRY CREEK PIONEER REGIONAL PARK

High Ridge Loop Trail

Pioneer Trail

connector

Meyers Ranch

Meyers Ranch Trail

1133'

Creek

Loop Trail

Tamarack Dr

238

Dry

High Ridge

Gossip Rock

Whipple Ave

Mission Blvd

Tolman Peak Trail

Tolman Peak

Peak Trail

Tolman

Peak

Trail

South Fork Trail

0   0.1   0.2   0.3   0.4   0.5 miles
0   200   400   600   800 meters

to Niles & Fremont

Dry Creek Pioneer Regional Park: Tolman Peak

This route explores a regional park gem—an oasis in the middle of one of the East Bay's most heavily industrial and residential areas. Scenery, views, and variety of habitat combine to make hiking to Tolman Peak more than just a challenging workout. Mileage and commitment, rather than steepness of terrain, earn for this hike its difficulty rating.

Best Time

Spring and fall; trails may be muddy in wet weather.

Finding the Trail

From Interstate 580 eastbound in Castro Valley, take the Hayward/Route 238 exit and follow signs for Hayward. From the first traffic light, continue straight, now on Foothill Blvd., for 1.7 miles to Mission Blvd, staying in the left lanes as you approach Mission Blvd. Bear left onto Mission Blvd. and go 3.5 miles to Garin Ave. Turn left and go 0.9 mile uphill to the entrance kiosk. At the kiosk bear right and proceed to parking areas; park in the lowest area if space is available.

From Interstate 580 westbound in Castro Valley, take the Strobridge exit and go 0.2 mile to the first stop sign. Turn right, go 0.1 mile to Castro Valley Blvd., and turn left. Follow Castro Valley Blvd. 0.5 mile to Foothill Blvd., turn left, and follow the directions above. Fees for parking and dogs when entrance kiosk is attended.

To find the trailhead from the northeast corner of the lower parking area, turn east and cross a creek

TRAIL USE
Hike, Run
LENGTH
9.6 miles, 4-6 hours
VERTICAL FEET
±1900'
DIFFICULTY
– 1 2 3 4 **5** +
TRAIL TYPE
Loop
SURFACE TYPE
Dirt

FEATURES
Dogs Allowed
Summit
Lake
Birds
Wildlife
Great Views
Secluded

FACILITIES
Visitor Center
Restrooms
Picnic Tables
Water
Phone

on a wooden bridge, then continue straight on a path into a picnic area. The route starts at the visitor center, a big red barn several hundred yards north.

Facilities

Visitor center; toilets; nearby you'll find picnic tables, water, phone.

Trail Description

From just south of the visitor center, you follow a dirt path heading east across a large meadow. When you come to a four-way junction with a gravel road,►1 continue straight and begin climbing the **High Ridge Loop Trail**, a dirt road. Soon the route levels, turns southeast, and then reaches a junction with the Meyers Ranch Trail, right.

Great Views

As you continue straight, a grand scene is revealed—San Francisco Bay National Wildlife Refuge, Coyote Hills, the Dumbarton and San Mateo bridges, Fremont, Newark, and Union City. A short climb to a notch between two low hills earns your first view of Mission Peak to the southeast, and the southern end of San Francisco Bay. Ahead is a junction with the Gossip Rock Trail, which goes left.►2 There is a rest bench here, but on a hot day you may want to walk the short distance to Gossip Rock and enjoy the shade of the large California bay laurel trees there.

Leaving the junction, the road descends through open grassland. Bear right at the next junction and continue steeply downhill. In a lovely valley, the Pioneer Trail departs right, and your route continues straight. At a T-junction,►3 the High Ridge Loop Trail turns right, but your route, the **Tolman Peak Trail**, goes left.

Turning left on a dirt-and-gravel road, you pass a stock pond and walk through Black Creek Valley.

Garin/Dry Creek visitor center, *in a restored barn, has displays of antique farm equipment and information about Hayward's ranching and farming history.*

Past a cattle pen, left, there is a place to sit and rest in a shady grove of eucalyptus. Beyond a gate, the route crosses a creek on a small bridge. Soon the Tolman Peak Trail turns left, but you continue straight on the dirt road you have been following, now called the **South Fork Trail.▶4** Just before reaching the regional park boundary, the South Fork Trail, now a single track, turns left and climbs across a steep hillside. Once out of the forest, the trail may be hard to spot: look for a line of matted grass.

As you begin to descend,▶5 look for a trail post with a sign for the **Tolman Peak Trail**. From here, a faint path leads right and uphill to Tolman Peak. (The 0.2-mile side trip to the very summit is fun but does

▲ Summit

not gain you any better views.) As you wind downhill on a moderate and then steep grade, you follow a small creek to a junction with the **South Fork Trail,**▶6 where you turn right and retrace your route through Black Creek Valley to the junction with the **High Ridge Loop Trail.**▶7

Now you continue straight, climbing on a gentle grade. Soon an unsigned road heads left, but you turn sharply right and descend to a fork. Here a dirt road goes left to a fence at the end of Tamarack Dr., but you veer right toward a trail post.▶8 This trail post marks the junction of the High Ridge Loop Trail and the Meyers Ranch Trail. Here you get on the **Meyers Ranch Trail** by going straight and slightly downhill.

The Meyers Ranch Trail, a dirt road, crosses Dry Creek on small bridges several times as the route ducks in and out of trees. Soon you come to a sign for **Meyers Ranch;**▶9 here you will see antique farm equipment, rusted, lying in the grass to your right. Planted poplars and fruit trees show this was once a homestead.

After leaving the Meyers Ranch site, look for a trail post on your left indicating DRY CREEK TRAIL.▶10 Turn left and descend this narrow path; just ahead is a narrow wooden bridge over **Dry Creek**. Several hundred feet past the bridge is a T-junction with the **Dry Creek Trail**, a single track.▶11 Here you turn right, toward Jordan Pond and the visitor center. Along this trail you will see numbered markers for the park's self-guiding nature trail, a great excursion for children and parents. A booklet keyed to the numbers can be bought or borrowed at the visitor center.

Your route now winds through a shady area and crosses the creek on another wooden bridge. After traversing a low ridge, you come to a grove of bay trees. Here one branch of the trail leads straight to a horse crossing at the creek, but you turn left and cross the creek on a wooden bridge.

Once across the creek, turn right and, at a big rock, join the path coming from the horse crossing. In an open area, a path heads left and uphill, but you continue straight to a fork: right for horses, straight for hikers. Another bridge takes you over the creek, and soon, heading straight, you come to a T-junction at **Jordan Pond.▶12**

Here the High Ridge Loop Trail goes left, but you turn right and begin circling the pond on a dirt road, through an area of picnic benches and fire grates. As you near the end of the pond, you come to a fork in the route: bear right to return to the visitor center and parking area.▶13

🚶	MILESTONES	
▶1	0.0	Take dirt path southeast, across four-way junction, to High Ridge Loop Trail
▶2	2.1	Trail to Gossip Rock on left
▶3	3.5	Left at T-junction on Tolman Peak Trail
▶4	4.4	Right on South Fork Trail
▶5	5.7	Trail to Tolman Peak on right; go straight on Tolman Peak Trail (dirt road)
▶6	6.5	Right at junction with South Fork Trail
▶7	7.4	Straight on High Ridge Trail
▶8	7.9	Right on Meyers Ranch Trail
▶9	8.4	Meyers Ranch
▶10	8.5	Left on connector to Dry Creek Trail
▶11	8.6	Right at T-junction with Dry Creek Trail
▶12	9.3	Jordan Pond; right at T-junction, then right at fork
▶13	9.6	Back at visitor center

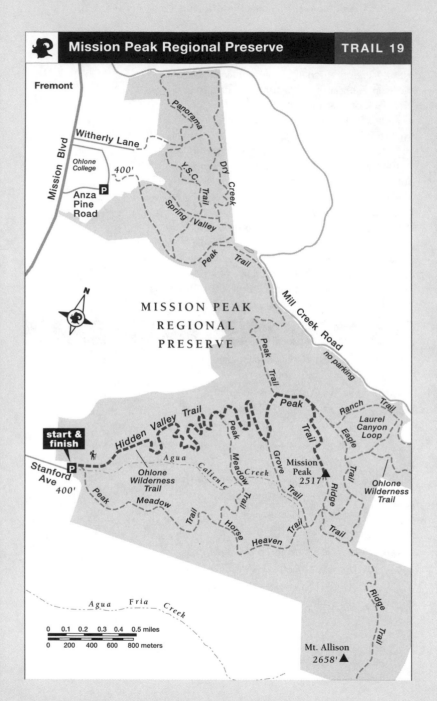

Fremont

Mission Blvd

Witherly Lane

Ohlone College

400'

Anza Pine Road

Panorama

Dry Creek

Y.S.C. Trail

Spring Valley

Peak Trail

MISSION PEAK
REGIONAL
PRESERVE

Mill Creek Road

no parking

N

Peak Trail

Peak Trail

Ranch Trail

Hidden Valley Trail

Peak

start & finish

Stanford Ave

400'

Ohlone Wilderness Trail

Agua

Caliente

Creek

Meadow Trail

Grove Trail

Mission Peak
2517'

Ridge

Eagle Trail

Laurel Canyon Loop

Ohlone Wilderness Trail

Peak

Meadow

Trail

Horse

Heaven

Trail

Trail

Ridge Trail

Agua Fria Creek

0   0.1 0.2 0.3 0.4 0.5 miles

0   200 400 600 800 meters

Mt. Allison
2658'

Mission Peak Regional Preserve: Mission Peak

A steady climb of more than 2000 feet in just over 3 miles, most of it on the Hidden Valley Trail, a well-graded dirt road, brings you to the top of Mission Peak, one of the East Bay's most dramatic summits, offering views of the entire Bay Area. Not a hike for hot weather, try to do this route just after a winter or spring storm, when the air is clear and the hills green. Even on a warm day, however, take extra clothes and a wind shell—this is a mountain environment which can quickly turn hostile.

Best Time

Fall through spring; pick a clear day with good visibility.

Finding the Trail

From Interstate 880 in Fremont, take the Mission Blvd./Warren Ave. exit and go northeast on Mission Blvd. 1.8 miles to Stanford Ave. Turn right and go 0.6 mile to a parking area at the end of Stanford Ave.

From Interstate 680 in Fremont, take the Mission Blvd./Warms Springs District exit and follow signs for Mission Blvd. eastbound. Once on Mission Blvd., follow it for 0.6 mile to Stanford Ave. Turn right and go 0.6 mile to the parking area at the end of Stanford Ave.

Trail Description

From the east side of the parking area, ▶1 the **Hidden Valley Trail**, a dirt road, heads uphill

---

TRAIL USE
Hike, Run, Bike
LENGTH
6.3 miles, 4 hours
VERTICAL FEET
±2250'
DIFFICULTY
– 1 2 3 4 **5** +
TRAIL TYPE
Out & Back
SURFACE TYPE
Dirt

FEATURES
Dogs Allowed
Summit
Birds
Great Views
Steep

FACILITIES
Restrooms
Water

▲ **Summit**

toward Mission Peak. After about 150 feet a dirt path branches left—there are gates across both routes. Once through the gates, the road and path run roughly parallel to each other, so you can take either one. If you follow the road, stay left at the first fork, a unsigned junction with the Peak Meadow Trail.►2 The road and the path soon rejoin, about 0.25 mile from the trailhead.

After about 0.3 mile, you reach an unsigned junction with a road heading right. Stay left and begin a gentle climb which soon becomes moderate. Right and downhill is the road coming up from the previous junction; it joins your route just past a gate, only to diverge again at the base of a rocky hill, where you stay left.

Your route passes through a wooded area, then bends south and continues to climb. You soon come to a short, steep section and then pass a junction with the Peak Meadow Trail, right. Now the road begins a series of switchbacks that will carry you to the summit. Ahead, the terrain around you becomes more rugged. You can see the park residence, a collection of several buildings used by EBRPD rangers, and looming above them to the southeast, Mt. Allison, bristling with communication towers.

Just below a band of cliffs you come to a T-junction. Your route, now a gravel road, turns left and—surprise!—climbs steeply toward the skyline ridge. Respite arrives, just as you crest the ridge, in the form of a broad, flat area. Several dirt paths head right, but you continue straight, getting your first view today of Mt. Diablo and Pleasanton Ridge. You pass through a gate in a barbed-wire fence and then reach a four-way junction where the Hidden Valley Trail ends. Here you turn right and follow the **Peak Trail.**►3

Ahead, to the east, the land drops away to the Alameda Creek drainage, then rises up on the other side to form the highlands of the Sunol/Ohlone

Hidden Valley Trail *ascends the west slope of Mission Peak.*

Wilderness. Soon you reach a fork in the route:▶4 left is the Eagle Trail, the continuation of the Ohlone Wilderness Regional/Bay Area Ridge Trails; right is your route, the continuation of the Peak Trail. Turn right and begin a gentle climb that soon turns steep, bringing you to the end of the road. From here, several dirt paths head southeast, steeply uphill to the summit of Mission Peak.▶5

Great Views

When you have finished enjoying this exhilarating and hard-won perch, retrace your route to the parking area.▶6

Some of the most notable landmarks visible from Mission Peak include Mt. Hamilton's Lick Observatory (4209'); Rose Peak (3817') in the Ohlone Wilderness; Flag Hill, behind the visitor center in Sunol Wilderness; Moffett Field in Mountain View; Mt. Tamalpais; San Francisco; and Coyote Hills Regional Park.

Regional Trails from Mission Peak

NOTE

The 28-mile **Ohlone Wilderness Regional Trail** passes through some of the East Bay's most scenic and remote territory. It starts at the Stanford Ave. parking area and follows your route up the west side of Mission Peak. From here it continues east to Sunol Wilderness, the Ohlone Wilderness, and Del Valle Regional Park near Livermore. The emblem for this trail, which you may see on trail posts here, is a white oak leaf in a red disk.

Near the summit, you join the **Bay Area Ridge Trail**, which runs north to Mission College and south to Ed R. Levin County Park.

MILESTONES

▶1   0.0   Take Hidden Valley Trail east
▶2   0.1   Left at junction with Peak Meadow Trail
▶3   2.5   Right at four-way junction with Peak Trail
▶4   2.7   Right at junction with Eagle Trail to stay on Peak Trail
▶5   3.15 Mission Peak summit
▶6   6.3   Retrace steps to parking area

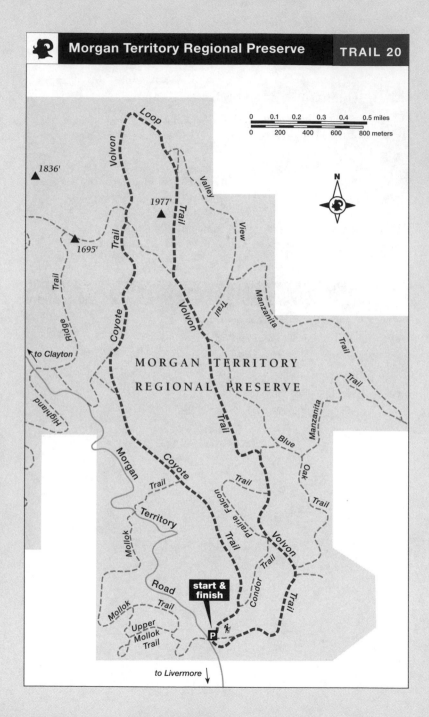

0   0.1   0.2   0.3   0.4   0.5 miles
0   200   400   600   800 meters

N

1836'

1977'

1695'

Loop

Volvon

Valley

View

Trail

Trail

Coyote

Manzanita

Trail

to Clayton

Ridge

Trail

Volvon

Trail

MORGAN TERRITORY

Highland

REGIONAL PRESERVE

Trail

Manzanita

Trail

Trail

Blue

Oak

Trail

Morgan

Coyote

Trail

Territory

Trail

Prairie Falcon

Trail

Mollok

Trail

Volvon

Condor Trail

Trail

Road

start & finish

Mollok

Trail

P

Upper

Mollok

Trail

to Livermore

Morgan Territory Regional Preserve: Bob Walker Ridge

This is one of the most remote and scenic parks in the East Bay, perched at 2000 feet on the southeastern edge of Mt. Diablo State Park, within sight of Livermore, Altamont Pass, and the Central Valley. Seclusion and wilderness make hiking here a special experience. This loop, which uses the Coyote, Volvon Loop, and Volvon trails, takes full advantage of these attributes, dropping into a deep canyon, then climbing lofty Bob Walker Ridge. This is a region of extremes: hot in summer, cold in winter, and potentially windy all year.

TRAIL USE
Hike, Run, Bike
LENGTH
5.9 miles, 4 hours
VERTICAL FEET
±1050'
DIFFICULTY
– 1 2 3 4 **5** +
TRAIL TYPE
Loop
SURFACE TYPE
Dirt

FEATURES
Dogs Allowed
Canyon
Autumn Colors
Birds
Great Views
Secluded

FACILITIES
Restrooms
Picnic Tables
Water

Best Time

Spring and fall

Finding the Trail

From Interstate 580 in Livermore, take the North Livermore exit and go north on North Livermore Ave., and then west on its continuation, Manning Rd. At 4.4 miles from the interstate, just after a sharp bend to the west, you turn right onto Morgan Territory Rd., and go 6.3 miles to the Volvon Staging Area, right. (Use caution: after 0.7 mile, Morgan Territory Rd. becomes a one-lane road with turnouts.)

From Marsh Creek Rd. in Clayton, turn right onto Morgan Territory Rd. and go southeast 9.4 miles to the Volvon Staging Area, left.

The trailhead is on the northeast edge of the parking area.

Trail Description

Morgan Territory's trail names are based on Native American history and tradition: Coyote is a mythic personality in Indian legends, and the Volvon were one of the East Bay groups that resisted the Spanish mission system.

As soon as you leave the large gravel parking area, you have a choice of two trails, Coyote and Volvon.▶1 Left is the Coyote Trail, a single track for hiking only; the Volvon Trail, a dirt road straight ahead, is open to hikers, horses, and bicycles.

Following the **Coyote Trail**, you descend to a stock pond, where you bear left, passing the Condor Trail. Beyond the pond, the trail, indistinct in places, descends through a narrow, rocky canyon. This is rugged terrain, colorful in fall, with a distinct wilderness feel. In the canyon bottom you pass a junction with the Mollok Trail, left.

Soon you come to a fork whose branches rejoin a short distance ahead at a gate. Passing through the gate, the route, sometimes just a matted path in the grass, stays in the middle of a large valley, and soon reaches another fork. This time, follow the right-hand branch and walk uphill. Ahead is T-junction with a dirt road.▶2 Here you turn right and climb north on a gentle and then moderate grade through oak savanna.

You are continuing on the Coyote Trail, and you will be on dirt roads until you return to the parking area. A trail, right, leads up Bob Walker Ridge to join the Volvon Trail.

You continue straight to a junction,▶3 where your route, the **Volvon Loop Trail**, goes right. When you reach the north end of **Bob Walker Ridge**, the route bends sharply right, presenting a vista that stretches east to the Central Valley and, on a clear day, the Sierra. Bob Walker Ridge and the Bob Walker Regional Trail honor a photographer and environmentalist whose efforts on behalf of EBRPD from 1984 until his death in 1993 led to additional land acquisitions in Morgan Territory Regional Preserve and Pleasanton Ridge Regional Park.

Now heading southeast, you pass on your left

 Great Views

the first of three connections to the Valley View Trail,▶4 the first two about 0.1 mile apart, the third about 0.8 mile farther along. Just ahead on the right is a good place for a picnic, with rocks to sit on.

Soon you reach a notch in the ridge, and a trail leading right and downhill to the Coyote Trail. Continuing straight, now on the **Volvon Trail**, you pass the Valley View and Blue Oak trails, left. Where the Hummingbird Trail goes straight, you follow the Volvon Trail sharply right.▶5 Soon you pass two junctions, about 0.2 mile apart, with the Prairie Falcon Trail, right. Just beyond the second of these is a junction with the Condor Trail, also right.

When you reach the second junction with the Blue Oak Trail,▶6 follow the Volvon Trail as it veers right, and in about 150 feet you come to a T-junction with a dirt-and-gravel road.▶7 Turn right here and begin an easy descent through open grassland. When you reach a fork,▶8 stay right and follow the gently rolling road until you can see the parking area. Bear left at the next fork and make a circuitous but moderate descent to the parking area.▶9

大	MILESTONES	
▶1	0.0	Left on Coyote Trail
▶2	1.6	Right at T-junction to stay on Coyote Trail
▶3	2.3	Right at T-junction on Volvon Loop Trail
▶4	3.5	Straight on Volvon Trail
▶5	4.5	Right at junction with Hummingbird Trail to stay on Volvon Trail
▶6	5.2	2nd junction with Blue Oak Trail; stay on Volvon Trail by veering right, then right again at T-junction with dirt-and-gravel road
▶7	5.5	Right at fork to stay on Volvon Trail
▶8	5.7	Left on single-track trail
▶9	5.9	Back at parking area

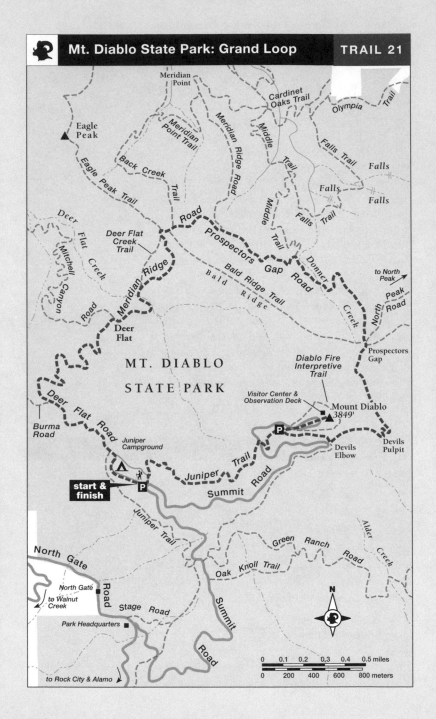

Meridian
Point

Cardinet
Oaks Trail

Olympia   Trail

Eagle
Peak

Meridian
Point Trail

Meridian
Ridge
Road

Middle
Trail

Falls Trail

Falls

Back Creek
Trail

Eagle Peak Trail

Road

Middle
Trail

Falls

Falls
Trail

Falls

Deer
Flat
Creek

Deer Flat
Creek
Trail

Prospectors
Gap
Road

Donner

Bald Ridge Trail

to North
Peak

Mitchell
Canyon

Meridian Ridge

Bald   Ridge

Creek

North
Peak
Road

Road

Deer
Flat

MT. DIABLO
STATE PARK

Diablo Fire
Interpretive
Trail

Prospectors
Gap

Burma
Road

Deer   Flat   Road

Visitor Center &
Observation Deck

Mount Diablo
3849'

Devils
Pulpit

Juniper
Campground

Juniper   Trail

Road

P

Devils
Elbow

start &
finish

P

Summit

Juniper Trail

North Gate

Green   Ranch   Road

Alder
Creek

Oak   Knoll Trail

North Gate
to Walnut
Creek

Road

Stage   Road

Summit

N

Park Headquarters

Road

to Rock City & Alamo

| 0 | 0.1 | 0.2 | 0.3 | 0.4 | 0.5 miles |

| 0 | 200 | 400 | 600 | 800 meters |

Mt. Diablo State Park: Grand Loop

A complete circle around Mt. Diablo, the East Bay's tallest peak, plus a trip to the summit, make this one of the region's premier hikes, and a great way to learn more about the trees, shrubs, and wildflowers that struggle for survival on the rugged mountain's upper reaches. This strenuous route uses Deer Flat, Meridian Ridge, and Prospectors Gap roads, and the North Peak, Summit, and Juniper trails.

Best Time

Fall through spring, but trails may be muddy in wet weather.

Finding the Trail

From Interstate 680 in Danville, take the Diablo Rd./Danville exit and follow Diablo Rd. 3 miles east to Mt. Diablo Scenic Blvd. Turn left onto Mt. Diablo Scenic Blvd.—which soon becomes South Gate Rd.—and go 3.7 miles to the South Gate entrance station. Continue on South Gate Rd. another 3.2 miles to Park Headquarters and a junction with North Gate and Summit roads. Turn right onto Summit Rd. and go 2.3 miles to Diablo Valley Overlook, a large parking area at a sharp bend in the road, just above Juniper Campground. The trailhead is on the north end of Diablo Valley Overlook.

Trail Description

From the north end of the parking area, ▶1 follow either of two paved roads downhill into the Juniper

TRAIL USE
Hike, Run
LENGTH
6.5 miles, 4 hours
VERTICAL FEET
±2200'
DIFFICULTY
– 1 2 3 4 **5** +
TRAIL TYPE
Loop
SURFACE TYPE
Dirt, Paved

FEATURES
Mountain
Summit
Wildflowers
Birds
Great Views
Photo Opportunity
Camping
Historic

FACILITIES
Visitor Center (summit)
Picnic Tables
Water
Restrooms

Stop a moment in Deer Flat, one of the prettiest spots on Mt. Diablo.

Campground. From the point where they join,►2 continue walking northwest on a gated dirt road, signed as **Mitchell Canyon Road** but called **Deer Flat Road** on the Mt. Diablo State Park trail map.

Passing Burma Road, left, you continue straight and then bear right as the road descends via well-graded S-bends, giving you a look at Mt. Diablo's 3849-foot summit, your goal. The road levels out in a little valley named **Deer Flat**, one of the prettiest spots on Mt. Diablo, especially in fall when bigleaf maple, California wild grape, and poison oak add touches of color to the scene. Soon you come to a junction►3 marking the end of Deer Flat Road. Here, Mitchell Canyon Road goes left, but your route, **Meridian Ridge Road**, turns right and heads for Murchio Gap.

Descending on a gentle grade from Deer Flat, the route turns north and begins to climb as it skirts **Bald Ridge**. With the grade now steep, you pass Deer Flat Creek Trail, left. A relentless climb in the open brings you to **Murchio Gap,**►4 an important junction with many trails. Clockwise from the left as you face north, they are Deer Flat Creek Trail, Eagle Peak Trail, Back Creek Trail, Meridian Ridge Road, and Bald Ridge Trail.

You follow **Meridian Ridge Road** east and gently downhill to a junction.►5 Here Meridian Ridge Road turns left, but your route, **Prospectors Gap Road**, goes straight. Where the Middle Trail joins from the left, near Big Spring, you descend slightly to within earshot of Donner Creek. Now comes a steep, rocky climb as you struggle toward

Variations on The Grand Loop

OPTIONS

For variation, use the Bald Ridge Trail instead of taking the Meridian Ridge and Prospectors Gap roads to get from Murchio Gap to Prospectors Gap.

Summit Museum

The stone building at the summit houses the Mount Diablo Interpretive association visitor center. It was created to hold information on the mountain's geology, flora and fauna. Unfortunately, at press time the center was closed because of budget constraints, with no reopening date set. Restrooms and water are still available, and you can climb to the observation deck for spectacular 360° views.

Prospectors Gap. A final pitch brings you, with relief, to **Prospectors Gap.►6** From here, Prospectors Gap Road drops steeply in front of you; North Peak Road heads left to North Peak; and your route, the **North Peak Trail**, goes uphill and right.

The trail, rutted and rocky in places, climbs across an open hillside and soon merges with an unsigned trail, right. As you switchback across a ridge, you are rewarded with a stunning 180° view, which takes in the west Delta, the Central Valley, Livermore, Pleasanton, the Sunol/Ohlone Wilderness, and Mission Peak.

Great Views

Now the route turns west toward Devils Elbow, a sharp bend in Summit Road. From here you can see the Summit Museum and communication towers on Mt. Diablo's summit. As you reach pavement at **Devils Elbow,►7** turn sharply right and begin climbing the **Summit Trail**, which rises through chaparral to the summit's lower parking area.►8 To reach Mount Diablo's 3849-foot summit from the lower parking area, turn right and follow either of two paved roads about 0.2 mile uphill.►9

> Looking west across Pine Canyon, you have expansive views of the hills of Oakland and Berkeley, with Mt. Tamalpais in distant Marin County visible on a clear day.

After resting and enjoying the scenery, retrace your steps to the lower parking area,►10 then continue walking west across pavement until you find a trail post marking the Juniper Trail, a single track heading downhill from the edge of the parking area. From here, make a steep, rugged descent on loose dirt, rocks, and railroad ties to Summit Road. Cross carefully, turn right, and walk uphill a short distance to a trail post, left, marking the continuation of the Juniper Trail.

You drop via a series of switchbacks and then continue to descend along the crest of a broad ridge, with a sea of chaparral on both sides of the trail. As the route flattens out at a saddle, you come to a junction with a trail to Moses Rock Ridge. A trail post with an arrow pointing left directs you to the continuation of the **Juniper Trail**, which descends through groves of bay and juniper to the parking area.►11

TRAIL 21 Mt. Diablo: Grand Loop Elevation Profile

🚶 MILESTONES

▶1 0.0 Go northwest on paved road through Juniper Campground
▶2 0.3 Straight on Deer Flat Rd.
▶3 1.4 Deer Flat; right on Meridian Ridge Rd.
▶4 2.2 Murchio Gap; angle right to stay on Meridian Ridge Rd.
▶5 2.4 Straight on Prospectors Gap Rd.
▶6 3.5 Prospectors Gap; right on North Peak Trail
▶7 4.6 Devils Elbow; right on Summit Trail
▶8 4.8 Lower parking area; right on paved road
▶9 5.0 Mt. Diablo summit
▶10 5.3 West end of lower parking area; take Juniper Trail
▶11 6.5 Back to parking area

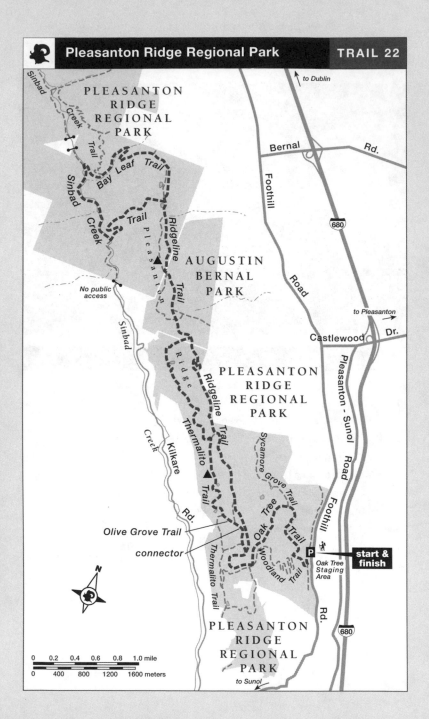

PLEASANTON
RIDGE
REGIONAL
PARK

Sinbad

Creek

Trail

Bay Leaf Trail

Sinbad

Creek

Trail

Pleasanton

Ridgeline Trail

No public
access

Sinbad

AUGUSTIN
BERNAL
PARK

to Dublin

Bernal   Rd.

Foothill

680

Road

to Pleasanton

Castlewood   Dr.

Creek

Kilkare

Rd.

Ridge

Ridgeline Trail

Thermalito Trail

Olive Grove Trail
connector

Thermalito Trail

PLEASANTON
RIDGE
REGIONAL
PARK

Sycamore

Grove Trail

Oak Tree

Trail

Woodland Trail

Pleasanton - Sunol Road

Foothill

P Oak Tree
Staging
Area

start &
finish

Rd.

680

PLEASANTON
RIDGE
REGIONAL
PARK

N

to Sunol

| 0 | 0.2 | 0.4 | 0.6 | 0.8 | 1.0 mile |

| 0 | 400 | 800 | 1200 | 1600 meters |

Pleasanton Ridge Regional Park

The hike along Pleasanton Ridge, while one of the longest and most challenging in this guide, is also one of the most rewarding. The views are outstanding, extending from Pleasanton, San Ramon, and Mt. Diablo to Sunol Valley, the Sunol/Ohlone Wilderness, and Mission Peak. The terrain is varied: the route passes through dense woodland, open grassland, and even a restored olive orchard. Bird and plant life flourish in this relatively undeveloped park.

Best Time

Fall through spring, but trails may be muddy in wet weather.

Finding the Trail

From Interstate 680 in Pleasanton, take the Sunol Blvd./Castlewood Dr. exit and go southwest on Castlewood Dr., staying straight where Pleasanton-Sunol Rd. bends left. After 0.3 mile, you reach Foothill Rd.; turn left and go south 1.6 miles on Foothill Rd. to the Oak Tree Staging Area, right. The trailhead is on the west side of the first parking area.

Trail Description

After walking a short distance west from the parking area on a dirt road, you come to a cattle gate; once through, bear left at a junction▶1 and begin climbing moderately on the **Oak Tree Trail**, also a dirt road.

The route ascends on a winding, open course, crossing a stream. As the it turns west, you pass a

TRAIL USE
Hike, Run, Bike
LENGTH
12.3 miles, 6-8 hours
VERTICAL FEET
±3000'
DIFFICULTY
– 1 2 3 4 **5** +
TRAIL TYPE
Loop
SURFACE TYPE
Dirt

FEATURES
Dogs Allowed
Canyon
Summit
Stream
Wildflowers
Birds
Great Views
Photo Opportunity
Secluded

FACILITIES
Restrooms
Picnic Tables
Water

**Enjoy the view!
Mission Peak is south;
San Antonio
Reservoir, with the
Sunol/Ohlone
Wilderness behind it,
is southeast; and
heavily forested Sunol
Ridge, topped by a
single communication
tower, rises above
Kilkare Canyon and
Sinbad Creek to the
west.**

junction, right, with the Sycamore Grove Trail. The route completes a 180° bend and now heads south, passing a junction with a grass-covered road, left, which is closed to bicycles.

Soon you emerge from a wooded area and reach a four-way junction near a barbed-wire fence.▶2 The trail merging from your left is the Woodland Trail. Straight ahead, and staying left of the fence, is an unsigned dirt road. Your route, the Oak Tree Trail, turns right and goes through an opening in the fence. About 30 feet beyond the fence is a trail post, and a choice of three dirt paths. You choose the middle one, the **Ridgeline Trail**.

The Ridgeline Trail makes a 180° bend to gain the ridgetop, passing an unsigned path, right. Bending left, the route reaches a fork marked by a trail post. Here you stay on the Ridgeline Trail by bearing right, heading generally northwest, and climbing past the olive grove on a moderate grade. Just beyond the grove is a drinking faucet, a watering trough for animals, and another fork, where you continue straight.

Rising steeply over rocky ground, your route eventually levels and comes into the open. Now you pass a junction with the Olive Grove Trail merging sharply from the left. Along the ridgetop, you climb over several high points, the first of which is just ahead. There is a picnic table atop one of these rounded summits.

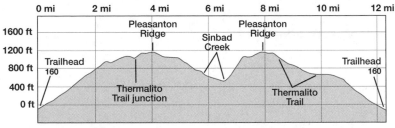

TRAIL 22 Pleasanton Ridge Open Space Preserve Elevation Profile

Soon you descend to a flat spot and a four-way junction. Your route continues straight, then bends right and climbs steeply to the summit of a grassy hill.

Continuing on the Ridgeline Trail, you climb steeply over several more hills. Finally, the route leaves the ridgetop, veering right and downhill through a cattle gate, then descends on a rutted and rocky road, soon entering the city of Pleasanton's **Augustin Bernal Park**. Now out of dense forest, you drop to a flat spot, which may be muddy, and a junction with the Thermalito Trail, a dirt road, left.▶3 There are drinking water and a trough for animals a short distance down the Thermalito Trail.

The Ridgeline Trail begins a moderate ascent, and soon the Valley View Trail merges from the right. (An equestrian trail departs left, just before the merge.) Ahead is a gate, marking the boundary between the city and regional parks. Beyond the gate is a junction: your route turns right and leads you through a beautiful oak savanna, with a fence marking the park boundary on your right. After a mostly level walk you merge with the dirt road and begin to gain elevation.

As the route breaks into the open, you pass a pond, left, and a junction with the Sinbad Creek Trail, left, part of your return route.▶4 For now continue straight, passing another small pond. At a junction near the park boundary, you go straight on the **Bay Leaf Trail**,▶5 then bend left and begin to descend. Soon the route turns sharply right and drops into a ravine on a moderate grade.

A Shorter Loop

An easier, 7.2-mile loop can be made by using the route description above but omitting the excursion on the Ridgeline, Bay Leaf, and Sinbad Creek trails ▶3-▶9; turn left at the junction of the Ridgeline and Thermalito trails.

The view south from Pleasanton Ridge *includes Mission and Monument Peaks (right).*

Now the route crosses two creeks that flow under the road through culverts. After an open section, you reach a junction right, with the single-track Sinbad Creek Trail.▶6 Your route follows the road, now also named the **Sinbad Creek Trail**, downhill. You soon reach **Sinbad Creek** at the bottom of **Kilkare Canyon**.▶7 Step across the creek on rocks and, at a T-junction with a dirt road, turn left. After a pleasant streamside stroll, you reach another T-junction,▶8 where you turn left, recross the creek, and begin climbing steeply out of the canyon on the Sinbad Creek Trail, a dirt road.

Passing a dirt road, left, you soon come to a T-junction with the **Ridgeline Trail**.▶9 Turn right on the Ridgeline Trail and retrace your route to the junction of the Ridgeline and Thermalito trails. When you reach that junction,▶10 turn right on the **Thermalito Trail**, a dirt road, and begin a moderate climb.

Now the route roller-coasters over rocky ground to a T-junction,▶11 where you stay right on the Thermalito Trail. Out in the open now, the road descends past a stock pond to a small ravine, which may hold water during wet weather. Crossing to the other side of the ravine, the route climbs slightly, bringing you to another pond, right, and a junction.▶12 Leaving the Thermalito Trail as it turns right, you continue straight on a **connector** to the Olive Grove Trail. Walking east about 100 yards, you get on the **Olive Grove Trail**▶13 by going straight. At the next junction, where the Olive Grove Trail swings right, go straight on a **connector** to the Ridgeline Trail.▶14 At the junction with the **Ridgeline Trail,**▶15 bear right and retrace your route to the parking area.▶16

Where there are oaks in the East Bay you are likely to find acorn woodpeckers.

🚶 MILESTONES

▶1	0.0	Take dirt road west to junction with Oak Tree Trail; turn left
▶2	1.3	Right at four-way junction to stay on Oak Tree Trail, then straight on Ridgeline Trail (middle of three dirt paths)
▶3	3.4	Thermalito Trail on left; go straight
▶4	4.5	Sinbad Creek Trail on left; go straight
▶5	4.9	Straight on Bay Leaf Trail
▶6	5.7	Straight on Sinbad Creek Trail (dirt road)
▶7	5.8	Cross Sinbad Creek, then left at T-junction to stay on Sinbad Creek Trail
▶8	6.5	Left at T-junction, cross creek to stay on Sinbad Creek Trail
▶9	7.4	Right at T-junction with Ridgeline Trail
▶10	8.5	Right on Thermalito Trail
▶11	9.8	Right at T-junction to stay on Thermalito Trail
▶12	10.5	Straight on connector to Olive Grove Trail
▶13	10.6	Straight on Olive Grove Trail
▶14	10.7	Straight on connector to Ridgeline Trail
▶15	10.8	Right on Ridgeline Trail, then follow Oak Tree Trail
▶16	12.3	Back at parking area

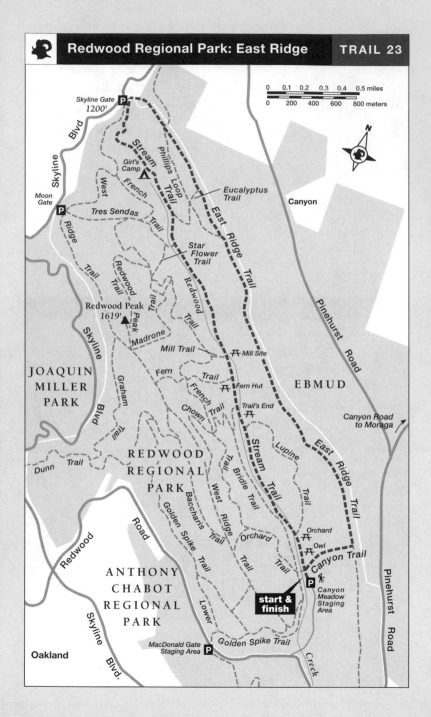

Skyline Gate
1200'

Skyline Blvd

Girl's Camp

West

French

Stream

Phillips Loop Trail

Eucalyptus Trail

Canyon

East Ridge Trail

Moon Gate

Tres Sendas

Ridge

Trail

Star Flower Trail

Redwood Trail

Redwood Peak 1619'

Redwood

Peak

Trail

Mill Trail

Mill Site

Madrone

Fern

Trail

Fern Hut

EBMUD

Skyline

Blvd

Graham

Trail

French Trail

Trail's End

JOAQUIN MILLER PARK

Chown

Pinehurst Road

Canyon Road to Moraga

Dunn   Trail

REDWOOD REGIONAL PARK

Stream Trail

Lupine

Trail

East Ridge Trail

Bridle Trail

Baccharis Trail

West Ridge

Trail

Orchard Trail

Orchard

Owl

Canyon Trail

Redwood

Golden Spike Trail

Trail

ANTHONY CHABOT REGIONAL PARK

Road

Lower

start & finish

Canyon Meadow Staging Area

Pinehurst Road

Oakland

Skyline Blvd.

MacDonald Gate Staging Area

Golden Spike Trail

Creek

N

0   0.1   0.2   0.3   0.4   0.5 miles
0   200   400   600   800 meters

Redwood Regional Park: East Ridge

This loop, using the East Ridge and Stream trails, pairs a vigorous hike along an exposed ridge with a secluded downhill ramble in the shade of tall redwoods, an unbeatable combination. Views from the East Ridge Trail, especially of the surrounding East Bay parklands, are superb, and the redwood forest along Redwood Creek, though merely a shadow of its former old-growth self, is nevertheless majestic. As an extra bonus, water is available not only at the trailhead, but also at Skyline Gate and various points along the Stream Trail.

TRAIL USE
Hike, Run
LENGTH
6.0 miles, 3-4 hours
VERTICAL FEET
±950'
DIFFICULTY
– 1 2 **3** 4 5 +
TRAIL TYPE
Loop
SURFACE TYPE
Dirt, Paved

FEATURES
Dogs Allowed
Stream
Birds
Great Views

FACILITIES
Restrooms
Picnic Tables
Water
Phone

Best Time

This trail is enjoyable all year.

Finding the Trail

From Interstate 580 southbound in Oakland, take the 35th Ave. exit, turn left and follow 35th Ave. east into the hills. After 0.8 mile 35th Ave. becomes Redwood Rd., and at 2.4 miles it crosses Skyline Blvd., where you stay in the left lane and go straight. At 4.6 miles from Interstate 580 you reach the park entrance; turn left and go 0.5 mile to the Canyon Meadow Staging Area.

From Interstate 580 northbound in Oakland, take the Warren Freeway/Berkeley/Hwy. 13 exit and go 0.9 mile to the Carson St./Redwood Rd. exit. From the stop sign at the end of the exit ramp, continue straight, now on Mountain Blvd., 0.2 mile, and bear right onto Redwood Rd. Go 3.2 miles to the park entrance; turn left and go 0.5 mile to the

Canyon Meadow Staging Area.

From Hwy. 13 southbound, take the Redwood Rd./Carson St. exit, turn left onto Redwood Rd. and follow the directions above.

Fees for parking and dogs when the entrance kiosk is attended. The trailhead is on the northwest end of the parking area.

Trail Description

The West Ridge Trail is the continuation of the East Bay Skyline/Bay Area Ridge Trail, and is open to bicycles all the way to Canyon Meadow, making a round trip on bicycle possible. From Skyline Gate to the Trail's End picnic area, the Stream Trail is closed to bicycles.

You head northwest, past a gate marked fire trail, on a paved path. Soon you reach a junction,►1 where a path heads left across Redwood Creek, but you turn right on the **Canyon Trail**, a dirt road. After a dirt road merges from the right, you climb on a moderate but well-shaded grade. Your route joins the **East Ridge Trail**, a wide dirt road, where you bear left.►2 The route follows a rolling course along the ridgeline, passing the Redwood Trail, right, and climbs to a rest bench.

Where Prince Road leads left and downhill, your route stays straight and climbs, soon reaching a fork with the Phillips Loop, left. Here you bear right, and continue climbing. Now heading through a corridor of pine, eucalyptus, and madrone, the route passes a junction with the Eucalyptus Trail, left, and begins to bend west. With the Skyline Gate parking area in view, you pass the Phillips Loop, left, and the **East Bay Skyline/Bay Area Ridge Trail**, right. Just before reaching the parking area, where water, toilets, a rest bench, and a phone are available, the route becomes paved. Ahead is a junction with the Stream and West Ridge trails.►3

Turn left on the **Stream Trail** and descend moderately to **Girls Camp**, a grassy meadow with picnic tables shaded by walnut trees.►4 Now on a gentle descent beside **Redwood Creek**, you pass the Eucalyptus Trail, left. Here the vegetation changes dramatically, and you now walk in a shady forest of

Second-growth redwoods *in Redwood Regional Park have gradually reclaimed hillsdes and canyons which were heavily logged in the 19th century.*

OPTIONS

More Trails in Redwood Regional Park

An alternate, more difficult loop of 7.7 miles can be made using the Stream, French, and Orchard trails. The French Trail and the West Ridge Trail (open to bikes) are part of the East Bay Skyline National Recreation Trail, a 31-mile route connecting Wildcat Canyon and Anthony Chabot regional parks.

magnificent redwoods growing straight and tall, towering overhead. A moderate descent soon brings you to a rest bench and a junction with the Tres Sendas Trail, right. In fall, thousands of breeding ladybugs cluster on the foliage near this junction, with others flying through the air, creating a fascinating spectacle.

⚑ Stream

You continue straight on the Stream Trail through deep forest, crossing several bridges over Redwood Creek. After a junction with Prince Road, left, you emerge briefly into an open area, then re-enter the redwood forest. Now you pass the Mill Trail, right, and two stone shelters at the **Mill Site** picnic area, left across the creek.

As you enjoy your level walk on the Stream Trail road, you pass a wooden bridge leading left across the creek, and the **Fern Hut** picnic area, right. Ahead the Fern Trail goes right, and another bridge crosses the creek. Continue straight past a junction with the Chown and Bridle trails, right, and another bridge over the creek. You reach pavement at the **Trail's End** picnic area,►5 and, after a short walk, leave the forest near the **Fern Dell** picnic area. A sign, right, points to the camper exit, used by drive-in camping groups, but you follow the paved road to the junction with the Canyon Trail; from there retrace your route to the parking area.►6

🚶 MILESTONES

►1	0.0	Take paved path northwest, then right on Canyon Trail
►2	0.4	Left on East Ridge Trail
►3	3.3	Skyline Gate; go left on Stream Trail
►4	3.7	Girls Camp
►5	5.2	Stream Trail becomes paved
►6	6.0	Junction with Canyon Trail, left; go straight to parking area

At the quarry overlook in *Sibley Volcanic Regional Preserve (Trail 24), hikers gaze east toward Mount Diablo.*

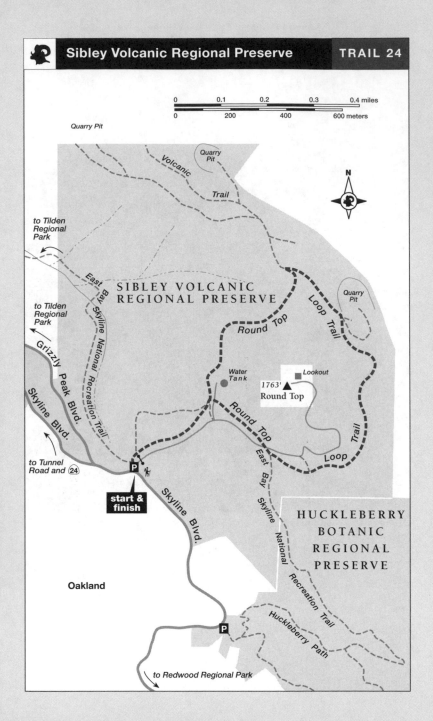

Sibley Volcanic Regional Preserve: Round Top Loop

This delightful loop circles Round Top, an extinct volcano and one of the highest peaks in the Oakland and Berkeley hills, and also provides access to a volcanic area that will be of interest to geology buffs. The preserve, named for Robert Sibley, director and president of EBRPD from 1948 to 1958, is one of the oldest East Bay regional parks. Originally called Roundtop, it was dedicated in 1936, just two years after the District was formed. The preserve was enlarged to its present size by additions of old Kaiser Sand and Gravel quarry sites.

The Sibley Volcanic Regional Preserve brochure and map, available free at the visitor center, has descriptions that correspond to numbered posts on the self-guiding Volcanic Trail. Because this is a short and easy hike, you may also have time to visit nearby Huckleberry Botanic Regional Preserve, just 0.4 mile south on Skyline Blvd.

Best Time

This trail is enjoyable all year

Finding the Trail

From Hwy. 24 just east of the Caldecott Tunnel, take the Fish Ranch Rd. exit and go uphill one mile to Grizzly Peak Blvd. Turn left and go 2.5 miles to Skyline Blvd. Turn left and go 0.1 mile to the preserve entrance, left. The trailhead is just west of the visitor center.

TRAIL USE
Hike, Run
LENGTH
1.6 miles, 1-2 hours
VERTICAL FEET
±400'
DIFFICULTY
− 1 **2** 3 4 5 +
TRAIL TYPE
Loop
SURFACE TYPE
Dirt

FEATURES
Dogs Allowed
Child Friendly
Birds
Great Views
Geologic Interest

FACILITIES
Visitor Center
Restrooms
Water

Facilities

The visitor center has exhibits explaining the area's volcanic past, as well as its plant and wildlife communities.

Trail Description

Bear left around the west side of the visitor center on a paved road.▶1 At a junction just past the center and just before a gate across the road, turn right and climb through a wooded area. You contour along a steep embankment to a junction, left, with a trail that leads back to the visitor center. In another 100 feet or so, you reach a four-way junction, marked by a trail post, where you turn left onto a wide dirt-and-gravel road that heads north and then northeast into the volcanic area.

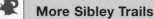
Geologic Interest

A mostly level walk over rocky ground takes you around the west and north sides of Round Top to a T-junction, where the Volcanic Trail heads left, and the **Round Top Loop Trail** continues right. Turning right and walking uphill, still on a dirt road, you soon come to a wonderful **viewpoint** above a quarry pit,▶2 with Mt. Diablo looming on the eastern skyline. Quarry

More Sibley Trails

OPTIONS

The self-guiding **Volcanic Trail** has numbered posts that are keyed to descriptions in The Sibley Volcanic Regional Preserve brochure and map, available free at the visitor center. Nearby **Huckleberry Botanic Regional Preserve**, just 0.4 mile south on Skyline Blvd., has a nature path with markers and an interpretive pamphlet available at the trailhead. The **East Bay Skyline National Recreation Trail**, a 31-mile route connecting Wildcat Canyon and Anthony Chabot regional parks, passes through Sibley Volcanic Regional Preserve.

operations here from the 1930s to the 1960s dug into the side of Round Top, exposing the basalt lava interior of the volcano, to the delight of geologists.

Just past the viewpoint, the continuation of the Round Top Loop Trail, here a dirt path, leaves the road, heads right and uphill, and makes a rising traverse across the grassy east side of Round Top. A side trail, left, offers access to another east-facing viewpoint. You descend to a cattle gate, curve right, and come to an open area. Ahead is an unsigned fork where you bear left.

The trail passes through a corridor of stately pines, reaching a junction, left, with the East Bay Skyline/Bay Area Ridge Trail, a route to Huckleberry Regional Preserve and Redwood Regional Park. Continue straight, and in about 125 feet, you arrive at Round Top Road. Cross the road and follow the Round Top Loop Trail across a paved road leading uphill to an EBMUD water tank. Just ahead is the four-way junction with the dirt-and-gravel road to the volcanic area. From this junction, continue straight—staying left at an upcoming fork—and retrace your route to the parking area.▶3

Because of its bulk and shape, Mt. Diablo could be mistaken for a volcano as well, but it is not, having been formed instead by a mass of rock pushing upward through sedimentary layers.

🚶 **MILESTONES**

▶1   0.0   Start
▶2   0.9   Quarry pit and viewpoint
▶3   1.6   Back at trailhead and visitor center

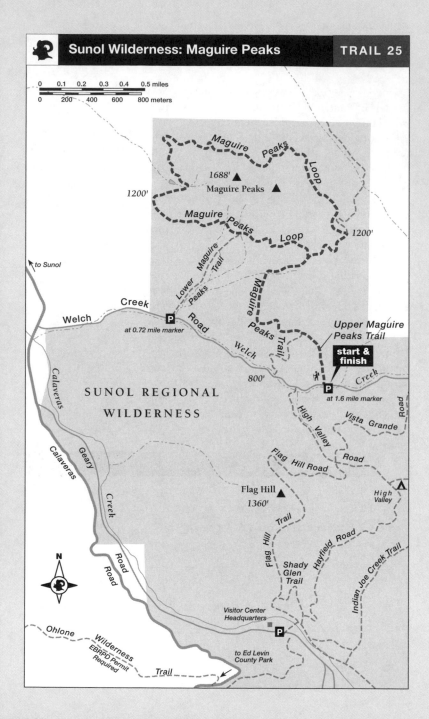

0   0.1   0.2   0.3   0.4   0.5 miles

0   200   400   600   800 meters

Maguire   Peaks   Loop

1688'

Maguire Peaks ▲

1200'

Maguire   Peaks   Loop

1200'

Lower   Maguire   Peaks   Trail

to Sunol

Creek

Welch   Road

P
at 0.72 mile marker

Maguire   Peaks   Trail

Upper Maguire
Peaks Trail

start &
finish

Welch

800'

Creek

P
at 1.6 mile marker

SUNOL REGIONAL

WILDERNESS

High   Valley

Vista   Grande

Road

Road

Calaveras

Flag   Hill Road   Road

Geary

Calaveras

Creek

Flag Hill ▲
1360'

High
Valley

Flag   Hill   Trail

Hayfield Road

Indian Joe Creek Trail

N

Road

Road

Shady
Glen
Trail

Visitor Center
Headquarters

P

Ohlone   Wilderness
EBRPD Permit
Required

Trail

to Ed Levin
County Park

Sunol Wilderness: Maguire Peaks

This circuit of Maguire Peaks explores a hidden corner of Sunol Wilderness, divided by Welch Creek Road from the main part of the park. The scenery is beautiful and serene, and the vistas from several vantage points are superb. Literally to top it off, you can make an ascent of Maguire Peaks west summit (1688′), a mountain climb in miniature. Parts of this route may be extremely muddy during wet weather.

Best Time

All year, but trails may be muddy in wet weather.

Finding the Trail

To park on Welch Creek Rd., you must have either a **parking permit**, available at the Sunol visitor center on Geary Rd., or a Regional Parks Foundation **membership card**: leave it on your dashboard.

From Interstate 680 southbound in Scotts Corner, take the Calaveras Rd. exit, and at a stop sign turn left onto Paloma Rd. Go back under I-680, stay in the left lane, and at the next stop sign continue straight, now on Calaveras Rd. Go south 3.9 miles to Welch Rd. Turn left and go to the 1.6 mile marker, where two turn-outs have space for about 6 to 8 cars total. The trailhead is on the north side of small parking area.

From Interstate 680 northbound in Scotts Corner, take the Calaveras Rd. exit, bear right onto Calaveras Rd., then follow directions above.

To reach the **Sunol visitor center**, proceed past Welch Creek Rd. another 0.3 mile, turn left on

---

TRAIL USE
Hike, Run, Bike
LENGTH
5.9 miles, 4 hours
VERTICAL FEET
±1950′
DIFFICULTY
− 1 2 **3** 4 5 +
TRAIL TYPE
Loop
SURFACE TYPE
Dirt

FEATURES
Permit Required
Dogs Allowed
Canyon
Summit
Wildflowers
Birds
Great Views
Secluded

FACILITIES
None

The taller of the two Maguire Peaks is the west peak (1688'), its grassy summit guarded by a rock rampart.

 Great Views

Geary Rd. and go 1.8 miles to the entrance kiosk. Then continue 0.1 mile to the visitor-center parking area, left. There are fees for parking and dogs.

Trail Description

From the parking area on Welch Creek Road,▶1 walk north down a small embankment and cross Welch Creek on rocks, finding a trail post and the **Upper Peaks Trail**, a single track heading north. About 50 feet past the trail post you step across a little tributary of Welch Creek, and then follow its left-hand bank upstream on a level grade. At a fork you bear left, away from the tributary, and begin to climb across a steep hillside on a generally northwest course.

Having gained elevation, you enter forest, then reach a clearing where you have a beautiful view north to Maguire Peaks, two rocky summits behind a foreground of rolling, grassy hills studded with oaks.

Now you follow an indistinct path, marked by metal trail posts, across grassland, to a T-junction with the **Maguire Peaks Trail**, a dirt road.▶2 A trail post here indicates a right turn for the Maguire Peaks Loop. Turning right, near the site of an old homestead, you follow the road bends sharply left and climbs moderately. As you turn a corner and head north, you again have a view of Maguire Peaks, both just under 1700 feet high. Now you begin to descend via moderately graded S-bends.

Reaching the bottom of a shady canyon, the route crosses a tributary of Welch Creek flowing

Biking Maguire Peaks

OPTIONS

Bicyclists should start from the visitor center and ride the Hayfield and High Valley roads to reach Welch Creek Rd., then follow the Maguire Peaks Trail to Maguire Peaks Loop.

Maguire Peaks *are a prominent landmark on the north edge of Sunol Regional Wilderness.*

through a culvert, and then begins to climb, soon coming to an unsigned junction where you continue straight. Leaving the dense forest behind and entering oak savanna, you arrive at a junction with the **Maguire Peaks Loop.▶3** Here you continue straight, still on an ascending dirt road, and after another 0.25 mile or so reach a junction, marked by a metal trail post with an arrow pointing left. Turn left, with Mt. Diablo just visible over hills to the north, and resume climbing.

The route, a dirt road, bends north, skirts the end of a ridge topped by the easternmost of the two Maguire Peaks, left, and then reaches level ground.

Circling around the north side of Maguire Peaks, you reach an open area where the view extends northwest to Pleasanton and Sunol ridges. The route climbs on a moderate grade, aiming for a flat spot in a ridge extending northwest from the west peak. The trail now turns left and follows the ridgetop toward Maguire Peaks.

To climb the west peak, just before the route turns right and begins to descend, find an unsigned path going straight and uphill,▶4 angling southeast up a steep hillside. After you gain the main ridge, staying well to the right of a severe drop-off, the grade eases. Soon you cross a rocky area, then tackle the final pitch up a grassy slope to the summit. A path leads across the summit to a 360° viewpoint.

Back on the Maguire Peaks Loop, you follow a winding course downhill, soon reaching level ground. Heading generally west, the route comes to the end of a long ridge, then bends around it to the south, crossing a culvert that drains a marshy area with a stock pond, right. Now you pass a junction with the Lower Maguire Peaks Trail, right. From here the route climbs gently to the junction of the Maguire Peaks Loop and the Maguire Peaks Trail.▶5 From here, turn right and retrace your route to the parking area.▶6

🚶 MILESTONES

▶1 0.0 Across Welch Creek, north on Upper Peaks Trail, bear left at fork
▶2 0.6 Right at T-junction with Maguire Peaks Trail
▶3 1.4 Straight on Maguire Peaks Loop
▶4 2.3 Unsigned path going southeast to west peak
       (out & back side trip)
▶5 4.5 Right on Maguire Peaks Trail
▶6 5.3 Straight on Upper Peaks Trail
▶7 5.9 Back at parking area

Kids and geese *meet at the Environmental Education Center in Tilden Regional Park, the starting point for Trail 26 (Wildcat Peak).*

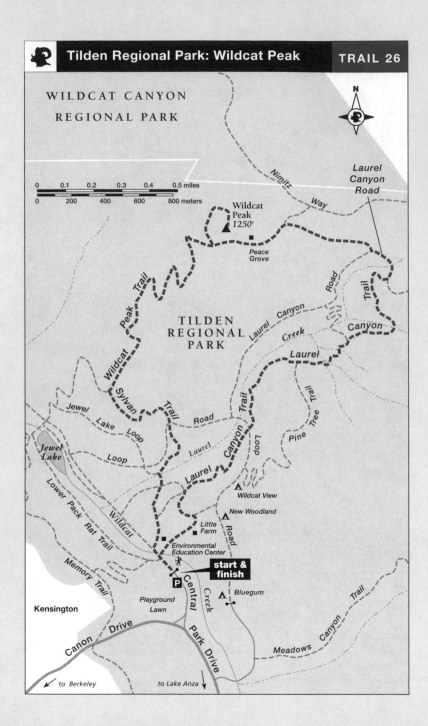

WILDCAT CANYON
REGIONAL PARK

N

Nimitz

Way

Laurel
Canyon
Road

0   0.1   0.2   0.3   0.4   0.5 miles
0   200   400   600   800 meters

Wildcat
Peak
1250'

Peace
Grove

Wildcat Peak Trail

TILDEN
REGIONAL
PARK

Laurel Canyon

Creek

Road

Trail

Canyon

Laurel

Sylvan

Trail

Jewel
Lake
Loop

Road

Laurel

Canyon Trail

Loop

Pine Tree Trail

Jewel
Lake

Loop

Lower Pack Rat Trail

Wildcat

Laurel

Wildcat View

New Woodland

Little
Farm

Memory Trail

Environmental
Education Center

Road

Kensington

start & finish

P

Playground
Lawn

Central

Creek

Bluegum

Park Drive

Canon Drive

Meadows

Canyon Trail

← to Berkeley

to Lake Anza ↓

Tilden Regional Park: Wildcat Peak

This scenic loop hike takes you from the Tilden Park Environmental Education Center to the summit of Wildcat Peak via the Jewel Lake, Sylvan, Peak and Laurel Canyon trails. Terrific views of the Bay Area and a variety of plants and birds keep this route interesting throughout. This route may be very muddy in wet weather.

TRAIL USE
Hike, Run
LENGTH
3.3 miles, 1-2 hours
VERTICAL FEET
±900'
DIFFICULTY
− 1 2 **3** 4 5 +
TRAIL TYPE
Loop
SURFACE TYPE
Dirt

FEATURES
Child Friendly
Canyon
Summit
Stream
Birds
Great Views

FACILITIES
Visitor Friend
Restrooms
Picnic Tables
Water
Phone

Best Time

All year, but trails may be muddy in wet weather.

Trail Approach

From Interstate 80 in Berkeley, take the University Ave. exit and go east 2.1 miles to Oxford St. Turn left and go 0.7 mile to Rose St. Turn right and go one block to Spruce St. Turn left and follow Spruce St. 1.8 miles to an intersection with Grizzly Peak Blvd. and Wildcat Canyon Rd. Cross the intersection and immediately turn left from Wildcat Canyon Dr. onto Canon Dr. There is a sign here for NATURE TRAIL, PONY RIDE, WILDCAT CANYON. Go downhill 0.3 mile to a junction with Central Park Dr. Turn left and go 0.1 mile to a large parking area.

The trailhead is behind the Environmental Education Center, which is a short walk north from the parking area on a paved path.

Trail Description

From the back deck of the **Environmental Education Center▶1** walk north across the lawn

Visible from the
summit of Wildcat
Peak are many Bay
Area landmarks,
including Mt.
Tamalpais, Mt. Diablo,
the Golden Gate
Bridge, Alcatraz and
Angel islands, and
San Pablo and
Briones reservoirs.

▲   Summit

and get on the **Jewel Lake Trail**, which you follow
for about 100 yards to a dirt road. Cross it and walk
about 50 yards on a wide dirt path until you come
to a trail post and a junction. Both the Jewel Lake
and Sylvan trails are left; the Laurel Canyon and
Pine Tree trails are right.

Turn left and continue on the Jewel Lake Trail as
it crosses two small streambeds on wooden planks,
and then a larger streambed on a wooden bridge.
Just after the bridge, you walk up a few wooden
steps and reach a junction.▶2 Turn right and follow
the **Sylvan Trail** as it climbs gently through forest.
Reaching Loop Road, you cross it and find the continuation of the Sylvan Trail heading northwest.
After about 0.5 mile you reach a junction and veer
right on the **Peak Trail**.▶3

In places the Peak Trail hugs a hillside that drops
steeply left. At a T-junction▶4 you turn left and
climb about 100 yards to the summit of **Wildcat
Peak** (1250'). East and below the summit is the
Rotary Peace Grove, a planting of giant sequoias.▶5
Because these trees are out of their habitat, they will
never attain giant status like their cousins in
Yosemite and Sequoia parks.

After spending time on the summit, retrace your
route to the last junction, then continue straight on
the **Peak Trail**, here a dirt road. Where a short connector to Nimitz Way goes left, you stay on the Peak
Trail, now a single track, After a short steep section
the route levels, takes you across an open hillside,
and then brings you via a few short switchbacks to
Laurel Canyon Road.▶6 You turn left on this road
and soon reach the start of the **Laurel Canyon
Trail**, a shady path that descends through a beautiful forested canyon.▶7

Turn right and carefully traverse the steep edge of Laurel Canyon. Soon you come to a small bridge that takes you across Laurel Creek to its south side. Now passing a trail to Laurel Canyon Road, right, you follow the Laurel Canyon Trail as it turns left and continues downhill on a moderate grade. Where the Pine Tree Trail heads left, you continue straight on a rolling course to **Loop Road.**▶8

Here you turn left and walk uphill. After about 100 feet, find the continuation of the **Laurel Canyon Trail**, marked by a trail post, heading right. Now you begin an easy descent through eucalyptus and coast live oak to a dirt road.▶9 Turn left and walk uphill, past an unsigned trail heading right. Just ahead is the fence at the corner of **Little Farm**. When you reach the fence, turn right and go about 0.2 mile downhill to the visitor center.▶10

Laurel Canyon Trail may be difficult in wet weather. For an alternate descent, turn right on Laurel Canyon Road, go downhill to Loop Road, and then follow the directions below.

🚶 MILESTONES

▶1 0.0 Take Jewel Lake Trail, then left to stay on it at junction with Laurel Canyon and Pine Tree trails
▶2 0.1 Right on Sylvan Trail
▶3 0.5 Right on Peak Trail
▶4 1.4 Left at T-junction to summit of Wildcat Peak (1250'), then retrace to previous junction and go straight on Peak Trail
▶5 1.6 Pass Rotary Peace Grove on left
▶6 1.9 Left on Laurel Canyon Rd.
▶7 2.0 Right on Laurel Canyon Trail
▶8 2.8 Left on Loop Rd., then right on Laurel Canyon Trail
▶9 3.1 Left on dirt road to Little Farm fence, then right
▶10 3.3 Back to visitor center

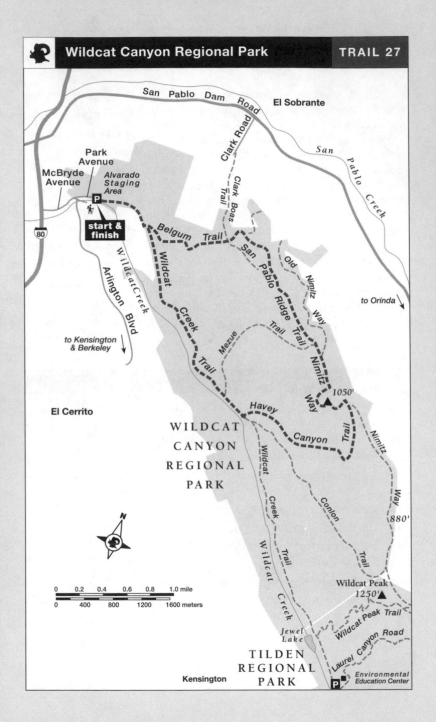

Wildcat Canyon Regional Park

TRAIL 27

San Pablo Dam Road

El Sobrante

Clark Road

San Pablo Creek

Park Avenue

McBryde Avenue

Alvarado Staging Area

Clark Boas Trail

start & finish

Belgum Trail

Wildcat Creek

Wildcat Creek

San Pablo Ridge Trail

Old Nimitz Way

to Orinda

Arlington Blvd

to Kensington & Berkeley

80

Mezue Trail

Nimitz Way

El Cerrito

1050'

Havey Canyon

Wildcat Canyon Trail

Nimitz Way

WILDCAT CANYON REGIONAL PARK

Wildcat Creek Trail

Conlon Trail

Nimitz Way

N

880'

0   0.2   0.4   0.6   0.8   1.0 mile
0   400   800   1200   1600 meters

Wildcat Creek Trail

Wildcat Peak 1250'

Wildcat Peak Trail

Jewel Lake

Laurel Canyon Road

TILDEN REGIONAL PARK

Kensington

Environmental Education Center

Wildcat Canyon Regional Park: San Pablo Ridge

This loop takes you from the lowlands of Wildcat Creek to the high, open slopes of San Pablo Ridge. You are rewarded for your efforts by some of the best views in the East Bay, including a 360° panorama from an old Nike missile site. Exposed to sun and wind for much of the way, this hike is best done when spring wildflowers bloom or after summer's heat has abated, when the hills are golden brown.

Best Time

Spring and fall; Havey Canyon closed to bikes and horses in wet weather.

Finding the Trail

From Interstate 80 eastbound in Richmond, take the Solano Ave. exit, which puts you on Amador St. Go 0.4 mile north to McBryde Ave. Turn right and follow McBryde Ave. 0.2 mile, staying in the left lane as you approach a stop sign. (Use caution at this intersection; traffic from the right does not stop.) Continue straight, now on Park Ave., for 0.1 mile to the Alvarado Staging Area, left.

From Interstate 80 westbound in San Pablo, take the McBryde Ave. exit, turn left onto McBryde, go over the freeway and follow the directions above from the intersection of McBryde and Amador.

You will find the trailhead at the east end of the parking area.

TRAIL USE
Hike, Run, Bike
LENGTH
7.0 miles, 3-4 hours
VERTICAL FEET
±1700'
DIFFICULTY
- 1 2 3 **4** 5 +
TRAIL TYPE
Loop
SURFACE TYPE
Dirt, paved

FEATURES
Dogs Allowed
Canyon
Summit
Stream
Wildflowers
Birds
Wildlife
Great Views
Photo Opportunity

FACILITIES
Restrooms
Picnic Tables
Water

Trail Description

Visit Wildcat Creek by turning right at the Mezue Trail junction and walking downhill about 100 yards on a dirt path.

The remnant of Wildcat Canyon Road, closed in the early 1980s by landslides, leads you east from the parking area.▶1 Renamed the **Wildcat Creek Trail**, the road, paved here but later dirt, runs southeast up the canyon to the Environmental Education Center in Tilden Regional Park.

As you climb gently, you pass the Belgum Trail, left,▶2 on which you will return. Continue straight, alternating on dirt and pavement, parallel to Wildcat Creek, right. Soon the pavement ends and you are walking on a dirt road between the tree-lined creek bed, right, and steep, open hills, left. At a junction with the Mezue Trail, left, are a drinking fountain and a watering trough for animals.

Your route continues straight, soon passing Rifle Range Road, right. Now you start to climb, arriving soon at a junction with the Havey Canyon and Conlon trails.▶3 Here you turn left up wooded **Havey Canyon**, following a tributary of Wildcat Creek, left. As the route abruptly breaks into the open, you see the open slopes of **San Pablo Ridge** rising ahead.

At the ridgetop, you reach a T-junction with **Nimitz Way**,▶4 a popular route shared by hikers, horseback riders, bicyclists, in-line skaters, and joggers. Turn left on this old paved road. You wind uphill on a gentle grade across hillsides decorated in spring by colorful wildflowers. When you reach a junction with a road heading right, take a few minutes to make the climb to an abandoned **Nike missile site**,▶5 a relic of the Cold War, that is

Trails from San Pablo Ridge

OPTIONS

Nimitz Way leads southeast to Tilden Regional Park, and from there you can use the East Bay Skyline/Bay Area Ridge Trail to connect to other regional parks along Skyline Blvd.

Wildcat Canyon Trail *ascends along Wildcat Creek to Tilden Regional Park.*

perched above. You will be rewarded with a rest bench, 360° views, and a chance to reflect on the fact that, for most people, Nike is a name no longer associated with the fear of nuclear war.

When the paved part of Nimitz Way ends, continue northwest on a dirt-and-gravel road, with San Pablo Reservoir to the right and far below. You come to a cattle pen and a choice of three dirt paths.▶6 The right-hand path is the continuation of Nimitz Way, heading downhill. The left-hand path is the Mezue Trail. The middle path, unnamed, rejoins the Mezue Trail just a few hundred feet ahead. Bear left on the **Mezue Trail**, and after about 100 yards or so, bear right at a fork,▶7 where the Mezue Trail heads left and the San Pablo Ridge Trail goes right.

Now the route climbs up and over a series of high points on San Pablo Ridge, then plunges steeply northwest to a junction with the **Belgum Trail**.▶8 Turning left on this dirt road, you soon pass the Clark-Boas Trail, right, and then an unsigned road, left. At an unsigned fork, you stay on the Belgum Trail by bearing left. The route now makes a well-graded descent via S-bends to a forest of coast live oak, bay, and eucalyptus, with a few palm trees thrown in for good measure. A paved section takes you to the junction with the **Wildcat Creek Trail**.▶9 Turn right and retrace your route to the parking area.▶10

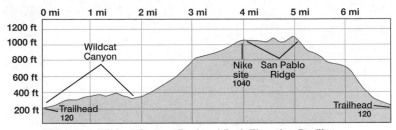

TRAIL 27 Wildcat Canyon Regional Park Elevation Profile

🚶 MILESTONES

- ►1　0.0　Take Wildcat Creek Trail (paved) east
- ►2　0.4　Belgum Trail on left; go straight
- ►3　2.1　Left on Havey Canyon Trail
- ►4　3.6　Left on Nimitz Way
- ►5　4.0　Road to Nike missile site on right
- ►6　4.4　Left on Mezue Way
- ►7　4.5　Right on San Pablo Ridge Trail
- ►8　5.7　Left on Belgum Trail
- ►9　6.6　Right on Wildcat Creek Trail
- ►10　7.0　Back at parking area

The view westward from San Pablo Ridge *takes in San Pablo Bay and the hills of Marin.*

CHAPTER 3

South Bay

South Bay

The South Bay, used here to mean that part of Santa Clara County near San Jose, includes not only California's third largest city but also some of the Bay Area's wildest terrain. Bordered by the Santa Cruz Mountains on the west, and the Diablo Range to the east, the broad and relatively flat Santa Clara Valley gives way dramatically on either side to chaparral-clad hills and then to forested slopes. Biologically rich and diverse, this is an area of extremes—summer temperatures here are often among the warmest in the Bay Area, but when cold winter storms arrive, the road to the University of California's Lick Observatory atop 4213-foot Mt. Hamilton may be closed by snow. Wildfires are not uncommon, especially in the Lexington Basin, which includes Sierra Azul, the southernmost preserve in the Midpeninsula Open Space District. Northern California's largest state park, Henry W. Coe, is nestled in rugged, remote country above Morgan Hill, southeast of San Jose.

Like other parts of the Bay Area, in the 1800s the South Bay saw an influx of people from all over the world, drawn by the fertile soil of the Santa Clara Valley, known as the "Valley of Heart's Delight," and the proximity to San Francisco Bay. The orchards and farms here provided an abundant harvest of fruits, nuts, vegetables, and grain. Loggers made camps in the rugged Santa Cruz Mountains and began cutting the plentiful coast redwoods that explorer John C. Frémont had noted when he camped near Los Gatos in 1846. Another extractive industry that left its mark on the South Bay was mining. At the New Almaden Mines, which operated from 1845 on into the 1970s and is today a county park, cinnabar ore was converted to mercury, an element used in the extraction of gold and silver from their ores. With the advent of the computer revolution, a new element, silicon, became the basis of the South Bay's economy and the reason for its rapid population growth.

Governing Agencies

The parks described in this chapter are managed by three government agencies. Henry W. Coe State Park has a map available for sale at the visitor center. Santa Clara County Parks has maps at its trailheads and downloadable maps on its Web site; these are also available by mail. Midpeninsula Regional Open Space District (MROSD) maps are available at its trailheads, by mail, and from its Web site. For contact information, see Appendix (p. 280).

Hikers amble along the Corral Trail in *Henry W. Coe State Park (Trail 30).*

South Bay

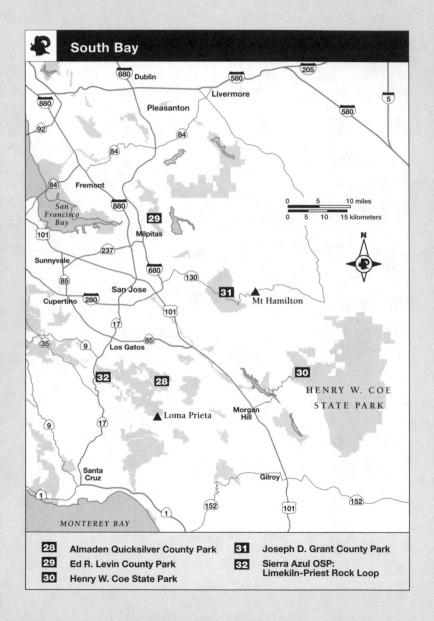

South Bay

680 Dublin 580 205 5

880 Livermore

92 Pleasanton 580

84

84

84 Fremont

San Francisco Bay 880 Milpitas 29

101

Sunnyvale 237

85 680 130

San Jose 31 ▲ Mt Hamilton

Cupertino 280

101

17

35 9 85

Los Gatos

32 28 30

HENRY W. COE STATE PARK

9 17 ▲ Loma Prieta Morgan Hill

Santa Cruz Gilroy

1 152 152

1 101

MONTEREY BAY

0 5 10 miles
0 5 10 15 kilometers

N

28	Almaden Quicksilver County Park	31	Joseph D. Grant County Park
29	Ed R. Levin County Park	32	Sierra Azul OSP: Limekiln-Priest Rock Loop
30	Henry W. Coe State Park		

TRAIL	Difficulty	Length	Type	USES & ACCESS	TERRAIN	FLORA & FAUNA	EXPOSURE	OTHER
28	5	7.0	Loop	Hiking, Trail Running, Dogs Allowed	Canyon, Summit, Stream	Birds	Great Views	Geologic Interest, Secluded, Historic
29	5	7.8	Loop	Hiking, Trail Running, Parking Fee (P)	Canyon, Summit, Stream	Birds, Wildlife	Great Views	
30	4	6.3	Loop	Hiking, Trail Running, Parking Fee (P)	Canyon, Stream	Wildflowers, Birds, Wildlife		Camping, Secluded, Historic
31	5	9.8	Loop	Hiking, Trail Running, Mountain Biking	Summit	Birds	Great Views	Camping, Secluded
32	3	5.2	Loop	Hiking, Trail Running, Mountain Biking, Dogs Allowed	Stream	Wildlife, Wildflowers, Birds	Great Views	Secluded, Historic

USE & ACCESS
- Hiking
- Trail Running
- Mountain Biking
- P — Parking Fee
- Permit
- Child Friendly
- Dogs Allowed
- Handicap Access
- Camping

TERRAIN
- Canyon
- Mountain
- Summit

WATER
- Stream
- Waterfall
- Beach
- Shore

FLORA & FAUNA
- Autumn Colors
- Wildflowers
- Birds
- Wildlife
- Tide Pools

DIFFICULTY
- 1 2 3 4 5 +
- less   more

OTHER
- Cool & Shady
- Great Views
- Photo Opportunity
- Secluded
- Historic
- Geologic Interest
- Moonlight Hiking
- Steep

South Bay

Bay trees *bloom in Spring with tiny, clustered, yellow blossoms.*

Joseph D. Grant County Park .... .203

Following a mostly rolling, ridgetop course, you enjoy views of the Diablo Range, crowned by nearby Mt Hamilton, and also the distant Santa Cruz Mountains. After visiting Antler Point, the trail dips to Deer Camp and then a marshy meadow, but soon resumes its quest of high places.

TRAIL 31

Hike, Run, Bike
9.8 miles, Loop
Difficulty: 1 2 3 4 **5**

Sierra Azul: Limekiln-Priest Rock .... .207

This loop visits the northwest corner of Sierra Azul, MROSD's largest, most remote preserve, called the Kennedy-Limekiln Area. Much of the journey is over serpentine soil, which gives rise to a fascinating community of shrubs and wildflowers. Early blooming shrubs, such as manzanita and currant, may add splashes of unexpected color as early as December, and bright red toyon berries attract numerous species of hungry songbirds.

TRAIL 32

Hike, Run, Bike
5.2 miles, Loop
Difficulty: 1 2 **3** 4 5

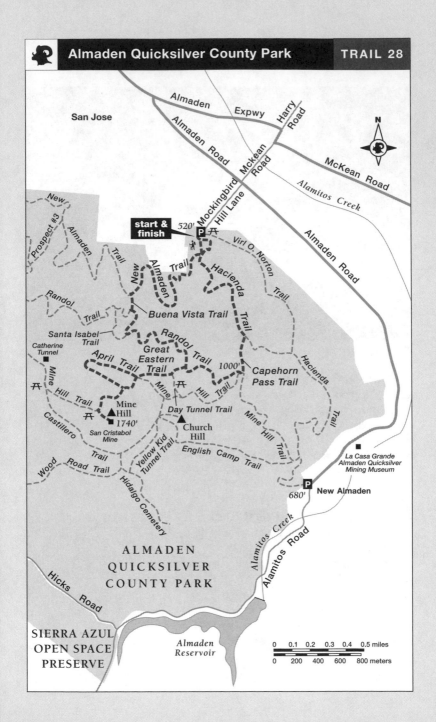

Almaden Quicksilver County Park   TRAIL 28

San Jose

Almaden Expwy
Harry Road
Almaden Road
McKean Road
McKean Road
Alamitos Creek

N

New
Prospect #3
Almaden Trail

Mockingbird Hill Lane

start & finish   520'
P

Virl O. Norton Trail

Almaden Road

Randol Trail

New Trail

Buena Vista Trail

Almaden Trail

Hacienda Trail

Santa Isabel Trail

Randol Trail

Great Eastern Trail

April Trail

Catherine Tunnel

Mine Hill Trail

Castillero Trail

Mine Hill Trail

Mine Trail

1000'

Capehorn Pass Trail

Hacienda Trail

Mine Hill

1740'

San Cristobal Mine

Day Tunnel Trail

Church Hill

Hill Trail

Mine Hill Trail

La Casa Grande Almaden Quicksilver Mining Museum

Wood Road Trail

Yellow Kid Tunnel Trail

Hidalgo Cemetery

English Camp Trail

New Almaden
P   680'

Hicks Road

ALMADEN QUICKSILVER COUNTY PARK

Alamitos Road

Alamitos Creek

SIERRA AZUL OPEN SPACE PRESERVE

Almaden Reservoir

0   0.1   0.2   0.3   0.4   0.5 miles
0   200   400   600   800 meters

Almaden Quicksilver County Park

Travel back in time on this strenuous route through one of the Bay Area's most famous mining areas, where at one time cinnabar ore was hauled out of the earth and converted to mercury in fiery brick furnaces. Today, oak woodlands, grasslands, and chaparral are the main attractions of this rugged and remote park.

Best Time

Fall through spring, but trails may be muddy in wet weather.

Trail Approach

From Hwy. 85 in San Jose, take the Almaden Expressway exit and go south 4.4 miles to Almaden Rd. Turn right, go 0.5 mile, then turn right on Mockingbird Hill Lane and go 0.4 mile to a paved parking area, left. The trailhead is on the south corner of the parking area.

Trail Description

A wide dirt path from the trailhead▶1 leads about 30 feet to a four-way junction. Here the New Almaden Trail goes straight, but you turn right on the **Hacienda Trail**. Soon another trail from the parking area joins from the right, and you begin climbing on a moderate and then steep grade.

After a short climb, you meet the New Almaden Trail, which crosses your route. You continue straight on a wide track that rises relentlessly and in

TRAIL USE
Hike, Run
LENGTH
7.0 miles, 4 hours
VERTICAL FEET
±1750'
DIFFICULTY
– 1 2 3 4 **5** +
TRAIL TYPE
Loop
SURFACE TYPE
Dirt

FEATURES
Dogs Allowed
Canyon
Summit
Stream
Birds
Great Views
Secluded
Steep
Historic
Geologic Interest

FACILITIES
Restrooms
Picnic Tables
Water

Mt. Umunhum, to the
southwest, was the
site of an Air Force
station during the
Cold War. You can still
see the concrete
building, used to
support a radar
system, on its summit.

places steeply. Finally you reach a flat spot, where a panorama stretches from the San Francisco Bay to Loma Prieta, the two-humped peak bristling with communication towers on the southern skyline.

Now you begin a roller-coaster ride that eventually subsides at a junction with the **Capehorn Pass Trail.**▶2 Turn right on this trail and descend. Soon you come to a junction with the **Randol Trail**, where you turn right.▶3

Piles of red rock beside the trail are mine tailings hauled out of nearby **Day Tunnel**, whose entrance is no longer visible. A picnic area is ahead on the left, beside a spring (non-potable water) surrounded by bigleaf maples, willows, and California bay trees. Just beyond the picnic area,▶4 the **Day Tunnel Trail**, veers left.

🚶 MILESTONES

▶1 0.0 Take dirt path south to four-way junction, then right on Hacienda Trail

▶2 1.2 Right on Capehorn Trail

▶3 1.5 Right on Randol Trail

▶4 2.0 Day Tunnel area, left on Day Tunnel Trail

▶5 2.3 Right on Great Eastern Trail

▶6 2.4 Right on April Trail

▶7 2.8 April Tunnel area

▶8 3.0 Right on Mine Hill Trail

▶9 3.4 Left on San Cristobal Trail to top of Mine Hill

▶10 3.5 Top of Mine Hill; retrace to junction of Mine Hill and April trails

▶11 4.0 Right to stay on Mine Hill Trail

▶12 4.2 Left on Great Eastern Trail, retrace to junction of Day Tunnel and Randol trails

▶13 4.6 Left on Randol Trail

▶14 5.5 Right on Buena Vista Trail

▶15 5.8 Right on New Almaden Trail

▶16 7.0 Back at parking area

Following this single track trail, you climb on a mostly moderate grade. At a junction with the **Great Eastern Trail**, unsigned, ▶5 you turn right and continue uphill on it to a T-junction with the **April Trail**. ▶6 Turning right on this dirt road, you descend gently, curve left, and then climb on a gentle grade.

Next you come to a replica of a building used to store explosives, called a powder house (The original, built in 1866, was destroyed by the 1989 Loma Prieta earthquake.) ▶7 When you reach the **Mine Hill Trail**, a dirt road, ▶8 turn sharply right and climb across a

Tailings piles *spill down the hillside below the mines, contrasting with the verdant hillsides.*

Several tunnels and mine shafts were dug in this area, including the April Tunnel, the Saint George Shaft, and the Victoria Shaft. Tailings mark the areas where these portals once provided entry to a dangerous, subterranean world.

forested hillside to a junction▶9 with the **San Cristobal Trail**, where you turn left. A picnic table atop **Mine Hill**▶10 commands a gorgeous view of San Jose, the Santa Clara Valley, and the summits of Mission and Monument peaks.

Now retrace your route to the junction of the Mine Hill and April trails.▶11 From here, follow the **Mine Hill Trail** as it curves right. Where the **Great Eastern Trail** joins on the left,▶12 you use it and then the **Day Tunnel Trail** to retrace your steps to the **Randol Trail.**▶13

Turning left on the Randol Trail, you follow the dirt road on a level but curvy course that wanders past a large pile of mine tailings. At a junction with the Santa Isabel Trail, you stay right, following the Randol Trail as it descends to meet the **Buena Vista Trail**, where you turn right.▶14

When you reach a junction with the **New Almaden Trail**, turn right.▶15 This trail, for hiking only, drops to a creek, which you cross on a plank bridge. A moderate climb soon puts you briefly atop a ridge, but then the trail curves downhill again and lands you in a ravine with a seasonal creek. You cross several more seasonal creeks, and then the trail snakes its way uphill to the four-way junction with the Hacienda Trail you passed near the start of this route. Continuing straight, you soon begin a series of S-bends that descend to the parking area.▶16

A Shorter Option

To make an easier, 4.4-mile loop, omit the excursion to Mine Hill ▶5-▶13 and continue along the Randoll Trail.

OPTIONS

Oak branches *frame a view of Sierra Azul from Almaden Quicksilver County Park (Trail 28).*

Mount Allison ▲
2658'

↗ to Mission Peak

Agua Fria Creek

Ridge

Trail

2543' ▲

MISSION PEAK
REGIONAL
PRESERVE

Monument
Peak
2594' ▲

1500'

Caliente

Trail

Agua

Scott

Creek

Monument Peak Trail

Monument Peak Road

2220'

Alameda Co.
Santa Clara Co.

Agua

Caliente

1000'

Trail

N

0   0.1 0.2 0.3 0.4 0.5 miles
0   200 400 600 800 meters

Calera Creek

Service

Trail

Calera

Creek

Road

Agua

Caliente

Trail

ED R. LEVIN
COUNTY PARK

start &
finish

Ⓟ

600'

Sandy Wool
Lake

Ⓟ

Tularcitos Trail

Calaveras Ridge

Downing Rd

Calaveras   Road

Evans   Road

PIO

Trail

Airpoint Trail

Ⓟ

Ⓟ

Arroyo

Calaveras Road

Los Coches Ridge   Trail

de los Coches

Milpitas

Ed R. Levin County Park

Explore the high ground on the border of Alameda and Santa Clara counties via this aerobic route, which uses the Agua Caliente and Monument Peak trails, and you will be rewarded with great views and the chance to spot aerial hunters such as hawks, falcons, and even golden eagles. Open grasslands dominate here, but you also cross wooded canyons holding Calera and Scott creeks. The climbing sometimes gets steep, and you may find yourself tracing mini-switchbacks across the dirt road that serves as your trail. As you gain elevation, the sight of Monument Peak and Mt. Hamilton, nearby landmarks, may spur you onward.

Best Time

Fall through spring, but trails may be muddy in wet weather

Finding the Trail

From I-680 in Milpitas, take the Calaveras Blvd./Milpitas exit and go east 1.9 miles to Downing Rd. Turn left and after 0.5 mile come to an entrance kiosk and self-registration station. Go another 0.9 mile to a paved parking area just north of Sandy Wool Lake. The trailhead is at the end of Downing Rd., about 100 yards northeast of the parking area.

Trail Description

You leave the trailhead▶1 and go east on the **Tularcitos Trail**, passing an information board. The

TRAIL USE
Hike, Run

LENGTH
7.8 miles, 5-6 hours

VERTICAL FEET
±2800'

DIFFICULTY
− 1 2 3 4 **5** +

TRAIL TYPE
Loop

SURFACE TYPE
Dirt

FFATURES
Dogs Allowed
Canyon
Summit
Stream
Birds
Wildlife
Great Views
Steep

FACILITIES
Restrooms
Picnic Tables
Water
Phone

trail, a dirt road closed to bikes and dogs, skirts a metal gate and then climbs gently to the first of two closely spaced junctions. At the first you continue straight. At the second, which you reach after a short, steep climb, you turn left on the **Agua Caliente Trail**, also a dirt road.▶2 There are a number of cattle gates on this route; make sure you close each one after passing through it.

Your road follows a rolling course, sometimes pitching steeply upward. After passing a hang-gliding area, left, you come to a four-way junction with a service road. You continue straight and then begin a series of switchbacks that take you uphill on a grade that alternates between moderate and steep. Now you descend to a wooded ravine that holds a tributary of Calera Creek. As you climb from this drainage, you are joined on the right by two unsigned dirt roads, not shown on the park map. At a junction with the **Monument Peak Trail**,▶3 you leave the Agua Caliente Trail and veer right. Just ahead is a four-way junction with the Monument Peak Road. Here you continue straight, passing a watering trough for horses and then a dirt road heading downhill, both left.

Climbing a steep, rocky track, you pass a dirt road joining sharply from the right. Your trail approaches Monument Peak Road, but the two routes soon diverge. Now the trail comes to **Calera Creek**, which you may have to step across on rocks. North of the creek, the trail finds level ground, and you begin to see the communication towers atop

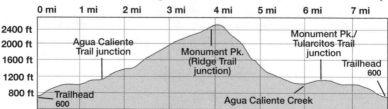

TRAIL 29 Ed R. Levin County Park Elevation Profile

Monument Peak, which is uphill and right. Soon the trail swings right and begins a steep, winding ascent. As you gain elevation, look for Mt. Hamilton, topped with observatory domes, to the southeast.

Slightly southwest of Monument Peak's summit, you leave Santa Clara County and enter the East Bay Regional Park District's **Mission Peak Regional Preserve**. A nearly level walk takes you past the headwaters of **Scott Creek**. With a communication tower looming overhead, you join a dirt-and-gravel road and head straight for a saddle and a junction.▶4 Here the road you are on bends right and enters a restricted area. The trail continuing straight

Look skyward for birds, especially hawks, falcons, kites, and golden eagles.

A eucalyptus tree *and signs mark the start of the Tularcitos Trail.*

is signed MISSION PEAK TO MONUMENT PEAK REGIONAL TRAIL, and is part of the Bay Area Ridge Trail. Your route, the **Agua Caliente Trail**, a multi-use dirt road, goes left. Climbing gently, you soon reach the route's high point, only about 50 feet lower than the summit of Monument Peak (2594'). Skirting a communication facility, the road veers left and descends on a grade that shifts between moderate and steep.

Eventually the grade eases and you make a winding descent into the wooded canyon holding **Scott Creek**. After crossing the creek, which drains through a culvert, you are faced with a short, steep climb. The road then bends sharply left and descends on a moderate and then steep grade. At a junction with the Calera Creek Trail,▶5 right, you stay on the Agua Caliente Trail to its junction with the Monument Peak Trail.▶6 From there, angle right and retrace your route to the parking area.▶7,▶8

🚶	MILESTONES	
▶1	0.0	Take Tularcitos Trail east
▶2	0.2	Left on Agua Caliente Trail
▶3	1.5	Right on Monument Peak Trail
▶4	3.9	Left on Agua Caliente Trail, left again at communication facility
▶5	6.0	Straight to stay on Agua Caliente Trail
▶6	6.3	Junction with Monument Peak Trail; veer right to stay on Agua Caliente Trail and retrace to Tularcitos Trail
▶7	7.6	Right on Tularcitos Trail
▶8	7.8	Back at parking area

Corral Trail *in Henry W. Coe State Park (Trail 30)*

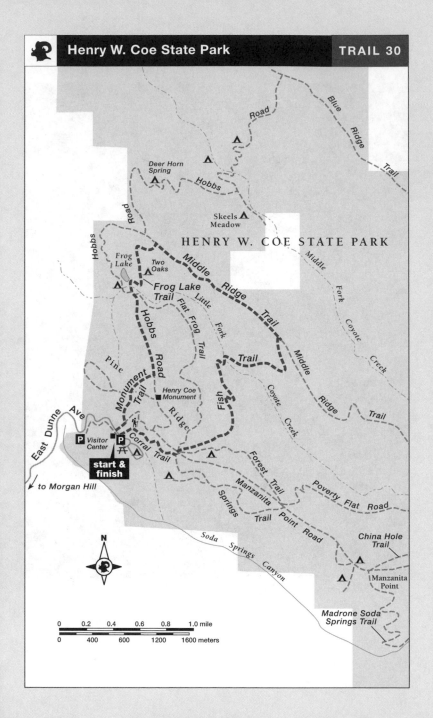

HENRY W. COE STATE PARK

Blue

Ridge

Trail

Road

Deer Horn
Spring

Hobbs

Skeels
Meadow

Middle

Road

Frog
Lake

Two
Oaks

Middle

Ridge

Fork

Coyote

Frog Lake
Trail

Hobbs

Trail

Flat Frog Trail

Little

Fork

Trail

Creek

Road

Pine

Monument

Henry Coe
Monument

Fish

Coyote

Middle

Trail

Ridge

Trail

Trail

Creek

East Dunne

Ave

Ridge

Trail

P

Visitor
Center

P

Corral

Trail

start &
finish

to Morgan Hill

Forest

Trail

Poverty Flat Road

Manzanita

Springs

Point

Road

China Hole
Trail

Trail

Soda

Springs

Canyon

Manzanita
Point

N

Madrone Soda
Springs Trail

| 0 | 0.2 | 0.4 | 0.6 | 0.8 | 1.0 mile |

| 0 | 400 | 600 | 1200 | 1600 meters |

Henry W. Coe State Park

This loop samples only a small corner of northern California's largest state park, but it should be enough to whet your appetite for further exploration of this magnificent area's rugged canyons, oak-studded ridges, and sky-scraping slopes. From the trailhead you ascend through stands of ponderosa pines, then drop steeply to Little Fork Coyote Creek. On Middle Ridge, you enjoy a long ramble until diverted by the Fish Trail, which drops into several canyons; an easy, shady walk that completes the circuit.

Best Time

Spring and fall are the best seasons.

Finding the Trail

From Hwy. 101 in Morgan Hill, take the East Dunne Ave./Morgan Hill exit and go northeast on East Dunne Ave. At 11.7 miles you reach the Coe Ranch entrance and the overflow parking area (a short trail leads from here to the main entrance). At 12.3 miles is the main entrance. There are fees for parking and camping; backpackers must register at the visitor center. The trailhead is several hundred feet back on East Dunne Ave., at the foot of Manzanita Point Rd.▶1

Trail Description

The visitor center, with books, maps, snacks and cold drinks is open weekends in fall and winter, and Friday–Sunday in spring and summer.

TRAIL USE
Hike, Run
LENGTH
6.3 miles, 3-4 hours
VERTICAL FEET
±1950'
DIFFICULTY
– 1 2 3 **4** 5 +
TRAIL TYPE
Loop
SURFACE TYPE
Dirt, Paved

FEATURES
Canyon
Stream
Wildflowers
Birds
Wildlife
Secluded
Historic
Camping

FACILITIES
Visitor Center
Picnic Tables
Restrooms
Water
Phone

Trail Description

This park has fine stands of ponderosa pines, a rarity in the Bay Area. Usually found in mountains, these stately trees are the most common pine in North America.

Climbing moderately on paved **Manzanita Point Road**, you soon reach a gate and a junction. Here you angle left onto the **Monument Trail**, a single track closed to bikes and horses.▶2 Switchbacks help you gain elevation to a four-way junction with the Ponderosa Trail.▶3 The **Henry W. Coe monument** is about 0.1 mile to your right, just across Hobbs Road.

From the four-way junction, continue on the Monument Trail to where it merges with **Hobbs Road**, on which you veer left.▶4 Making a long descent on a moderate and then steep grade, you eventually step across Little Fork Coyote Creek and then reach a junction. Here you turn sharply right onto the **Frog Lake Trail**,▶5 a single track closed to bikes and horses. After a few tight switchbacks, you meet Hobbs Road at **Frog Lake**.▶6 Turning right, you cross the earthen dam that made the lake, pass a trail that circles the lake, and then start to climb by switchbacking right.

Passing a trail to Two Oaks Camp, right, you wind your way gently uphill to a T-junction with the **Middle Ridge Trail**.▶7 Turning right, you climb gently across an open field and then begin to descend on a moderate grade through stands of gray pine and blue oak. Beyond a saddle, the trail rises steeply, then descends through a corridor of chaparral that includes giant manzanitas.

At a junction with the **Fish Trail**,▶8 you turn right and leave the ridge you have been following. In

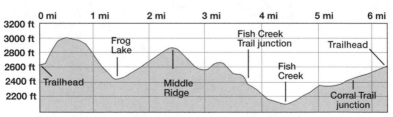

TRAIL 30 Henry W. Coe State Park Elevation Profile

places the trail is merely a ledge cut in the hillside, so use caution. A rolling course brings you to **Little Fork Coyote Creek**, which you step across on rocks. Now the trail zigzags uphill and then contours across a hillside that slopes left. After passing a seasonal creek in a mossy, fern-filled ravine, you climb steeply via switchbacks to a saddle. Now a gentle descent over open and then forested ground puts you in a narrow canyon that holds a tributary of Little Fork Coyote Creek.

Leaving the canyon, the trail climbs to a broad ridgetop and several junctions with a welter of trails. First is a four-way junction with the self-guiding Forest Trail, left, and the Flat Frog Trail, right. Then, past an information board, you come to Manzanita Point Road and a short connector, just across it, to the Corral Trail.▶9 Cross the road, and in a few hundred feet you reach the **Corral Trail**, on which you turn right. You enjoy a level walk across a forested hillside that falls steeply to the headwaters of Soda Springs. The trail ducks into and swings out of ravines cut into the hillside. Climbing on a gentle grade, you reach open ground, curve left, and cross a bridge over a branch of Soda Springs. Just ahead is the parking area at park headquarters.▶10

This park is infested with wild pigs, and you may see evidence beside the trail of their destructive rooting.

🚶	**MILESTONES**

▶1	0.0	Take Manzanita Point Rd. (paved) northeast
▶2	0.1	Left on Monument Trail
▶3	0.4	Trail to Coe monument on right
▶4	0.6	Left on Hobbs Rd.
▶5	1.4	Right on Frog Lake Trail
▶6	1.6	Frog Lake
▶7	2.4	Right on Middle Ridge Trail
▶8	3.8	Right on Fish Trail
▶9	5.7	Cross Manzanita Point Rd., then right on Corral Trail
▶10	6.3	Back at parking area

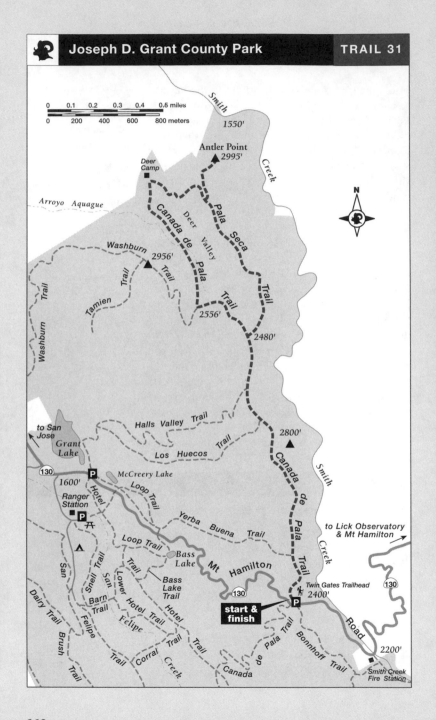

Smith

1550'

Antler Point
2995'

Deer Camp

Arroyo Aquague

Creek

Canada de Pala

Washburn

Deer Valley

2956'

Pala Seca

N

Tamien Trail

Washburn Trail

Washburn Trail

Trail

2556'

Trail

2480'

Halls Valley Trail

2800'

to San Jose

Grant Lake

Los Huecos Trail

Canada de Pala Trail

Smith

130

McCreery Lake

1600'

Ranger Station

Loop Trail

Yerba Buena Trail

to Lick Observatory
& Mt Hamilton

Hotel Trail

Loop Trail

San Trail

Bass Lake

Mt Hamilton

Creek

Snell Trail

Lower Hotel Trail

Bass Lake Trail

Twin Gates Trailhead
2400'

130

San Felipe Trail

Barn Trail

Hotel Trail

130

start & finish

Felipe Trail

Dairy Trail

Corral Creek Trail

de Pala Trail

Bonnhoff Trail

Road

2200'

Brush Trail

Canada

Smith Creek Fire Station

Joseph D. Grant County Park

Following a mostly rolling, ridgetop course on the Canada de Pala and Pala Seca trails, you enjoy views of the Diablo Range, crowned by nearby Mt. Hamilton, and the distant Santa Cruz Mountains. After visiting Antler Point, the trail dips to Deer Camp and then a marshy meadow, but soon resumes its quest of high places. Closing the loop around Deer Valley, you retrace your route to the parking area.

Best Time

Fall through spring

Finding the Trail

From I-680 in San Jose, take the Alum Rock exit, go northeast 2.2 miles to Mt. Hamilton Rd., and turn right. At 7.7 miles you reach the entrance to the park's main area. Continue another 3.4 miles to a paved parking area, left, for the Twin Gates Trailhead. The trailhead is on the west side of the parking area.

Trail Description

From the trailhead▶1 you go through a metal gate and then climb moderately on the **Canada de Pala Trail**, a dirt road. The road bends right and gains the top of a ridge. Mt. Hamilton, a hulking giant topped by 4373-foot Copernicus Peak, rises to your east. The white domes clustered around Mt. Hamilton's summit belong to University of California's Lick Observatory.

TRAIL USE
Hike, Run, Bike
LENGTH
9.8 miles, 4-6 hours
VERTICAL FEET
±1650'
DIFFICULTY
– 1 2 3 4 **5** +
TRAIL TYPE
Loop
SURFACE TYPE
Dirt

FEATURES
Summit
Birds
Great Views
Camping
Secluded

FACILITIES
Restrooms
Picnic Tables
Water
Phone

Soon the grade eases, and you enjoy a rolling course over mostly open, grassy terrain. At a junction with the Yerba Buena Trail, left, you continue straight, with a rest bench and a stock pond, both left. After passing through a cattle gate, you descend an eroded stretch of road to a junction, left, with the Los Huecos Trail, a dirt road. Steadily losing elevation, you reach the Halls Valley Trail, left, and then a saddle in the ridge you've been following.

At a junction where the Canada de Pala Trail bends left,►2 you continue straight, now on the **Pala Seca Trail**. This trail, also a dirt road, climbs moderately and then steeply, still following the crest of a ridge. A rest bench, right, invites you to stay awhile and relish the scenery.

The road levels, curves right, and then begins to descend. Twin summits are just ahead, the right one being **Antler Point**. You reach it via the **Antler Point Trail**, a single track angling right.►3 This trail wanders across a hillside and soon reaches an unsigned fork. You bear right and climb gently to a rest bench at the end of the trail.►4 The view northward from Antler Point takes in a rugged ensemble of canyons, ravines, and ridges that make up some of the wildest land in the Bay Area.

After enjoying this invigorating scene, retrace your route to the Pala Seca Trail.►5 Now you make a hard right on the dirt road, pass a rest bench, and

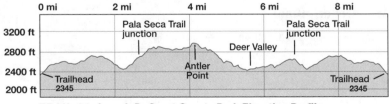

TRAIL 31 **Joseph D. Grant County Park Elevation Profile**

begin to descend via S-bends. In places the road is rocky, eroded, and perhaps muddy where a creek trickles across. After losing elevation, you climb on a gentle grade to a barbed-wire fence and a cattle gate. Once through the gate, you pass **Deer Camp**, site of a renovated cabin.►**6** Here the Pala Seca Trail ends and you join without fanfare the **Canada de Pala Trail**. Resuming the descent, you drop steeply into a ravine, where the creek you crossed earlier is confined to a culvert. Climbing out of this drainage, you cross a ridge and enter beautiful, wide Deer Valley. Soon you are beside a creek, right, that creates a marshy tract of sedges and rushes. A culvert carries the creek under the road and puts it on your left.

A wet meadow, left, marks the head of the creek. An extensive ground squirrel colony is nearby. Now you come to a junction with the Washburn Trail, a dirt road heading right. You continue straight and climb out of the valley at its south end. Soon you reach a cattle gate, and just beyond is the junction with the **Pala Seca Trail.**►**7** From here, bear right and retrace your route to the parking area.►**8**

From the Canada de Pala Trail you can see two Bay Area mountain ranges–the Diablo Range and the Santa Cruz Mountains.

🚶 MILESTONES

►1	0.0	Take the Canada de Pala Trail
►2	2.6	Straight on Pala Seca Trail
►3	4.2	Right on trail to Antler Point
►4	4.4	Antler Point, retrace to previous junction
►5	4.6	Right on Pala Seca Trail
►6	5.3	Deer Camp, straight on Canada de Pala Trail
►7	7.2	Right to stay on Canada de Pala Trail, retrace to parking area
►8	9.8	Back at parking area

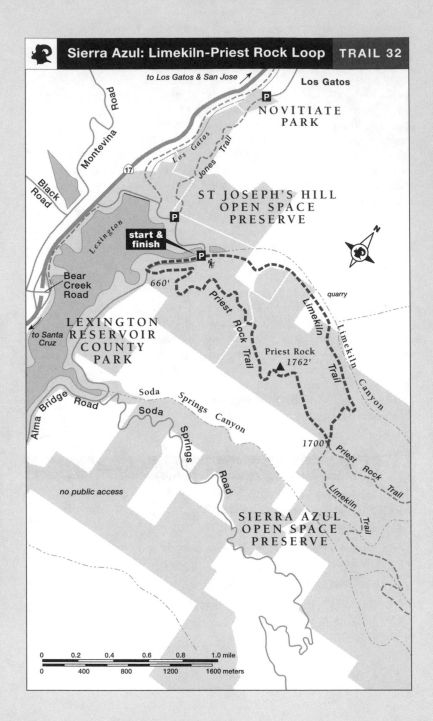

to Los Gatos & San Jose

Los Gatos

NOVITIATE PARK

Montevina Road

Black Road

Los Gatos

Jones Trail

17

ST JOSEPH'S HILL OPEN SPACE PRESERVE

N

Lexington

start & finish

Bear Creek Road

660'

LEXINGTON RESERVOIR COUNTY PARK

to Santa Cruz

Priest Rock Trail

Priest Rock 1762'

quarry

Limekiln Trail

Limekiln Trail

Limekiln Canyon

Alma Bridge Road

Soda

Soda

Springs

Canyon

Springs

Road

1700'

Priest Rock Trail

Limekiln Trail

no public access

SIERRA AZUL OPEN SPACE PRESERVE

| 0 | 0.2 | 0.4 | 0.6 | 0.8 | 1.0 mile |
| 0 | 400 | 800 | 1200 | 1600 meters |

Sierra Azul
Open Space Preserve:
Limekiln-Priest Rock Loop

This loop, which starts and ends in Lexington Reservoir County Park, visits the northwest corner of MROSD's largest, most remote preserve. Much of the journey is over serpentine soil, which gives rise to a fascinating community of shrubs and wildflowers. Early blooming shrubs, such as manzanita and currant, may add splashes of unexpected color as early as December, and the bright red toyon berries attract numerous species of ever-hungry songbirds. Often blazingly hot in summer, this route is perfect for a winter ramble if it's not made muddy by rain.

TRAIL USE
Hike, Run, Bike
LENGTH
5.2 miles, 2-3 hours
VERTICAL FEET
±1300'
DIFFICULTY
– 1 2 **3** 4 5 +
TRAIL TYPE
Loop
SURFACE TYPE
Dirt

Best Time

This trail is best fall through spring, but trails may be muddy in wet weather.

Finding the Trail

From Hwy. 17 northbound, exit at Alma Bridge Rd., south of Los Gatos. At 0.7 mile, you pass a parking area, right, for Lexington Reservoir. At 1.2 miles, stay right at a fork with the entrance road to Lexington Quarry. Roadside parking is just ahead on the right side of Alma Bridge Rd. The trailhead is at gate SA22, on the southeast side of the road across from this parking area.

    From Hwy. 17 southbound, take the Bear Creek Rd. exit south of Los Gatos. After 0.1 mile, you come to a stop sign at a four-way junction. Turn right, cross over Hwy. 17, and turn left to get on Hwy. 17 northbound. Go 0.4 mile to Alma Bridge Rd., turn right and follow the directions above.

FEATURES
Dogs Allowed
Stream
Autumn Colors
Wildflowers
Birds
Great Views
Secluded
Historic

FACILITIES
None

Trail Description

Clumps of leather oak, a low shrub with curved and prickly leaves, indicate the presence of serpentine soil.

From the trailhead,▶1 you begin climbing northeast on the **Limekiln Trail**, a formerly paved road that is part of Lexington Reservoir County Park's trail system. Almost immediately, you come to a fence and a gate marked FIRE LANE. Passing through a gap in the fence, you climb the rough and rocky road on a moderate grade. A creek flows through Limekiln Canyon, which is downhill and left. Still climbing, now on a gentle grade, you follow a winding course up a hillside that drops steeply left.

Now the road turns left and crosses a creek that drains into Limekiln Canyon, named for furnaces used to reduce limestone to lime. A handful of these operated in the canyon from the late 1800s until the 1930s. The road here may be very wet and muddy. This is a landslide-prone area, and there are young manzanita bushes growing atop piles of debris, helping to stabilize the soil. After climbing out of the slide area, the road swings right.

Now you descend into a cool and shady forest. Soon you reach the preserve boundary and begin a moderate-to-steep climb over very rocky ground. Through openings in the trees, left, you can see the Lexington Quarry, a massive rock quarry. With the deep valley and chaparral-clad hills of Limekiln Canyon to your left, you continue your uphill trek.

OPTIONS

Exploring Further in Sierra Azul

The **Priest Rock Trail**, a rugged dirt road, climbs northeast from its junction with the Limekiln Trail▶2 nearly 1000 feet in 1.5 miles, to a junction with the Kennedy Trail. From there, you can make a 4.6-mile loop back to the Limekiln-Priest Rock junction▶2 by turning right onto the Kennedy Trail and right again onto the Limekiln Trail. The 6.2-mile Woods Trail joins this loop to a parking area at gate SA06 on Hicks Road.

Just beyond a fence and a gate is a junction.▶2 Here, the Limekiln Trail continues straight, and the **Priest Rock Trail**, a dirt road, goes left and right.

You turn right on the Priest Rock Trail. A gentle ascent ends with a short, steep pitch, and now you are on level ground. An unsigned dirt road joins sharply from the left, and then a short trail to a viewpoint departs right.

Crossing under a set of power lines and a tower, the road bends sharply left. A fence is just to the right of the road, and **Priest Rock**, a modest formation, rises behind it, half hidden in the chaparral. Now the road begins to

Cyclists *rest at the junction of the Limekiln and Priest Rock Trails.*

snake its way downhill, and soon you reach gate SA23 and the preserve boundary. Your road continues into **Lexington Reservoir County Park**, and you descend on a grade that alternates between gentle, moderate, and steep. Leveling briefly, the road then climbs gently through a possibly wet area. Passing a dirt road, left, you continue winding downhill to the bottom of the Priest Rock Trail. Here, at gate SA21, you turn sharply right to meet paved **Alma Bridge Road**.▶3 Cross it carefully, turn right, and walk northeast along the road shoulder about 0.4 mile to the parking area.▶4

Enjoy a fine view that stretches north from San Jose to the East Bay Hills and Mt. Diablo.

🚶 **MILESTONES**

▶1   0.0 Take Limekiln Trail northeast
▶2   2.3 Right on Priest Rock Trail
▶3   4.8 Right on Alma Bridge Rd.
▶4   5.2 Back at parking area

CHAPTER 4

Peninsula

Windy Hill *overlooks the Peninsula, San Francisco Bay, and Mt. Diablo (Trail 44).*

Peninsula

The Peninsula is the great thumb of land between the Pacific Ocean and San Francisco Bay, encompassing San Francisco and San Mateo counties, and the northwestern part of Santa Clara County. Most parks and open spaces here are associated with the Santa Cruz Mountains, in an area stretching from Saratoga Gap northwest to Montara Mountain. Others are scattered from San Francisco to Silicon Valley. The land has a rich history, having been used by Native Americans, Spanish missionaries, and Mexican settlers. The slopes of the Santa Cruz Mountains in the 19th century held ranches and vineyards, and also echoed with the thud of the logger's ax as the coast redwood forest was decimated for lumber to build San Francisco and other cities.

The terrain on the Peninsula is varied. On the west side of the Santa Cruz Mountains, you find deep, forested canyons, stream-filled ravines, and grassy ridges. On the east side are oak woodlands, mixed-evergreen forests, grasslands, and salt marshes. In the 1960s, development along the Hwy. 101 corridor threatened to push into the hills, but this was stopped when voters in 1972 approved creation of the Midpeninsula Regional Open Space District (MROSD), which now administers nearly 50,000 acres of Peninsula open space. Add this to a network of federal, state, county, and local parks, and you have one of the finest places to enjoy outdoor activities in the Bay Area. Even heavily populated areas such as San Francisco, Sunnyvale, and Santa Clara have trailheads nearby. Many parks and open spaces on the Peninsula are contiguous, making long hiking, bicycling, and running routes possible.

Governing Agencies

The parks described in this chapter are managed by three government agencies, all listed in Appendix B. Maps for the Presidio of San Francisco are available at the Presidio's visitor centers and from the Golden Gate National Recreation Area's Web site. Trail maps for the central and southern Peninsula, produced by the Trail Center, are available from Wilderness Press, www.wildernesspress.com. Midpeninsula Regional Open Space District maps are available at its trailheads, by mail, and from its Web site. Maps for San Mateo County Parks are available at trailheads and by mail. For contact information, see Appendix (p. 280)

Peninsula

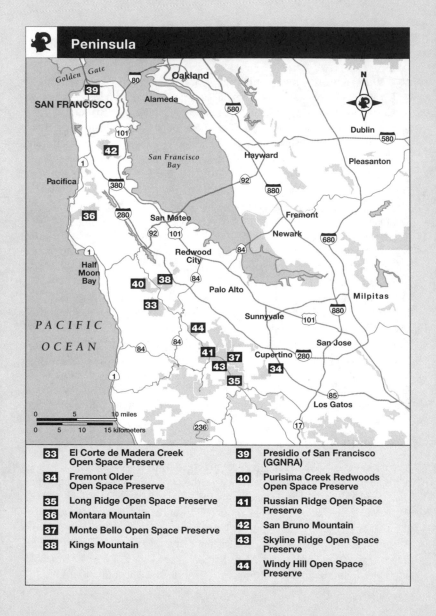

Peninsula

33 El Corte de Madera Creek
Open Space Preserve

34 Fremont Older
Open Space Preserve

35 Long Ridge Open Space Preserve

36 Montara Mountain

37 Monte Bello Open Space Preserve

38 Kings Mountain

39 Presidio of San Francisco
(GGNRA)

40 Purisima Creek Redwoods
Open Space Preserve

41 Russian Ridge Open Space
Preserve

42 San Bruno Mountain

43 Skyline Ridge Open Space
Preserve

44 Windy Hill Open Space
Preserve

Peninsula

TRAIL	Difficulty	Length	Type	Hiking	Trail Running	Mountain Biking	Parking Fee	Permit	Dogs Allowed	Child Friendly	Canyon	Mountain	Summit	Stream	Waterfall	Autumn Colors	Wildflowers	Birds	Wildlife	Cool & Shady	Great Views	Photo Opp.	Secluded	Historic	Camping	Geologic Interest	Steep
33	3	4.3	loop	✓	✓	✓					✓			✓		✓		✓		✓						✓	✓
34	3	3.1	loop	✓	✓	✓			✓	✓		✓					✓	✓			✓						
35	3	4.6	loop	✓	✓	✓					✓	✓	✓			✓		✓		✓	✓		✓				
36	4	7.2	↗	✓	✓	✓	P				✓						✓				✓						
37	4	6.0	loop	✓	✓	✓					✓	✓	✓			✓	✓	✓			✓	✓			✓		
38	5	7.9	loop	✓	✓		P				✓							✓	✓	✓				✓			
39	2	2.6	loop	✓	✓	✓			✓	✓				✓			✓	✓			✓	✓			✓		
40	5	10.1	loop	✓	✓	✓					✓			✓		✓	✓	✓		✓	✓			✓	✓		
41	3	4.6	loop	✓	✓	✓						✓					✓	✓	✓		✓	✓					
42	3	3.1	loop	✓	✓		P			✓	✓	✓					✓	✓			✓	✓					
43	3	3.4	↗	✓	✓	✓								✓			✓	✓			✓						
44	5	8.0	loop	✓	✓						✓			✓		✓	✓	✓		✓	✓			✓			

USE & ACCESS
- Hiking
- Trail Running
- Mountain Biking
- P Parking Fee
- Permit
- Child Friendly
- Dogs Allowed
- Handicap Access
- Camping

TERRAIN
- Canyon
- Mountain
- Summit

WATER
- Stream
- Waterfall
- Beach
- Shore

FLORA & FAUNA
- Autumn Colors
- Wildflowers
- Birds
- Wildlife
- Tide Pools

OTHER
- Cool & Shady
- Great Views
- Photo Opportunity
- Secluded
- Historic
- Geologic Interest
- Moonlight Hiking
- Steep

DIFFICULTY
- 1 2 3 4 5 +
less   more

Peninsula

TRAIL 33

Hike, Run, Bike
4.3 miles, Loop
Difficulty: 1 2 **3** 4 5

El Corte de Madera Creek 221

An unusual sandstone formation called tafoni is the main attraction of this loop through the north end of the preserve. Towering Douglas-firs and coast redwoods, a sea of chaparral, and a lush riparian corridor near the headwaters of El Corte de Madera Creek are some of the other attractions visitors will enjoy here.

TRAIL 34

Hike, Run, Bike
3.1 miles, Loop
Difficulty: 1 2 **3** 4 5

Fremont Older 225

Varied terrain and superb views from Hunters Point make this route a favorite among South Bay hikers. In spring, the grasslands come alive with wildflowers, while the secluded canyon traversed by the Seven Springs Trail offers shady respite on a warm day. Remnants of walnut and apricot orchards hearken back to Santa Clara Valley's heyday as an agricultural paradise.

TRAIL 35

Hike, Run, Bike
4.6 miles, Loop
Difficulty: 1 2 **3** 4 5

Long Ridge 231

Superb views are the reason to wander uphill from the shady confines of Peters Creek to the dramatically situated Wallace Stegner memorial bench high atop Long Ridge. On a clear day, the scene extends westward over the Pescadero Creek watershed, taking in thousands of acres of protected lands, which are truly a living monument to the open space movement.

Starting in a eucalyptus forest and then wandering through chaparral and coastal scrub, you finally attack the ramparts of Montara Mountain, actually a long ridge with several summits. Views of the Santa Cruz Mountains, the East Bay hills, and some San Francisco landmarks reward your efforts.

TRAIL 36

Hike, Run, Bike
7.2 miles, Out & Back
Difficulty: 1 2 3 **4** 5

This challenging but supremely rewarding loop climbs from the riparian corridor along Stevens Creek to the windswept grasslands of Monte Bello Ridge, capped by Black Mountain. The route includes a self-guiding nature trail and a trip across the San Andreas Fault.

TRAIL 37

Hike, Run, Bike
6.0 miles, Loop
Difficulty: 1 2 3 **4** 5

This route explores the rugged terrain just north-west of Huddart County Park, and the contrast between the county park and it's GGNRA neighbor couldn't be more extreme. Trading picnic areas and sports fields for a serene forest of coast redwoods, you climb the aptly named Lonely Trail to Kings Mountain, then descend through the heavily wooded county park, a favorite among equestrians.

TRAIL 38

Hike, Run
7.9 miles, Loop
Difficulty: 1 2 3 **4** 5

San Bruno Mountain 267

This exploration takes you to an island of open space surrounded by a sea of residential and industrial development. Despite this urban setting, the mountain's rugged canyons and ridges host a remarkable array of rare and/or endangered species. When not fogbound, the trails here afford views of San Francisco and beyond, and the spring wildflower displays are sensational.

TRAIL 42

Hike, Run
3.1 miles, Loop
Difficulty: 1 2 **3** 4 5

Skyline Ridge 271

Rising from the forested environs of Alpine Pond, the ridge trail takes you to a breezy realm of grassland and chaparral, where views of Butano Ridge, Portola Redwoods State Park, and the Pacific coast await. The spring wildflowers here are superb, and it is easy to see why this stretch of trail, which is part of the Bay Area Ridge Trail, is a favorite among Peninsula hikers.

TRAIL 43

Hike, Run, Bike
3.4 miles, Out & Back
Difficulty: 1 2 **3** 4 5

Windy Hill 275

This adventurous semi-loop explores one of the MROSD's best-loved preserves. Dropping about 1000 feet in 3 miles, you follow cool and shady Hamms Gulch downhill through a lush forest, only to win back lost elevation via switchbacks, and then contour on a course roughly parallel to Skyline Blvd. for an easy last lap to the parking area.

TRAIL 44

Hike, Run
8.0 miles, Loop
Difficulty: 1 2 3 4 **5**

El Corte de Madera Creek Open Space Preserve

An unusual sandstone formation called tafoni is the main attraction of this invigorating loop at the north end of the preserve. Towering Douglas-firs and coast redwoods, a sea of chaparral, and a lush riparian corridor near the headwaters of El Corte de Madera Creek are some of the other attractions visitors will enjoy here.

Best Time

All year, but trails may be muddy in wet weather.

Finding the Trail

From the junction of Skyline Blvd. and Hwy. 84 in Sky Londa, take Skyline Blvd. northwest 3.9 miles to the Caltrans parking area at Skeggs Point. The trailhead is at gate CM01, on the southwest side of Skyline Blvd. about 100 yards northwest of the parking area. Walk carefully along the east shoulder until opposite this gate, then cross when it is safe.

Trail Description

A metal gate and a wood fence mark the trailhead.▶1 An information board with a map holder, an open space preserve sign, and a trail sign are just past the gate. From here, you follow the **Tafoni Trail**, a dirt road that soon begins to climb on a moderate grade past towering Douglas-firs. The road then levels and curves right, bringing you to a junction, where you continue straight.▶2 The hillside on your right falls steeply right into the canyon holding the headwaters

TRAIL USE
Hike, Run, Bike
LENGTH
4.3 miles, 2-3 hours
VERTICAL FEET
±1300'
DIFFICULTY
− 1 2 **3** 4 5 +
TRAIL TYPE
Loop
SURFACE TYPE
Dirt

FEATURES
Canyon
Stream
Autumn Colors
Birds
Cool & Shady
Secluded
Geologic Interest

FACILITIES
Restrooms
Picnic Tables

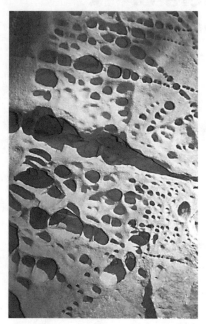

Tafoni *originated as undersea sand deposits.*

of El Corte de Madera Creek. Turning right at a T-junction and climbing on a gentle grade, you travel parallel to a ridgetop that is uphill and left. Soon you come to a saddle and a four-way junction in a small clearing.▶3 Here, the Fir Trail is left and straight, and the Tafoni Trail is right. Bear right on the Tafoni Trail, a dirt road, and descend on a gentle grade.

At a junction signed SANDSTONE FORMATION, you turn right on a single-track trail that is closed to bikes and horses.▶4 Soon you come to an observation deck from where you can see the eroded **sandstone formations**, a form of rock that is called tafoni.▶5 The terrain around the formations is very steep: please stay on the trail or the observation deck at all times.

When you have finished enjoying this unusual area, return to the **Tafoni Trail** and turn right.▶6 The road curves right and descends. Now on a ridgetop, you follow a rolling course which soon leads to a long, moderate descent. The road bends right, climbs for a while, and then descends along a ridge. A fenced restoration area will force you to turn right, as the Tafoni Trail

Vista Point

OPTIONS

From the junction of the Fir and Tafoni trails,▶3 you can make an easy, 0.25-mile excursion to Vista Point, where views of the San Mateo coast and the Pacific Ocean await. Go straight on the Fir Trail, a dirt road, then stay right at two forks ahead.

becomes a single track. Beside the trail are huge redwood stumps surrounded by family circles of second-growth trees, remnants of the area's logging past.

Now you merge with the **El Corte de Madera Creek Trail,**▶7 which joins sharply from the left. Continuing almost straight, you follow the single-track trail gently uphill through dense forest. Soon the trail curves right. **El Corte de Madera Creek** lies at the bottom of the steep drop to your left. You descend and follow the trail as it bends sharply left and brings you to a bridge across El Corte de Madera Creek.

Geologic Interest

Across the bridge, you reach a T-junction with a dirt road; you turn right to continue on the El Corte de Madera Creek Trail. As you climb steadily in a shady, steep-walled canyon, the creek wanders back and forth under the road through culverts. The road soon bends right and brings you to the junction with the Tafoni Trail, where you began this loop.▶8 From here, turn left and retrace your route to Skyline Boulevard trailhead.▶9 When walking back to the parking area, carefully cross Skyline Blvd. and walk on the east shoulder of the highway.

🚶 **MILESTONES**

▶1   0.0 Take Tafoni Trail southwest
▶2   0.1 El Corte de Madera Creek Trail on right; go straight
▶3   1.3 Stay on Tafoni Trail by veering right at four-way junction with Fir Trail
▶4   1.4 Trail to sandstone formation on right (no bikes)
▶5   1.5 Sandstone formation and observation deck; retrace to junction
▶6   1.6 At previous junction, turn right on Tafoni Trail
▶7   2.5 Straight on El Corte de Madera Creek Trail
▶8   4.2 Left on Tafoni Trail, retrace to trailhead
▶9   4.3 Back at trailhead

Regnart Road

Woodhills Trail

Seven Springs Trail

Trail

Hunters Point

Ranch Road

Seven Springs Trail

Hayfield Trail

Cora Older Trail

Hayfield Trail

to Stevens Creek County Park

Creekside Trail

Prospect Road

Prospect Road

to Cupertino

P

start & finish

FREMONT OLDER
OPEN SPACE
PRESERVE

Coyote Ridge Trail

Maisie's Peak

Toyon Trail

Bay View Trail

Toyon Trail

Vista Loop Trail

to Stevens Creek County Park

| 0 | 0.1 | 0.2 | 0.3 miles |

| 0 | 200 | 400 meters |

N

Fremont Older
Open Space Preserve

The varied terrain found in the northeast corner of this preserve, and the superb views from Hunters Point, make this semi-loop route a favorite among South Bay hikers, bicyclists, and runners. In spring, the grasslands visited on the Cora Older and Hayfield trails come alive with wildflowers, while the secluded canyon traversed by the Seven Springs Trail offers shady respite on a warm day. Remnants of walnut and apricot orchards hearken back to Santa Clara Valley's heyday as an agricultural paradise.

Best Time

Fall through spring, but trails may be muddy in wet weather

Trail Approach

From Hwy. 85 at the Cupertino-San Jose border, take the De Anza Blvd. exit, go south 0.5 mile to Prospect Rd., and turn right. After 0.4 mile you come to a stop sign, where you stay on Prospect Rd. by turning left and crossing a set of railroad tracks. When you reach the junction of Prospect Rd. and Rolling Hills Rd., follow Prospect Rd. as it bends sharply left. At 1.8 miles, you reach the preserve entrance and the parking area, left. (The parking area is adjacent to Saratoga Country Club, and a sign here warns you to beware of flying golf balls and to park at your own risk.) The trailhead is on the north side of Prospect Rd., across from the parking area.

TRAIL USE
Hike, Run, Bike
LENGTH
3.1 miles, 2-3 hours
VERTICAL FEET
±800'
DIFFICULTY
− 1 2 **3** 4 5 +
TRAIL TYPE
Loop
SURFACE TYPE
Dirt

FEATURES
Dogs Allowed
Child Friendly
Summit
Wildflowers
Birds
Great Views

FACILITIES
Restrooms

225

Trail Description

The view from Hunters Point takes in San Jose, the Santa Clara Valley, Mt. Hamilton, Mt. Umunhum, and most of the southern end of San Francisco Bay, the East Bay hills and Mt. Diablo. On a clear day, you can even see Mt. Tamalpais and the San Francisco skyline.

From the trailhead,►1 which has two information boards and a map holder, you follow the **Cora Older Trail** uphill and right. After about 100 feet, the single-track trail switchbacks left, then winds uphill and crosses several culverts draining seasonal creeks. Turning left and crossing an open hillside, you soon reach a T-junction.►2 Here, you go right on a dirt road and after several hundred feet arrive at another junction.►3 From this junction, the road curves left, but you angle right on the **Seven Springs Trail**, a single track.

With a ravine holding a seasonal creek on your left, you enter a cool and shady forest. Soon the ravine widens to a valley, whose north-facing slope holds the remnants of an orchard. Winding your way downhill, you pass stands of walnut trees and then meander through a brushy area. The trail turns left, crosses a culvert draining the seasonal creek, and then reaches a four-way junction.

Here, Ranch Road joins from the left, and a road signed STOP, DO NOT TRESPASS goes right. Your route, the Seven Springs Trail, continues across the junction and then angles right. Now you climb up toward the

🚶	**MILESTONES**	
►1	0.0	Take Cora Older Trail
►2	0.4	Right on dirt road at T-junction
►3	0.5	Right on Seven Springs Trail
►4	2.1	Merge with Ranch Rd., then right on Hayfield Trail
►5	2.2	Right at junction with Woodhills Trail, climb to Hunters Point, then retrace to previous junction
►6	2.3	Straight on Hayfield Trail
►7	2.5	Left on dirt road
►8	2.6	Right on Cora Older Trail, retrace to parking area
►9	3.1	Back at parking area

Looking south *from Fremont Older Preserve toward Black Mtn.*

preserve boundary and a ridgetop. A level stretch and then a gentle descent bring you to two junctions.▶4 At the first, a fork, you bear left. At the second, you continue straight. Your trail soon merges with **Ranch Road**, which again comes sharply from the left. Bear right and just ahead meet the **Hayfield Trail**. Turning right, you soon come to a fork where the Woodhills Trail goes left. Here, you veer right and, after about 100 feet, find yourself atop **Hunters Point.**▶5

Great Views

After enjoying a rest and the superb scenery, retrace your route to the junction with the Woodhills Trail, and then to the next junction, just west of where the Seven Springs Trail and Ranch Road merge.▶6 Here, you follow the **Hayfield Trail** as it angles right and descends on a moderate grade. You now pass two dirt roads, both right. The first is unsigned, but the second is signed REGNART ROAD, 0.2 MILE.

Continuing straight, you follow a rolling course to a junction with a trail signed PROSPECT ROAD PARK-ING, 0.8 MILE. Here you turn left,▶7 and, after several hundred feet, you reach the junction with the Seven Springs Trail, where you began this loop. Now you turn right on the Cora Older Trail▶8 and retrace your route to the parking area.▶9

Fremont Older's Home

HISTORY

Fremont Older Preserve was named for a crusading San Francisco newspaper editor, who, with his wife Cora, lived here for many years. You can visit the Olders' home, "Woodhills," which was completed in 1914 and is on the National Register of Historic Places, during the annual house and garden tour, which usually takes place in the spring. Call the MROSD office for details: (650) 691-1200.

A family enjoys the view *from atop Hunters Point.*

More Fremont Older Trails

You can visit the preserve's highest point, Maisie's Peak, via the Hayfield and Coyote Ridge trails.▶7 Trails from this preserve connect with ones in neighboring Stevens Creek County Park, making longer routes possible.

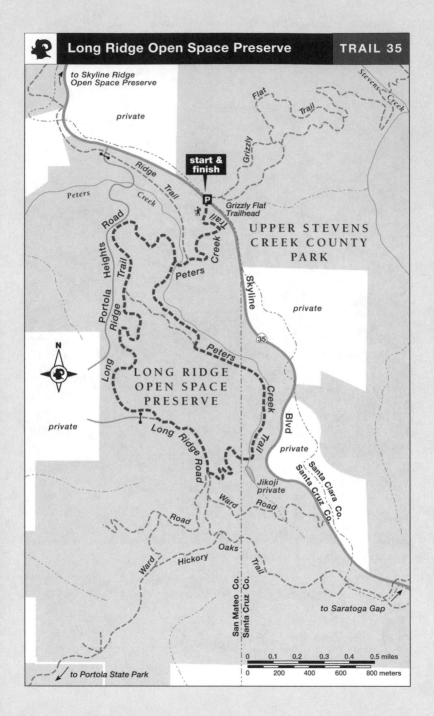

to Skyline Ridge
Open Space Preserve

private

Flat

Trail

Stevens

Creek

Grizzly

Ridge

Trail

start &
finish

P

Grizzly Flat
Trailhead

Peters

Creek

Road

Portola Heights

Long Ridge Trail

Peters

Creek

Trail

UPPER STEVENS
CREEK COUNTY
PARK

Skyline

private

35

Peters

LONG RIDGE
OPEN SPACE
PRESERVE

N

private

Long Ridge Road

Long

Creek

Trail

Blvd

private

Santa Clara Co.
Santa Cruz Co.

Jikoji
private

Ward

Road

Ward

Road

Hickory

Oaks

Trail

San Mateo Co.
Santa Cruz Co.

to Saratoga Gap

| 0 | 0.1 | 0.2 | 0.3 | 0.4 | 0.5 miles |

| 0 | 200 | 400 | 600 | 800 meters |

to Portola State Park

Long Ridge
Open Space Preserve

Superb views are the reason to wander uphill from the shady confines of Peters Creek to the dramatically situated Wallace Stegner memorial bench high atop Long Ridge. On a clear day, the scene extends westward over the Pescadero Creek watershed, taking in thousands of acres of protected lands, which are truly a living monument to the open space movement.

Best Time

All year, but trails may be muddy in wet weather. Peters Creek, Long Ridge and Ridge trails are closed seasonally to bikes and horses.

Finding the Trail

From the junction of Skyline Blvd. and Page Mill Rd./Alpine Rd. south of Palo Alto, take Skyline Blvd. southeast 3.1 miles to a roadside parking area on the left. This parking area, sometimes called Grizzly Flat, serves both Long Ridge OSP and Upper Stevens Creek County Park. The trailhead is on the southwest side of Skyline Blvd., across from the parking area.

Trail Description

At the trailhead▶1 is a fence with a gate that prevents access by bikes and horses during wet weather. About 50 feet beyond this fence are two information boards and a map holder. From here, you follow the **Peters Creek Trail** as it wanders

TRAIL USE
Hike, Run, Bike
LENGTH
4.6 miles, 2-3 hours
VERTICAL FEET
±850'
DIFFICULTY
− 1 2 **3** 4 5 +
TRAIL TYPE
Loop
SURFACE TYPE
Dirt

FEATURES
Canyon
Summit
Stream
Autumn Colors
Birds
Great Views
Cool and Shady
Secluded

FACILITIES
None

A still-prolific apple orchard beside the Peters Creek Trail blooms beautifully in spring and in the fall is often heavily loaded with several varieties of apples.

 Stream

across a hillside that falls away to the right. Soon this single track trail swings left and descends into a cool, dark forest of mostly Douglas-fir and California bay.

At a junction, a trail merges sharply from the right. This is the Ridge Trail, which heads north to Skyline Ridge Open Space Preserve. The Ridge Trail and the Peters Creek Trail (from this point on) are both part of the Bay Area Ridge Trail. Dogs are prohibited beyond this point on the Peters Creek Trail. You continue straight, and after several hundred feet cross the trail's namesake creek on a bridge. Continue straight at the next junction, where the Long Ridge Trail joins from the right.▶2 Soon you pass a dirt road, right, which connects to the Long Ridge Trail.

From here, you continue straight on the **Peters Creek Trail**, now a dirt road. At an unsigned junction, a dirt road forks left and crosses a bridge over a wet area. Several hundred feet ahead, another dirt road angles left and joins it. Soon you cross Peters Creek, which flows under the road through a culvert.

Where a gated dirt road angles left to the preserve boundary, you turn right and cross an earthen dam. Built in the 1960s, this 200-foot-long dam turned part of Peters Creek into the cattail-fringed lake on your left. On the far side of the dam, Peters Creek drains water from the lake, and you cross the creek on a wooden bridge. Now the trail zigzags uphill through forest, to a fence with a gate that pre-

Trail Options

OPTIONS

Long Ridge OSP borders on Upper Stevens Creek County Park and Portola Redwoods State Park, making extended loops and point-to-point routes possible.

vents access by bikes and horses during wet weather. Just beyond the gate is a four-way junction atop Long Ridge.▶3 Here, you meet Ward Road, a dirt road, just where it makes a sharp bend and nearly doubles back on itself. On the outside of the bend, **Long Ridge Road**, also dirt, heads along the ridgetop. You turn right and follow the spectacularly situated road, which affords a fabulous view that extends westward across the Pescadero Creek drainage to the Pacific Ocean.

Leaving the ridgetop, you enjoy a rolling course through mostly open terrain that brings you in about 0.5 mile to the **Wallace Stegner memorial bench**, which honors one of California's best-loved writers and open-space advocates.▶4

Your route, the single-track **Long Ridge Trail**, veers right from the road. After about 100 feet you come to another seasonal closure gate. Once past it, you enter dense forest and contour across a hillside that falls away to the right.

Crossing a saddle, you descend to a junction in a clearing.▶5 Go straight and continue on Long Ridge Trail When you reach the junction with the Peters Creek Trail you passed earlier, turn left▶6 and retrace your route to the parking area.▶7

Since 1979, the pond at the headwaters of Peters Creek has been the property of a Buddhist group, now known as Jikoji, which runs a nearby meditation center.

🚶	**MILESTONES**

▶1	0.0	Take Peters Creek Trail
▶2	0.5	Long Ridge Trail on right
▶3	2.1	Right at four-way junction on Long Ridge Rd.
▶4	2.6	Stegner memorial bench on left; veer right on Long Ridge Trail
▶5	3.4	Straight across clearing to stay on Long Ridge Trail
▶6	4.1	Left on Peters Creek Trail, retrace to trailhead
▶7	4.6	Back at trailhead

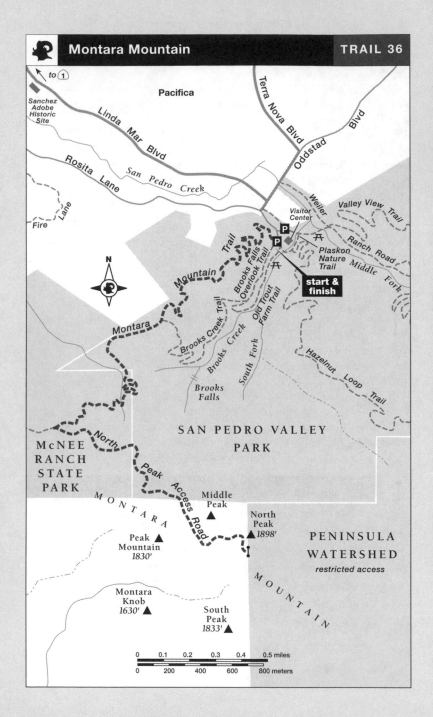

Montara Mountain

TRAIL 36

to (1)

Sanchez Adobe Historic Site

Pacifica

Linda Mar Blvd

Terra Nova Blvd

Oddstad Blvd

Rosita Lane

Fire Lane

San Pedro Creek

Visitor Center

Weiler

Valley View Trail

Ranch Road

Plaskon Nature Trail

Middle Fork

start & finish

Mountain Trail

Brooks Falls Overlook Trail

Brooks Creek Trail

Montara

Old Trout Farm Trail

Brooks Creek

South Fork

Hazelnut Loop Trail

Brooks Falls

SAN PEDRO VALLEY PARK

North Peak Access Road

McNEE RANCH STATE PARK

M O N T A R A

Middle Peak ▲

North Peak ▲ *1898'*

PENINSULA WATERSHED
restricted access

Peak Mountain ▲ *1830'*

Montara Knob *1630'* ▲

South Peak *1833'* ▲

M O U N T A I N

| 0 | 0.1 | 0.2 | 0.3 | 0.4 | 0.5 miles |
| 0 | 200 | 400 | 600 | 800 meters |

Montara Mountain

This route starts in a eucalyptus forest in San Pedro Valley Park. Soon you are wandering uphill through chaparral and coastal scrub, until you finally attack the ramparts of Montara Mountain itself, actually a long ridge with several summits. The cleverly constructed trail makes good use of the terrain, so the climbing is not difficult. Views of the Santa Cruz Mountains, the East Bay hills, and some San Francisco landmarks reward your efforts.

Best Time

All year; expect fog in summer.

Trail Approach

From the junction of Hwy. 1 and Linda Mar Blvd. in Pacifica, go southeast 1.9 miles on Linda Mar Blvd. to Oddstad Blvd. Turn right and then immediately left into the park. Pay your fee at the entrance kiosk then turn right and go to a paved parking area, right. (If this area is full, there is a second lot on the other side of the visitor center.) The trailhead is on the west side of the parking area, just right of the restrooms. ▶1

Trail Description

Take a paved path from the trailhead and then turn left onto a trail that leads to a junction. Here the Brooks Creek and Old Trout Farm trails go left, but you veer right, onto the **Montara Mountain Trail**. The single-track trail heads gently uphill through a eucalyptus forest to a paved road, and gains elevation

TRAIL USE
Hike, Run, Bike
LENGTH
7.2 miles, 3-4 hours
VERTICAL FEET
±1650'
DIFFICULTY
− 1 2 3 **4** 5 +
TRAIL TYPE
Out & Back
SURFACE TYPE
Dirt

FEATURES
Mountain
Wildflowers
Great Views

FACILITIES
Restrooms
Picnic Tables
Phone
Water
Visitor Center
(open weekends)

Montara Mountain's *chaparral-clad slopes form a scenic background to Pacifica.*

steadily. Soon you have a view of the Pacific Ocean, framed by the San Pedro Valley. Soon you climb above the eucalyptus forest for your first good look from the trail at Montara Mountain, topped with communication towers. The trail takes advantage of a ridgetop to gain higher ground.

Curving right, the trail passes a rest bench, left. The view from here extends northeast to Sweeney Ridge and east to the San Francisco Water Department's Peninsula Watershed. Where the Brooks Creek Trail goes left, you continue straight on the Montara Mountain Trail.▶2

OPTIONS

Brooks Falls Overlook

On the way down, when you reach the junction with the Brooks Creek Trail,▶2 turn right and follow it and the Brooks Falls Overlook Trail back to the parking area. During the rainy season, **Brooks Falls** drops about 175 feet in three tiers from the north side of Montara Mountain.

The trail, here rocky and eroded, runs atop a ridge as it prepares to attack Montara Mountain. Soon, without fanfare, you enter **McNee Ranch State Park.▶3** When you reach a junction with the **North Peak Access Road** (shown on the county park map as **Montara Mountain Road**), join it by veering left.▶4 This road is open to bicycles, so use caution.

Near the peaks the road levels out on a flat between the summits. You continue straight to a gate at the **Peninsula Watershed** boundary.▶5 Montara Mountain's **North Peak** is just uphill and left, on private property. Mt. Hamilton, with its white observatory domes, graces the distant skyline. Southeast, you have an uninterrupted vista of the Santa Cruz Mountains down to Mt. Umunhum. To the north, you can pick out features of San Francisco such as the Sunset District, Twin Peaks, and Golden Gate Park. The Berkeley hills, capped by Vollmer Peak and Round Top, are also visible.

From here, retrace your route to the parking area in San Pedro Valley.▶6

Montara Mountain is actually a long ridge crowned by a handful of summits, including North Peak (1898'), South Peak (1833'), and Scarper Peak (1944').

 Great Views

🚶	**MILESTONES**	
▶1	0.0	Take paved path west, then left on dirt path and right on Montara Mountain Trail
▶2	1.4	Brooks Creek Trail on left
▶3	2.1	McNee Ranch State Park boundary
▶4	2.5	Left on North Peak Access Rd.
▶5	3.6	Road's end, retrace to parking area
▶6	7.2	Back at parking area

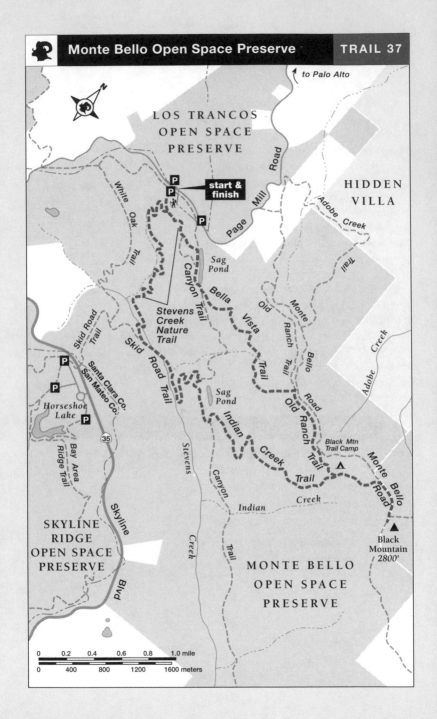

to Palo Alto

LOS TRANCOS
OPEN SPACE
PRESERVE

HIDDEN
VILLA

start & finish

White Oak Trail

Page Mill Road

Adobe Creek

Sag Pond

Canyon Trail

Bella Vista Trail

Old Ranch Trail

Monte Bello Road

Stevens Creek Nature Trail

Skid Road Trail

Skid Road Trail

Santa Clara Co.
San Mateo Co.

Horseshoe Lake

Sag Pond

Indian Creek Trail

Old Ranch Trail

Black Mtn Trail Camp

Adobe Creek

Bay Area Ridge Trail

Stevens

Indian Canyon

Indian Creek

Monte Bello Road

Skyline Blvd

Creek

Canyon Trail

SKYLINE
RIDGE
OPEN SPACE
PRESERVE

MONTE BELLO
OPEN SPACE
PRESERVE

Black Mountain 2800'

0   0.2   0.4   0.6   0.8   1.0 mile
0   400   800   1200   1600 meters

Monte Bello
Open Space Preserve

This challenging but supremely rewarding loop gains and then loses about 1000 feet on its journey from the riparian corridor along Stevens Creek to the windswept grasslands of Monte Bello Ridge. The route takes you across the San Andreas fault and then up the ridge that forms the scenic backdrop for Sunnyvale, Cupertino, and Mountain View. The views from Black Mountain, the summit of Monte Bello Ridge, are superb, and the descent along the Old Ranch and Bella Vista trails offers some of the best hiking on the Peninsula.

Best Time

Spring and fall; Stevens Creek may be impassable in wet weather.

Finding the Trail

From I-280 in Los Altos Hills, take the Page Mill Rd./Arastradero Rd. exit and go south on Page Mill Rd. 7.2 miles to a parking area on your left.

From the junction of Skyline Blvd. and Page Mill Rd. southwest of Palo Alto, take Page Mill Rd. north 1.4 miles to a parking area on your right.

The trailhead is on the south corner of the parking area.▶1

Trail Description

Passing two information boards and a map holder, you follow the self-guiding **Stevens Creek Nature Trail**, a single track, as it wanders through open

TRAIL USE
Hike, Run, Bike
LENGTH
6.0 miles, 3-4 hours
VERTICAL FEET
±1400'
DIFFICULTY
– 1 2 3 **4** 5 +
TRAIL TYPE
Loop
SURFACE TYPE
Dirt

FEATURES
Canyon
Mountain
Stream
Autumn Colors
Wildflowers
Birds
Great Views
Photo Opportunity
Geologic Interest
Camping

FACILITIES
Restrooms

239

Skid Road was once traversed by teams of oxen dragging huge Douglas-firs felled by loggers. To make the going easier, the road was inlaid with flat-topped logs called "skids," which were doused with water to reduce friction. In 19th-century Western towns, the neighborhood frequented by loggers, which usually contained saloons, flophouses, and brothels, was often called Skid Road or Skid Row.

grassland. Along the way you'll find interpretive signs describing the flora, fauna, and geology of this wonderful preserve.

At a junction marked by a trail post and a rest bench,▶2 you stay on the Stevens Creek Nature Trail by veering sharply right. Now descending via switchbacks, you soon enter a mixed evergreen forest. A canyon, right, holds a seasonal tributary of Stevens Creek. A sharp left-hand bend brings you to a set of wooden steps leading down to **Stevens Creek**. After crossing Stevens Creek on rocks (this may be impossible during wet weather), you climb an eroded bank to get back on the trail. A moderate climb that soon levels brings you to a junction with the **Skid Road Trail**, where you bear left.▶3

Now a bridge takes you across Stevens Creek, and then the route temporarily narrows to single-track width. A moderate climb brings you to a bridge over a tributary that falls from Monte Bello Ridge. Curving right and climbing steeply, the trail takes you across a precipitous hillside and soon returns to dirt-road width.

Now ascending via S-bends, you reach a fence with a gate that prevents access to the Skid Road Trail by bikes and horses during wet weather. In a clearing, you find a T-junction with the **Canyon Trail**, a dirt road.▶4 Here you turn right.

The Canyon Trail angles left and almost immediately begins a steep climb. At a T-junction,▶5 the Canyon Trail turns right, but you switch to the **Indian Creek Trail**, also a dirt road, by veering left.

TRAIL 37 Monte Bello Open Space Preserve Elevation Profile

The view across Stevens Creek headwaters *follows the San Andreas fault.*

From Black Mountain, on a clear day, you can see most of the San Francisco Bay Area, bounded by Mt. Tamalpais, Mt. Diablo, and Mt. Hamilton. San Jose, Santa Clara, and the southern shoreline of San Francisco Bay lie at your feet.

Now you begin a long, steady climb up the side of **Monte Bello Ridge**.

The road eventually reaches two closely spaced junctions. At the first, a single-track trail leads left to Monte Bello Road. At the second, a dirt road veers left.▶6 To reach the **Black Mountain backpack camp** and a well-deserved rest spot, turn left on this dirt road. After about 100 feet, you come to a T-junction with a gravel road where you turn left to reach the camp.For backpack camp reservations, call the MROSD office: (650) 691-1200.

To press on to the summit of Black Mountain, stay on the Indian Creek Trail as it curves right and climbs past the turn-off to the backpack camp. The Indian Creek Trail ends at the next junction,▶7 where you join **Monte Bello Road** by bearing right. Continuing straight past the Black Mountain Trail, left, you soon stand atop **Black Mountain**, marveling at the 360° views from the broad, rocky, and treeless vantage point.▶8

After enjoying this splendid summit, retrace your route to the backpack camp turn-off.▶6/▶9 Here you swing right and after about 100 feet meet the gravel road at the T-junction mentioned above. Turn left and walk through the backpack camp. Just past the camp, you pass the single-track connector to the Indian Creek Trail, left. Continuing straight, you follow the ridgetop to a four-way junction.▶10 Here, Monte Bello Road joins sharply from the right and

Monte Bello Trail Options

OPTIONS

To shorten the route, you can omit the 3.5-mile excursion to Black Mountain by turning left on the **Canyon Trail**▶4 to the junction of the Canyon and Bella Vista trails,▶12 then follow the main route.

The **Black Mountain Trail**, which meets Monte Bello Road near the summit of Black Mountain,▶8 descends north to connect Monte Bello and Rancho San Antonio open space preserves.

continues by veering right. Your route, though, is the single track **Old Ranch Trail**, which angles left.

At the next junction,▶11 you swing left onto the **Bella Vista Trail**, another single track. When you reach the **Canyon Trail**, a dirt road, angle right.▶12 After passing a rest bench, right, you come to a junction with a hiking-only trail on the left. Continue straight for about 100 yards and then turn left on the **Stevens Creek Nature Trail**, a single track also closed to bikes and horses.▶13

Now you pass through an old orchard of mostly English walnut trees, soon reaching a junction, left, with the previously mentioned hiking-only trail. Here, you bear right and leave the orchard behind, making a rising traverse across an open slope. When you reach the junction where you started this loop, simply retrace your route the short distance to the parking area.▶14

| 大 | **MILESTONES** |

▶1	0.0	Take Stevens Creek Nature Trail
▶2	0.1	Right to Stay on Stevens Creek Nature Trail
▶3	1.2	Left on Skid Rd. Trall
▶4	1.8	Right on Canyon Trail
▶5	2.0	Left on Indian Creek Trail
▶6	3.0	Road to backpack camp on left
▶7	3.2	Right on Monte Bello Rd.
▶8	3.4	Black Mountain Trail on left, summit of Black Mountain (2800'); retrace to backpack camp junction
▶9	3.8	Right on dirt road, then left at T-junction with gravel road
▶10	4.0	Left on Old Ranch Trail
▶11	4.5	Left on Bella Vista Trail
▶12	5.3	Right on Canyon Trail
▶13	5.6	Left on Stevens Creek Nature Trail
▶14	6.0	Back at parking area

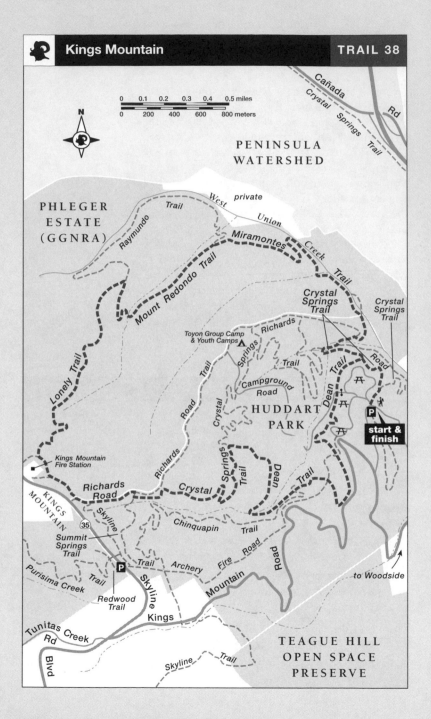

PENINSULA
WATERSHED

Cañada
Crystal Springs Trail
Rd

0   0.1   0.2   0.3   0.4   0.5 miles
0   200   400   600   800 meters

N

PHLEGER
ESTATE
(GGNRA)

West   private
Union   Creek

Trail

Raymundo

Miramontes

Trail

Mount Redondo Trail

Crystal
Springs
Trail

Crystal
Springs
Trail

Richards

Lonely Trail

Toyon Group Camp
& Youth Camps

Springs

Trail

Road

Dean Trail / Road

Campground
Road

HUDDART
PARK

start &
finish

Crystal

Kings Mountain
Fire Station

Richards
Road

Road

Richards

Crystal

Springs

Trail

Dean

Trail

KINGS
MOUNTAIN

Skyline

35

Chinquapin

Trail

Summit
Springs
Trail

Trail

Archery

Fire

Road

Mountain

Road

Purisima Creek

Trail

P

Redwood
Trail

Skyline

Kings

to Woodside

Tunitas Creek
Rd

Blvd

Skyline

Trail

TEAGUE HILL
OPEN SPACE
PRESERVE

Kings Mountain

This route explores the rugged terrain just north-west of Huddart Park, and the contrast between the county park and it's Phleger Estate neighbor could not be more extreme. Trading picnic areas and sports fields for a serene forest of coast redwoods, you climb the rugged eastern side of Kings Mountain on the aptly named Lonely Trail, then descend through the heavily wooded county park, a favorite among equestrians.

Best Time

All year, but trails may be muddy in wet weather

Finding the Trail

From I-280 in Woodside, take the Woodside Rd./Woodside/Hwy. 84 exit and go southwest 1.6 miles to Kings Mountain Rd. Turn right, go 2.1 miles to the Huddart Park entrance, and turn right. At 0.2 mile there is an entrance kiosk and self-registration station. There are parking areas on both sides of the road just ahead. The trailhead is a few hundred feet north of the parking areas, on the east side of a paved road that is signed for Zwierlein, Werder, Madrone, and Miwok picnic areas. ▶1

Trail Description

The trailhead has information boards, a map holder, and water. You follow a single track that curves right and descends to a left-hand switchback amid stands of coast redwood, Douglas-fir, coast live oak, and

---

TRAIL USE
Hike, Run
LENGTH
7.9 miles, 3-5 hours
VERTICAL FEET
±1500'
DIFFICULTY
– 1 2 3 4 **5** +
TRAIL TYPE
Loop
SURFACE TYPE
Dirt

FEATURES
Canyon
Stream
Birds
Wildlife
Cool & Shady
Secluded

FACILITIES
Restrooms
Picnic Tables
Phone
Water

245

tanbark oak. Soon the Bay Tree Trail departs sharply to the right, and you have a sports field, picnic area, and restrooms on your left. Now reach a junction with the **Crystal Springs Trail,**▶2 where you bear left and follow a rolling course. You pass the Dean Trail, your return route, left.▶3

Now the trail descends on a gentle grade, via more switchbacks, into a canyon holding a seasonal tributary of **West Union Creek**, shown on the park map as **McGarvey Gulch Creek**. A junction awaits you at the canyon bottom.▶4 You don't cross the creek, but instead go straight on a **connector**, where soon you merge with the **Richards Road Trail** and turn sharply left,▶5 crossing a culvert that holds the creek. At a junction, you leave the road by veering right onto the **Miramontes Trail**, a single track.▶6 The trail gradually bends left and descends to West Union Creek, which is right.

 Canyon

Your trail climbs via switchbacks to a junction.▶7 You continue straight, now on the single-track **Mount Redondo Trail**. At the next junction, the Raymundo Trail goes straight and your route, the **Lonely Trail**, heads left.▶8

Soon you begin to work your way across a canyon wall that drops steeply left. You are now high on the eastern flank of Kings Mountain, a long ridge extending from near Hwy. 92 southeast to Bear

---

Semi-Loop Trip

OPTIONS

An easier, slightly shorter (6.9 mile) route is to follow the Raymundo Trail from its junction with the Lonely Trail▶8 and descend along West Union Creek to the junction of the Mount Redondo and Miramontes trails.▶7 Then retrace your route to the parking area.▶1

Gulch Road. Skyline Blvd., one of California's pre-mier scenic routes, runs along the ridge's summit.

After a brief respite, you resume a steady climb beside a deep ravine, left. The trail is a narrow track perched on a steep hillside. With the communica-tion towers of the Kings Mountain Fire Station just uphill, you follow a rolling course parallel to Skyline Blvd., passing a trail that joins from the right.

At the boundary of **Huddart County Park**, you go straight on the **Richards Road Trail**, a dirt road.▶**9** After passing the Skyline Trail, right, you turn right onto the **Summit Springs Trail**.▶**10** After several hundred feet, you find the Crystal Springs Trail, left, and a rest bench. Here you follow the **Crystal Springs Trail**, left, past a gate that prevents access by horses during wet weather. The wide path descends gently along a ridge and then through for-est. At a junction with the **Dean Trail**, turn sharply right and continue descending.▶**11**

 Secluded

Just before reaching a bridge over a seasonal creek, you pass McGarvey Flat, a lovely spot with a picnic table and several rest benches hewn from logs. A level walk brings you to a four-way junction (shown incorrectly on the Huddart map).▶**12** Here, you have three choices. Your route, the Dean Trail, veers left. Stay on the Dean Trail as it twice crosses the Archery Fire Road.

At the edge of a paved road near the Miwok pic-nic area, the Dean Trail turns sharply left and then begins a series of switchbacks, descending past the Madrone picnic area. Stay on the Dean Trail, here a wide path, as it makes a curving descent past more picnic areas. At a T-junction with the **Crystal Springs Trail**,▶**13** you turn right and retrace your route to the trailhead.▶**14**

▶1 0.0 Take single-track trail northeast; Bay Tree Trail on right

▶2 0.2 Left on Crystal Springs Trail

▶3 0.4 Dean Trail on left

▶4 0.7 Straight on connector to Richards Road Trail

▶5 0.8 Merge with Richards Road Trail, then left across creek

▶6 0.9 Right on Miramontes Trail

▶7 2.3 Straight on Mount Redondo Trail

▶8 3.1 Left on Lonely Trail

▶9 4.3 Left on Richards Road Trail

▶10 4.9 Right on Summit Springs Trail, then left on Crystal Springs Trail

▶11 5.7 Right on Dean Trail

▶12 6.3 Left at four-way junction to stay on Dean Trail

▶13 7.5 Right at T-junction on Crystal Springs Trail, retrace start of route

▶14 7.9 Back at trailhead

The Golden Gate Promenade/Bay Trail *follows the north shore of the Presidio (Trail 39), connecting the Golden Gate Bridge with Marina Green and Fort Mason.*

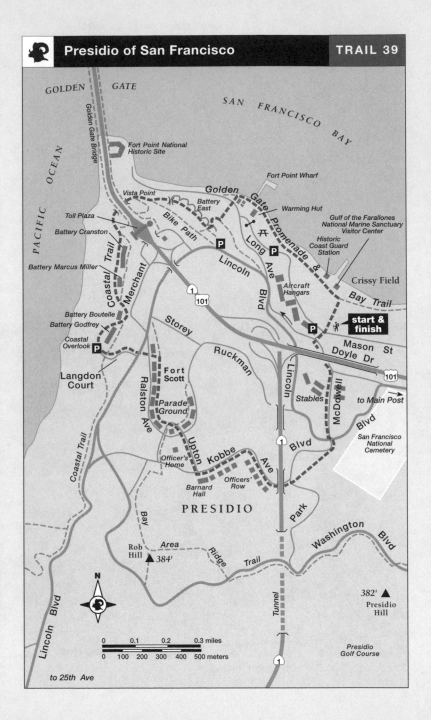

GOLDEN GATE

SAN FRANCISCO BAY

PACIFIC OCEAN

Golden Gate Bridge

Fort Point National Historic Site

Fort Point Wharf

Vista Point

Golden Gate Promenade

Battery East

Warming Hut

Toll Plaza

Bike Path

Gulf of the Farallones National Marine Sanctuary Visitor Center

Battery Cranston

Long Ave

Historic Coast Guard Station

Battery Marcus Miller

Coastal Trail

Merchant

Lincoln

Blvd

Aircraft Hangars

Crissy Field

Bay Trail

1 101

Storey

Battery Boutelle
Battery Godfrey

P

start & finish

Coastal Overlook

P

Ruckman

Mason St
Doyle Dr

Langdon Court

Ralston Ave

Fort Scott

Lincoln

101

to Main Post

Parade Ground

Stables

McDowell

Blvd

San Francisco National Cemetery

Coastal Trail

Upton

Kobbe

Ave

1 Blvd

Officer's Home

Barnard Hall

Officers' Row

PRESIDIO

Bay

Area

Park

Rob Hill ▲ 384'

Ridge

Trail

Washington Blvd

N

Tunnel

382' ▲
Presidio Hill

Lincoln Blvd

| 0 | 0.1 | 0.2 | 0.3 miles |
| 0 | 100 | 200 | 300 | 400 | 500 meters |

1

Presidio Golf Course

to 25th Ave

Presidio of San Francisco

The only urban route in this book, this loop through the Presidio of San Francisco is both an enjoyable walk back in time, and a hopeful look forward at the effort to reclaim and restore developed lands for public enjoyment. Along the way you pass military buildings from the late 19th and early 20th centuries, vantage points with views of the Golden Gate, San Francisco Bay, and beyond, and a warming hut where food, drinks, books, maps, and other information are available. The Presidio was transferred by the Army to the National Park Service in 1994, terminating more than 200 years of military history dating back to the Spanish era.

Best Time

All year; expect fog in summer

Finding the Trail

From the Presidio's Marina Gate entrance at the west end of Marina Blvd., go west on Mason St. 1 mile to a paved parking area, left.▶1

Trail Description

From the west end of the parking area, head west several hundred feet on **Mason Avenue** to its junction with **Crissy Field Avenue**. Turn sharply left and follow Crissy Field Avenue uphill, passing under Doyle Drive/U.S. 101, to a junction with **McDowell Avenue**.▶2 Here you angle right and

TRAIL USE
Hike, Run, Bike
LENGTH
2.6 miles, 1-2 hours
VERTICAL FEET
±300'
DIFFICULTY
– 1 **2** 3 4 5 +
TRAIL TYPE
Loop
SURFACE TYPE
Dirt, Paved

FEATURES
Dogs Allowed
Child Friendly
Shore
Wildflowers
Birds
Great Views
Photo Opportunity
Historic

FACILITIES
Restrooms
Phone
Picnic Tables
Water
Concessions

251

The Presidio Pet Cemetery *is located beneath the Doyle Drive/U.S. 101 bridge.*

climb moderately past the **Presidio stables** and the GGNRA's archives and records center.

Carefully crossing Lincoln Blvd., you take **Park Blvd**. gently uphill to a junction.▶3 Here you angle left on a dirt path that rises steadily through a forest of Monterey cypress and eucalyptus, both planted here. Meeting Park again and crossing it,▶4 you take **Kobbe Avenue** past **Officers Row**, a set of beautiful homes built in 1912. Climbing gently, you pass Barnard Hall, an imposing brick building named for John G. Barnard, Chief Engineer of Construction of Fortifications of San Francisco Harbor and Fort Point, 1853-1854.

At a four-way junction, you turn right on **Upton Avenue**,▶5 following a sidewalk on its left side. Some of the officers' homes in the Presidio are quite lavish, with spacious lawns and exotic landscaping. Where Upton veers right, you continue straight across Ralston Avenue, and then enter **Fort Winfield Scott**.▶6

Turn left and keep the parade ground on your

🏠 **Historic**

right. As you walk along the left side of the parade ground, views stretch to the Golden Gate Bridge, Angel Island, and Mt. Diablo. With a sports field on your right, you turn left on the **Juan Bautista de Anza National Historic Trail**, also part of the Bay Area Ridge Trail.▶7 You walk on pavement between two buildings (numbers 1207 and 1208), cross Ralston, and then come to Lincoln.▶8 Cross carefully, and then follow **Langdon Court** about 50 feet to a trail post. You jog left, then veer right through a parking area, heading toward the Pacific Ocean.

At the west end of the parking area, you follow a paved road that soon changes to dirt and gravel. Turning right at a trail post, you get on the **Coastal Trail**, a wide dirt-and-gravel path that is part of the Anza/Bay Area Ridge Trail.▶9 The low concrete bunkers beside the trail were built from 1891 to 1900 for coastal defense. At the end of World War II, the guns in these bunkers were removed. Near the bunkers the trail forks: hikers stay left, bicyclists stay right.▶10 You follow the rocky and eroded hiking trail to another fork, where the left branch is signed for the Anza/Bay Area Ridge Trail.

Staying left here, and right at the next fork, where a trail goes left to a viewpoint, you skirt the coastal cliffs and descend via wooden steps. Now on level ground, you merge with the trail for bicyclists, which joins sharply from the right.▶11 Ahead is a paved path which goes under the **Golden Gate Bridge**. You get on it and angle left. Use caution: The paved path is shared by bicyclists, joggers, walkers, and others.

Beyond the bridge the trail forks, and you stay left, enjoying a view that reaches from the Golden Gate to the East Bay hills. You pass a trail, left to **Battery East**, which dates from 1876, and a picnic area. A brick path goes right and uphill to the Golden Gate Bridge gift shop. You descend to a junction with a trail, left, signed for FORT POINT.▶12

The fort is named for Winfield Scott, who served in the army from before the War of 1812 until the Civil War. He is best known for his command of U.S. troops during the Mexican-American War.

 Great Views

Crissy Field was once a landing strip for airplanes.

 Shore

Here you turn left and in a clearing come to a four-way junction. Battery East is left, and a trail to a parking area is right. You continue straight and descend steeply over rough ground, passing a trail, right. Aided by steps, you soon reach Marine Drive, the paved road to Fort Point.

Cross the road, and when you reach a seawall, turn right on a paved path, part of the **Golden Gate Promenade** and the **San Francisco Bay Trail.**►13 Nearby are restrooms, water, and a warming hut with food, drinks, books, maps, and other information.►14 Beyond the warming hut, the path changes to dirt and gravel. Information boards along the way tell you about the geology and history of the Golden Gate. A path cuts sharply right, going back to the warming hut. You pass a picnic area, right, and then reach a five-way junction beside Long Avenue.

Here you continue straight on the dirt-and-gravel path. An historic **Coast Guard station** and the **Gulf of the Farallones National Marine Sanctuary visitor center** are left. You are passing through an area that has been extensively restored and landscaped with native plants. Several hundred feet past the visitor center, you turn right,►15 climb a few steps and then cross **Crissy Field**, formerly a landing strip for planes. After about 100 yards you reach Mason, which you cross to return to the parking area.►16

MILESTONES

▶1   0.0 West on Mason Ave. to Crissy Field Ave., then left

▶2   0.1 Right on McDowell Ave.

▶3   0.3 Cross Lincoln Blvd., take Park Blvd. uphill, then right on dirt path

▶4   0.5 Cross Park, straight on Kobbe Ave. past Officers Row

▶5   0.8 Right on Upton Ave.

▶6   0.9 Enter Fort Scott, go left around parade ground

▶7   1.1 Left on Juan Bautista de Anza National Historic Trail

▶8   1.2 Cross Lincoln Blvd., go straight on Langdon Court,
          then through parking area

▶9   1.3 Right on Coastal Trail

▶10   1.4 Left at fork on hiking-only trail

▶11   1.6 Left on paved path under Golden Gate Bridge

▶12   1.8 Left on trail signed for Fort Point; Battery East is left

▶13   2.0 Right on Golden Gate Promenade beside seawall

▶14   2.1 Pass Warming Hut, right

▶15   2.5 Right on trail across Crissy Field

▶16   2.6 Back at parking area

Trails from the Golden Gate

OPTIONS

From the Golden Gate Bridge, the Coastal Trail goes south and then southwest to Baker Beach, Lands End, and the Cliff House. Eastward, the Golden Gate Promenade/ Bay Trail extends past Fort Mason to Aquatic Park. Northward, the Bay, Ridge, and Coastal trails follow the bridge's east sidewalk to Marin County.

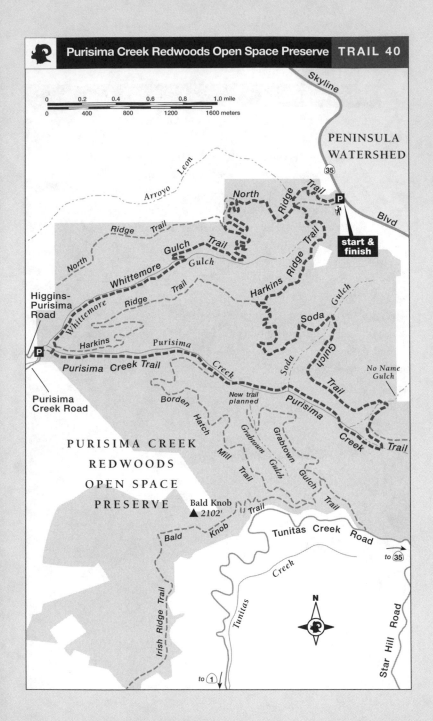

0   0.2   0.4   0.6   0.8   1.0 mile
0   400   800   1200   1600 meters

Skyline

PENINSULA WATERSHED

35

North

Ridge

Trail

P

start & finish

Blvd

Arroyo

Leon

Ridge   Trail

North

Whittemore   Gulch   Trail

Gulch

Harkins   Ridge   Trail

Higgins- Purisima Road

Whittemore   Ridge   Trail

Soda   Gulch

P

Harkins

Purisima

Creek

Soda

Gulch

No Name Gulch

Purisima   Creek   Trail

Purisima Creek Road

Purisima

Creek

Trail

Borden

New trail planned

Hatch

Grabtown   Gulch

Grabtown   Gulch   Trail

PURISIMA CREEK REDWOODS OPEN SPACE PRESERVE

Mill

Trail

Bald Knob
▲ 2102'

Trail

Tunitas   Creek   Road

to 35

Bald   Knob

Creek

N

Irish Ridge Trail

Tunitas

Star Hill Road

to 1

Purisima Creek Redwoods Open Space Preserve

One of the premier routes on the Peninsula, this challenging loop explores the north half of this expansive preserve. Dropping more than 1500 feet to Purisima Creek, you pass the giant stumps of old-growth redwoods, and can imagine yourself going back in time to an era when the canyons here echoed with the sounds of men and machinery hard at work harvesting a seemingly limitless resource. Completing the loop via a vigorous climb, you pass through a Douglas-fir forest and then a zone of coastal scrub, which make this one of the most botanically diverse routes in this book.

Best Time

All year, but trails may be muddy in wet weather.

Finding the Trail

From the junction of Skyline Blvd. and Hwy. 92, take Skyline Blvd. southeast 4.5 miles to a parking area on the right. The trailhead is on the southwest corner of the parking area.

Trail Description

From the trailhead,▶1 go through a gap in a wood fence, passing two information boards and a map holder on your right. After 100 feet or so you reach a junction with the **North Ridge Trail**, part of the Bay Area Ridge Trail, as are some of the other trails on this route. Here you bear right.

TRAIL USE
Hike, Run, Bike
LENGTH
10.1 miles, 4-6 hours
VERTICAL FEET
±1600'
DIFFICULTY
- 1 2 3 4 **5** +
TRAIL TYPE
Loop
SURFACE TYPE
Dirt

FEATURES
Canyon
Stream
Autumn Colors
Wildflowers
Birds
Cool & Shady
Great Views
Secluded
Historic

FACILITIES
Restrooms
Phone

> The Borden Hatch Mill site is now a jungle-like area of ferns, thimbleberry, and hazelnut, all presided over by lofty redwoods.

You switchback downhill to a four-way junction.▶2 You go straight, now on the **Harkins Ridge Trail**. This trail, a wide dirt path, is open to horses and bikes. After following the trail through several bends, you reach open ground on a scrubby hillside that drops to the right. Now you reach a T-junction with a closed road, left. Here, you turn right and descend a dirt road. After a steep, eroded pitch, the road curves right, levels, and leads to a junction.▶3

Here you turn left on the **Soda Gulch Trail**, a single track closed to bikes and horses that leads downhill into the realm of the redwoods. When you reach **Soda Gulch**, you turn sharply right and cross a wood bridge. After traversing an open hillside, you cross an an tributary of Purisima Creek at the bottom of a steep canyon.

You zigzag uphill to a junction with the **Purisima Creek Trail**,▶4 and bear right. You follow this old dirt road as it curves left and descends to Purisima Creek, which flows under the road through a culvert. Soon a bridge takes you across **Purisima Creek**, which is now left. The creek from Soda Gulch joins from the right and you cross it on the next bridge.

You descend on a moderate grade to the creek and cross it on a bridge, soon passing a junction with the Borden Hatch Mill Trail, left.▶5 The trail is named for the old Borden & Hatch Mill, one of the two best-known mills that used to operate in the canyon (the other was the Pharis Shingle Mill).

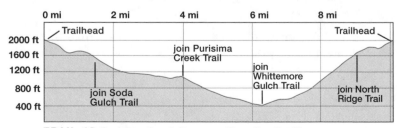

TRAIL 40 Purisima Creek Preserve Elevation Profile

Just before the Higgins Purisima parking area,▶6 you turn right and cross Purisima Creek on a wood bridge. About 50 feet ahead is a second T-junction. Here, the Harkins Ridge Trail goes right, but you follow the **Whittemore Gulch Trail**, a rocky dirt road, to the left. (Use caution: this trail is popular with bicyclists; it is closed seasonally to bike and horses).

 Historic

Soon you pass a fence with a gate that prevents access by bikes and horses during wet weather. The road curves right, narrows to a single track, and begins to climb. **Whittemore Gulch**, holding a tributary of Purisima Creek within its steep and narrow walls, is left.

A small bridge takes you across the creek in Whittemore Gulch, and then you climb, aided by switchbacks, past a short connector to the North Ridge Trail. After more twists and turns, you come to another seasonal-closure gate and then a T-junction with the **North Ridge Trail.**▶7 Now you bear right on this dirt road and enjoy a mostly level walk. At the four-way junction where you started this loop,▶8 turn left onto the hiking-only trail and retrace your route uphill to the parking area.▶9

🚶 MILESTONES

▶1 0.0 Take dirt road southwest, then right on North Ridge Trail

▶2 0.5 Straight at four-way junction on Harkins Ridge Trail

▶3 1.4 Left on Soda Gulch Trail

▶4 4.0 Right on Purisima Creek Trail

▶5 5.3 Borden Hatch Mill Trail on left; continue straight

▶6 6.3 Right across bridge, then left on Whittemore Gulch Trail

▶7 9.1 Right at T-junction on North Ridge Trail

▶8 9.6 Left at four-way junction, retrace to parking area

▶9 10.1 Back at parking area

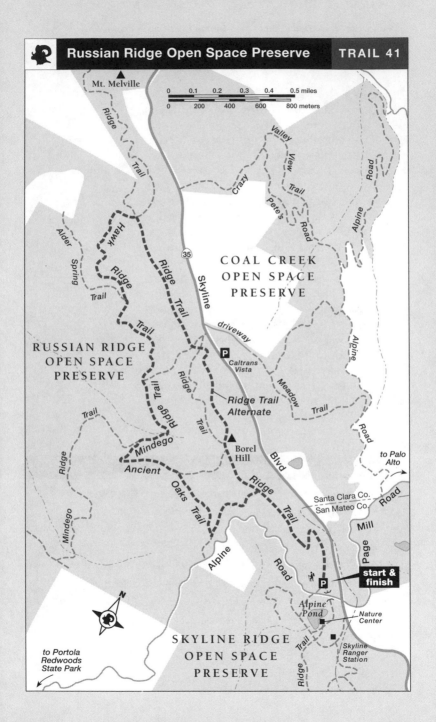

Mt. Melville

0   0.1   0.2   0.3   0.4   0.5 miles
0   200   400   600   800 meters

Ridge Trail

Crazy

Valley

View

Trail

Pete's

35

Road

Alpine

Road

Skyline

COAL CREEK
OPEN SPACE
PRESERVE

Hawk

Ridge

Alder

Spring

Trail

Ridge

Trail

Ridge Trail

Alpine

driveway

P

Caltrans
Vista

RUSSIAN RIDGE
OPEN SPACE
PRESERVE

Ridge

Trail

Meadow

Ridge Trail
Alternate

Trail

Trail

Road

Borel
Hill

Ridge

Blvd

Mindego

Trail

Ancient

to Palo
Alto

Ridge

Oaks

Santa Clara Co.

Trail

Trail

San Mateo Co.

Road

Mindego

Mill

Page

Road

Alpine

Road

start &
finish

P

N

Alpine
Pond

Nature
Center

to Portola
Redwoods
State Park

SKYLINE RIDGE
OPEN SPACE
PRESERVE

Trail

Skyline
Ranger
Station

Ridge

Russian Ridge
Open Space Preserve

This remarkable ramble through what many consider the Peninsula's most scenic preserve uses the
Ridge, Ancient Oaks, Mindego Ridge, Alder Spring,
and Hawk Ridge trails to sample a wide variety of
habitats, from oak forests perched on Pacific-facing
slopes to dazzling wildflower meadows atop Borel
Hill, whose displays intensify week by week during
spring. Birders will definitely want to have binoculars handy to pick out soaring hawks and falcons,
right along with various Bay Area landmarks. Part of
this semi-loop route follows the Bay Area Ridge
Trail, which runs along the spine of Russian Ridge,
parallel to Skyline Blvd.

Best Time

All year, but spring wildflowers are the prime attraction; trails may be muddy in wet weather.

Finding the Trail

From the junction of Skyline Blvd. and Page Mill
Rd./Alpine Rd. south of Palo Alto, take Alpine Rd.
west about 100 yards to a parking area on the right.
This parking area serves both Russian Ridge and
Skyline Ridge open space preserves. On busy days
parking may be unavailable. Additional parking
with access to the preserve's trails is available at the
Caltrans Vista Point parking area 1.1 miles northwest on Skyline Blvd. The trailhead is on the west
side of the parking area.▶1

TRAIL USE
Hike, Run, Bike
LENGTH
4.6 miles, 2-3 hours
VERTICAL FEET
±1050'
DIFFICULTY
– 1 2 **3** 4 5 +
TRAIL TYPE
Loop
SURFACE TYPE
Dirt

FEATURES
Summit
Wildflowers
Birds
Wildlife
Great Views
Photo Opportunity

FACILITIES
Restrooms

261

Trail Description

Your route, the single-track **Ridge Trail**, heads northwest from the trailhead. This is part of the Bay Area Ridge Trail. In this preserve, there is also a 0.5-mile segment of dirt road called the Ridge Trail, which climbs up and over Borel Hill, in this book designated as the Ridge Trail (alternate).

Russian Ridge is famous for its springtime displays of wildflowers, with sometimes more than 50 species seen on docent-led hikes. Lupine, clarkia, checker mallow, red maids, California buttercup, fiddleneck, purple owl's clover, Johnny jump-ups, mule ears, tidy-tips, and California poppies are among the most common grassland species found here. In the preserve's cool, forested canyons, you may find shade-loving plants like trillium, fairy bells, mission bells, and hound's tongue.

Aided by several switchbacks, you steadily gain elevation and are rewarded by ever-improving views east across the San Andreas fault to Monte Bello Ridge and Black Mountain, and southeast to Mt. Umunhum and Loma Prieta. After about 0.5 mile, you turn left at a junction▶2 with a dirt road **connector** to the Ancient Oaks Trail. Now you follow this road curving left past a wooded ravine. With Alpine Road immediately left, you meet a junction with the **Ancient Oaks Trail**.▶3 Turning right on a single track, you enjoy a splendid view of the Pacific Ocean as you make a rising traverse across a grassy hillside.

The trail curves left, levels briefly, and then starts to descend. Now a connector to the Ridge Trail joins on the right, but you continue straight. Following a ridgetop downhill, you skirt a steep hillside, left, that drops into a canyon.

Westerly winds from the Pacific push fog inland to Russian Ridge, where it helps provide water for plants during the dry season. Moisture dripping

Bicyclists *ascend multi-use Ridge Trail toward Borel Hill. Black Mountain is on the horizon (left).*

from trees may cause the ground underfoot to be wet and slippery.

Losing elevation, you come to a junction with the **Mindego Ridge Trail**, on which you veer right.▶4 This dirt road wanders over level ground to a junction with the **Alder Spring Trail**.▶5 Now you turn left and follow a dirt road through open grassland.

You enjoy a level walk, with views of Mindego Hill and, on a clear day, the Pacific Ocean. Now descending on a moderate grade, the road alternates between wooded and open areas. At a junction with the **Hawk Ridge Trail**, you go straight.▶6 The top-of-the-world feeling is enhanced as the trail rises toward a gap in the crest of Russian Ridge.

At a four-way junction with the **Ridge Trail**, a turn right on this dirt road.▶7 Ahead about 1 mile is Borel Hill, the geographic high point of this route. When you reach a four-way junction with the Mindego Ridge Trail,▶8 you continue straight and begin a moderate climb. After about 75 feet, a single-track segment of the Ridge Trail veers right, but you stay on the **Ridge Trail (alternate)**, an eroded track that soon starts to snake its way uphill.

Near the summit of **Borel Hill** is truly a sea of wildflowers, a carpet of color. At a four-way junction,▶9 a trail goes right to a vantage point, but you turn left for the final push to the summit, where a sign shows you are 2572 feet above sea level. From this dramatic perch, most of the San Francisco Bay Area is revealed.

When you are ready to leave, put the elevation sign at your back and follow the trail in front of you. It soon joins the **Ridge Trail (alternate)** at a T-junction. You turn left and, after about 100 feet, merge with the **Ridge Trail.** ►10 The next junction ►11 is with the connector to the Ancient Oaks Trail you used near the start of this trip. From here, retrace your route and descend to the parking area. ►12

🚶 MILESTONES

►1   0.0 Take Ridge Trail northwest

►2   0.5 Left on connector to Ancient Oaks Trail

►3   0.8 Right on Ancient Oaks Trail

►4   1.5 Right on Mindego Ridge Trail

►5   1.8 Left on Alder Spring Trail

►6   2.2 Straight on Hawk Ridge Trail

►7   2.8 Right at four-way junction on Ridge Trail (dirt road)

►8   3.3 Straight at four-way junction on Ridge Trail (dirt road-alternate)

►9   3.8 Left to Borel Hill (2572'), then south to Ridge Trail (dirt road) and left at T-junction

►10 3.9 Straight at junction with Ridge Trail (single track)

►11 4.1 Straight at junction with connector to Ancient Oaks Trail and retrace to parking area

►12 4.6 Back at parking area

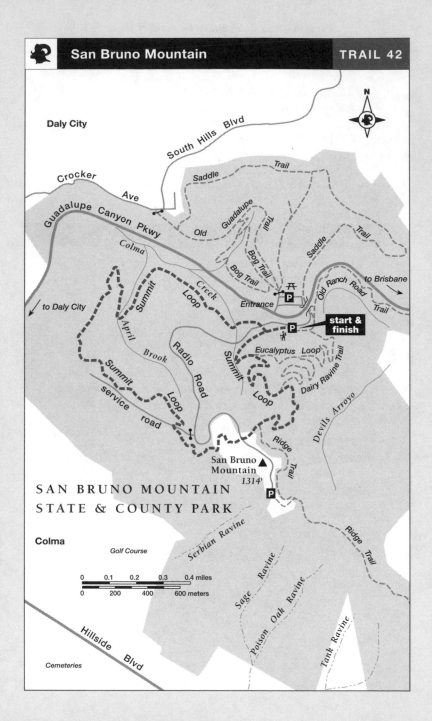

Daly City

South Hills Blvd

Crocker Ave

Guadalupe Canyon Pkwy

Saddle Trail

Old Guadalupe Trail

Colma

Saddle Trail

Bog Trail

Bog Trail

Creek Loop

to Brisbane

Entrance

Old Ranch Road

Trail

to Daly City

Summit

April Brook

Radio Road

Summit Loop

start & finish

Eucalyptus Loop

Dairy Ravine Trail

Summit service road

Loop

Devils Arroyo

Ridge Trail

San Bruno Mountain 1314'

SAN BRUNO MOUNTAIN
STATE & COUNTY PARK

Colma

Golf Course

Serbian Ravine

Sage Ravine

Poison Oak Ravine

Ridge Trail

Tank Ravine

0   0.1   0.2   0.3   0.4 miles
0   200   400   600 meters

Hillside Blvd

Cemeteries

San Bruno Mountain State & County Park

This exploration of San Bruno Mountain State and County Park via the Summit Loop Trail takes you to an island of open space surrounded by a sea of residential and industrial development. Despite this urban setting, the mountain's rugged canyons and ridges host a remarkable array of rare and/or endangered species. Among these are several species of butterflies and more than a dozen plants, including three manzanitas. When not fogbound, the trails here afford views of San Francisco and beyond, and the spring wildflower displays are sensational (most of the year, something is in bloom).

Best Time

All year; often foggy and windy; trails may be muddy in wet weather.

Finding the Trail

From Hwy. 101 northbound in San Francisco, take the Third St. exit (not well signed). Go 0.5 mile to Paul Ave., turn left, go 0.1 mile to San Bruno Ave., and turn left again. At 0.9 mile San Bruno Ave. joins Bayshore Blvd. Continue straight another 1.5 miles to Guadalupe Canyon Pkwy. and turn right. Go 2.2 miles to the park entrance, right. Just past the entry kiosk, turn right, passing the main parking area, pass under the bridge, and go 0.2 mile to a paved parking area on the south side of Guadalupe Canyon Pkwy. The trailhead is on the south side of the parking area.

From Hwy. 101 southbound in San Francisco,

TRAIL USE
Hike, Run
LENGTH
3.1 miles, 2-3 hours
VERTICAL FEET
±700'
DIFFICULTY
– 1 2 **3** 4 5 +
TRAIL TYPE
Loop
SURFACE TYPE
Dirt

FEATURES
Mountain
Summit
Wildflowers
Birds
Great Views
Photo Opportunity

FACILITIES
Restrooms
Picnic Tables
Water
Phone

267

Eucalyptus trees are not native to California, and these hearty and adaptable trees present a problem for land managers. Logging here in the 1990s removed some of the mountain's eucalyptus trees, but public pressure stopped this effort.

take the Cow Palace/Third St. exit, staying right toward the Cow Palace. At 0.3 mile you reach Bayshore Blvd. and go straight. Go another 1.8 miles to Guadalupe Canyon Pkwy., turn right, and follow the directions above.

Facilities

None at the trailhead; restrooms, picnic tables, phone, and water are at the main parking area.

Trail Description

After passing an information board and a map holder, you come to a junction▶1 and turn right on the **Summit Loop Trail**, a single track (shown as **Summit Trail** on the park map). Soon you reach a junction where the Summit Loop Trail divides.▶2 Here you stay left and climb through a eucalyptus forest.

After a switchback left, you pass the Eucalyptus Loop Trail, left,▶3 and bear right to stay on the Summit Loop Trail. As you gain elevation, the views of San Francisco, San Francisco Bay, and the East Bay hills become more and more dramatic. Where the Dairy Ravine Trail angles left,▶4 stay right on the Summit Loop Trail.

Gaining a ridgetop, you pass the Ridge Trail, left.▶5 Continue on the Summit Loop Trail to the paved road that climbs from the park entrance to just below the mountain's summit.▶6 Your route resumes on the other side of the road, just right of a metal gate across a paved driveway.

San Bruno Mountain itself is actually a long ridge, topped by communication towers, which angles northwest toward Daly City from Brisbane. The mountain, often fog-bound and buffeted by high winds, resembles an island rising above an urban sea of industrial and residential development. The mountain is home to more than a dozen rare or endangered plants, including several species of manzanita. The park also provides habitat for four species of endangered or threatened butterflies—San Bruno elfin, Mission blue, Callippe silverspot, and Bay checkerspot.

The trail zigzags its way downhill on a gentle grade past communication towers and satellite dishes to a paved road, which you cross. You traverse a canyon wall, descend a ridgetop, then follow the trail as it bends sharply right and slices across a hillside.

At the bottom of the canyon, the trail bends left, then veers right to cross **April Brook**. Now heading downstream, your route soon curves right, climbs on a moderate grade, and then levels. Several plank bridges help you cross areas that may be wet. You cross a paved road and then reach the junction where you began this loop.▶7 From here, turn left and retrace your route to the parking area.▶8

⫟ MILESTONES

▶1   0.0 Go past information board, then right on Summit Loop Trail

▶2   0.1 Left on Summit Loop Trail

▶3   0.3 Eucalyptus Loop Trail on left; stay right

▶4   0.7 Dairy Ravine Trail on left; go straight

▶5   0.9 Ridge Trail on left; go straight

▶6   1.0 Cross paved road, continue southwest on Summit Loop Trail

▶7   3.0 Cross paved road, then left at junction,
              and retrace to parking area

▶8   3.1 Back at parking area

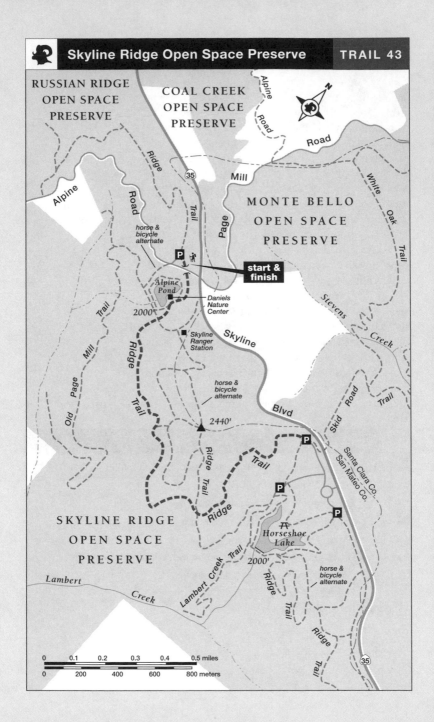

Skyline Ridge Open Space Preserve   TRAIL 43

RUSSIAN RIDGE OPEN SPACE PRESERVE

COAL CREEK OPEN SPACE PRESERVE

MONTE BELLO OPEN SPACE PRESERVE

start & finish

Alpine Road

Alpine Road

35

Mill

Page Trail

Ridge Road

horse & bicycle alternate

Alpine Pond

Daniels Nature Center

2000'

Skyline Ranger Station

Skyline

Stevens Creek

White Oak Trail

Old Page Mill Trail

Ridge Trail

horse & bicycle alternate

2440'

Blvd

Ridge Trail

Skid Road

Trail

Santa Clara Co.
San Mateo Co.

SKYLINE RIDGE OPEN SPACE PRESERVE

Ridge Trail

Ridge

Horseshoe Lake

2000'

horse & bicycle alternate

Lambert Creek

Lambert Creek Trail

Ridge Trail

Ridge Trail

35

| 0 | 0.1 | 0.2 | 0.3 | 0.4 | 0.5 miles |
| 0 | | 200 | 400 | 600 | 800 meters |

Skyline Ridge
Open Space Preserve

This out-and-back jaunt along the Ridge Trail rises from the forested environs of Alpine Pond to a breezy realm of grassland and chaparral where views of Butano Ridge, Portola Redwoods State Park, and the Pacific coast await. The spring wildflowers here are superb, and it is easy to see why this stretch of trail, which is part of the Bay Area Ridge Trail, is a favorite among hikers young and old alike. This trip can easily be combined with a circuit of cattail-fringed Alpine Pond, which is near the trailhead, or a loop around Horseshoe Lake, which is near the turn-around point.

TRAIL USE
Hike, Run, Bike
LENGTH
3.4 miles, 2-3 hours
VERTICAL FEET
±250'
DIFFICULTY
– 1 2 **3** 4 5 +
TRAIL TYPE
Out & Back
SURFACE TYPE
Dirt

FEATURES
Child Friendly
Shore
Wildflowers
Birds
Great Views

FACILITIES
Nature Center
Restrooms

Best Time

All year, but trails may be muddy in wet weather.

Finding the Trail

From the junction of Skyline Blvd. and Page Mill Rd./Alpine Rd. south of Palo Alto, take Alpine Rd. west about 100 yards to a parking area on the right. This parking area serves both Skyline Ridge OSP and Russian Ridge OSP. On busy days parking may be unavailable. Additional parking with access to the preserve's trails is available at the parking area for Horseshoe Lake, 0.9 mile southeast on Skyline Blvd. The trailhead is on the south side of the parking area.

Trail Description

A set of steps and also a wheelchair-accessible path lead down from the parking area to an information

271

Much of the land that became Skyline Ridge Open Space Preserve (and also Russian Ridge Open Space Preserve) was at one time owned by a politician named James Rolph, Jr., or "Sunny Jim," as he was known to his constituents.

board.►1 Just ahead, your route, the **Ridge Trail**, passes under Alpine Road through a tunnel. The Ridge Trail is part of the Bay Area Ridge Trail, and from here to the parking area serving Horseshoe Lake it is closed to bikes and horses. (**Bicyclists** and **equestrians** headed for Horseshoe Lake and beyond must use a trailhead just across Alpine Road, and then follow an alternate trail.

After passing a gravel road that joins from the left, you soon arrive at **Alpine Pond** and the **Daniels Nature Center**.►2 Just past the nature center you come to a fork. Here the Pond Loop Trail goes right, but you follow the Ridge Trail, a single track, to the left. Now the trail crosses a culvert, angles right, and arrives at a four-way junction with a paved road. You continue straight, soon passing an unsigned trail and a fenced building, both uphill and left.

Emerging from forest, you make a rising traverse across an open hillside that drops right. The trail makes a couple of bends, crosses a culvert, and the curves around the rock outcrop, which is left. From a vantage point with a rest bench, where the Pacific may be in view, you climb steadily on a moderate grade into a zone of chaparral.

A stretch of level leads you through a wooded area, but this soon gives way to extensive groves of manzanita and stands of silk tassel. The trail here is merely a ledge carved from the slope. As the trail winds sharply left, you begin to get sweeping views that extend southeast toward Mt. Umunhum. Monte

Skyline Ridge Trails

OPTIONS

Skyline Ridge OSP is bordered by Russian Ridge, Monte Bello, and Long Ridge open space preserves, making many route options possible. The Bay Area Ridge Trail runs through Russian Ridge, Skyline, and Long Ridge open space preserves. The loop around **Horseshoe Lake** adds 1.2 miles to the main hike.

Bello Ridge, topped by Black Mountain, is northeast. At a four-way junction with the alternate trail for bicyclists and equestrians, you continue straight. ▶3

Crossing a culvert, the route bends sharply right and then wanders downhill, eventually reaching a clearing. Just ahead are two information boards and a **parking area** ▶4 Past the information boards, the Ridge Trail bends sharply right and continues mile to nearby **Horseshoe Lake**, which has a lovely loop trail. From the Horseshoe Lake trailhead, retrace your route back along the Ridge Trail to the parking area. ▶5

Daniels Nature Center *has an observation deck overlooking Alpine Pond.*

🚶 MILESTONES

▶1 0.0 Take Ridge Trail south through tunnel

▶2 0.2 Alpine Pond, Daniels Nature Center; stay left on Ridge Trail

▶3 1.2 Four-way junction with bike/horse trail; go straight

▶4 1.7 Horseshoe Lake trailhead, retrace to parking area

▶5 3.4 Back at parking area

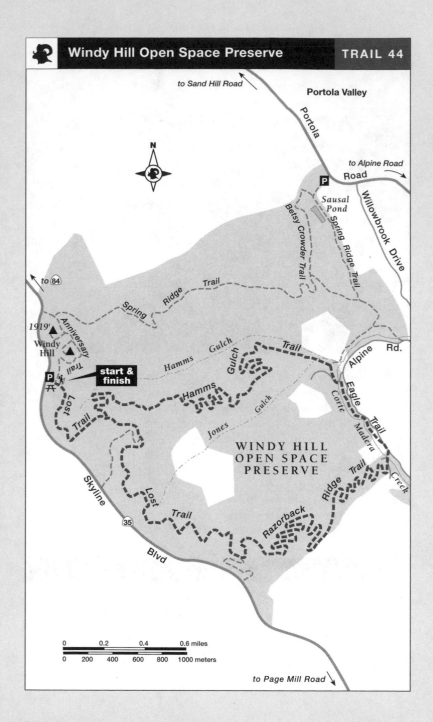

to Sand Hill Road

Portola Valley

Portola

P

to Alpine Road

Road

Sausal Pond

Willowbrook Drive

N

to 84

Betsy Crowder Trail

Spring Ridge Trail

Spring Ridge Trail

1919'
Windy Hill

Anniversary Trail

P

start & finish

Lost Trail

Hamms Gulch Trail

Gulch Trail

Gulch Trail

Hamms

Hamms Gulch

Jones Gulch

Alpine Rd.

Eagle Trail

Corte Madera

Creek

WINDY HILL
OPEN SPACE
PRESERVE

Razorback Ridge Trail

Skyline

35

Lost Trail

Blvd

| 0 | 0.2 | 0.4 | 0.6 miles |

| 0 | 200 | 400 | 600 | 800 | 1000 meters |

to Page Mill Road

Windy Hill Open Space Preserve

This adventurous semi-loop explores one of MROSD's best-loved preserves. Dropping about 1000 feet in 3 miles, you follow cool and shady Hamms Gulch downhill through a lush forest of Douglas-fir, California buckeye, and bigleaf maple to the banks of lovely Corte Madera Creek before climbing back to Skyline Blvd. Bring binoculars to catch glimpses of forest birds flitting through the trees, and scan the skies for raptors such as hawks and falcons. Native plant enthusiasts will be delighted by the variety of trees and shrubs found along this route. As its name implies, there is often wind at the upper reaches of this preserve, and also, in summer, fog.

TRAIL USE
Hike, Run

LENGTH
8.0 miles, 4-5 hours

VERTICAL FEET
±1650'

DIFFICULTY
– 1 2 3 4 **5** +

TRAIL TYPE
Loop

SURFACE TYPE
Dirt

FEATURES
Canyon
Stream
Autumn Colors
Wildflowers
Birds
Cool & Shady
Great Views
Secluded

FACILITIES
Restrooms
Picnic Tables

Best Time

This trail is best all year; often foggy and windy.

Finding the Trail

From the junction of Skyline Blvd. and Hwy. 84 in Sky Londa, take Skyline Blvd. southeast 2.3 miles to a parking area on the left. The trailhead is on the northeast corner of the parking area.

Trail Description

Once past the picnic area, which has three information boards and a map holder, you come to a split-rail fence with a gap. Beyond the fence are two trails: the Anniversary Trail to Windy Hill, left, and the **Lost Trail**, right, part of the Bay Area Ridge

Great Views

Trail.▶1 You turn right and, after about 100 feet, reach another fence, this one with a gate that controls equestrian use. During wet weather horses are prohibited and the gate is closed.

Now your single-track trail climbs on a gentle grade, with views that range from the Stanford Campus and Palo Alto to the East Bay hills and Mt. Diablo. At a junction with the **Hamms Gulch Trail**, a single track,▶2 you turn sharply left and begin descending via switchbacks through dense forest.

Soon you reach a fence and another equestrian gate. Just beyond the fence, the Hamms Gulch Trail veers right and is joined on the left by a connector to the Spring Ridge Trail.▶3 You stay on the Hamms Gulch Trail, and after several hundred yards reach a bridge over a creek flowing through **Jones Gulch**. Crossing the bridge, you come to a paved road in about 100 feet.

To the right is the preserve boundary, so you turn left and then cross **Corte Madera Creek** on a stone bridge.▶4 Once across the creek, look right to find the start of the **Eagle Trail**, which is maintained by the town of Portola Valley and closed to bikes. Follow this single-track trail as it parallels the rocky bed of Corte Madera Creek, which is right. Soon the trail reaches **Alpine Road**, which you follow for about 100 yards, then regain the trail as it descends right.

Again returning to Alpine Road, you follow it for several hundred feet to a **paved driveway** on the right. Crossing Corte Madera Creek on a bridge, the driveway turns right, but you continue straight and climb a dirt-and-gravel road. After a short, moderate climb, you leave the road by veering right on the **Razorback Ridge Trail**, a single track marked with a trail post and an arrow.

After about 50 feet the trail curves right and comes to an equestrian gate. Now the moderate but relentless climb continues, thankfully, via switch-

Windy Hill's *twin, grassy summits and wooded slopes are prominent landmarks along the skyline on the central Peninsula.*

backs in the shade. The deep canyon holding Damiani Creek is to your left, and now you begin a long, rising traverse which brings you to a vantage point with a view of Windy Hill.

Now switchbacks take you back and forth across the crest of a forested ridge. At a junction with the **Lost Trail,**►5 you angle right, pass a watering trough for horses, and then enjoy a mostly level grade. Now following a ridge downhill, you give up several hundred feet of hard-won elevation near the head of Jones Gulch before leveling again.

A trail sign, left, confirms that you are following the Lost Trail toward Hamms Gulch. On a scrub-covered hillside, you cross under a set of power lines and then reach a four-way junction with a dirt-and-gravel road. Continuing straight across the junction, you climb on a gentle grade to meet the Hamms Gulch Trail on the right.►6 From here, retrace your route to the parking area.►7

🚶 MILESTONES

- ►1 0.0 Take Lost Trail, right
- ►2 0.4 Left on Hamms Gulch Trail
- ►3 3.0 Right to stay on Hamms Gulch Trail, then across bridge and left on paved road to Eagle Trail (alternates with Alpine Rd.)
- ►4 3.6 Across Corte Madera Creek on bridge, climb dirt-and-gravel road to Razorback Ridge Trail, right.
- ►5 5.9 Right on Lost Trail
- ►6 7.6 Hamms Gulch Trail on right, retrace to parking area
- ►7 8.0 Back at parking area

Appendices

Governing Agencies

Chapter 1: North Bay

National Park Service (NPS)
Golden Gate National Recreation Area (GGNRA)
(415) 561-4700   www.nps.gov/goga
Point Reyes National Seashore
(415) 464-5100   www.nps.gov/pore

California State Parks (CSP)
(800) 777-0369   http://parks.ca.gov

Marin County Open Space District (MCOSD)
(415) 499-6387   www.marinopenspace.org

Marin Municipal Water District (MMWD)
Sky Oaks Ranger Station   (415) 945-1181
www.marinwater.org/resourcemanagement.html#recreation

Skyline Park Citizens Association (Napa)
(707) 252-0481   www.skylinepark.org

Sonoma County Parks and Recreation   www.parks.sonoma.net

Chapter 2: East Bay

California State Parks (CSP)   (800) 777-0369   http://parks.ca.gov

Mt. Diablo State Park
Information   (925) 837-2525
Reservations   (800) 444-7275
Mt. Diablo Interpretive Association   (925) 927-7222   www.mdia.org

East Bay Regional Park District (EBRPD)
Information   (510) 562-7275   www.ebparks.org
Reservations:
   Oakland Area   (510) 636-1684
   Hayward Area   (510) 538-6470
   Contra Costa County   (925) 676-0192
   Livermore Area   (925) 373-0144

Chapter 3: South Bay

California State Parks (CSP)   (800) 777-0369   http://parks.ca.gov

Henry W. Coe State Park
Information   (408) 779-2728   www.coepark.org
Reservations, campsites   (800) 444-7275
Reservations, backcountry First come, first served

Santa Clara County Parks
Information   (408) 355-2200   www.parkhere.org
Reservations   (408) 355-2201   www.gooutsideandplay.org

Midpeninsula Regional Open Space District (MROSD)
(650) 691-1200   www.openspace.org

Chapter 4: Peninsula

Golden Gate National Recreation Area (GGNRA)
(415) 561-4700   www.nps.gov/goga

Midpeninsula Regional Open Space District (MROSD)
(650) 691-1200   www.openspace.org

San Mateo County Parks
Information (650) 363-4020   www.eparks.net
Reservations (650) 363-4021

Outfitters

North Bay

Sonoma Outfitters   145 Third St., Santa Rosa (800) 290-1920
REI   213 Corte Madera Town Center, Corte Madera   (415) 927-1938
REI   2715 Santa Rosa Ave, Santa Rosa   (707) 540-9025

East Bay

Marmot Mountain Works   3049 Adeline St., Berkeley   (510) 849-0735
REI   1338 San Pablo Ave., Berkeley   (510) 527-4140
REI   1975 Diamond Blvd., Ste. B100, (The Willows Shopping Center), Concord   (925) 825-9400
REI   43962 Fremont Blvd., Fremont   (510) 651-0305
Sunrise Mountaineering   2455 Railroad Ave., Livermore   (925) 447-8330

San Francisco and the Peninsula

Lombardi Sports   1600 Jackson St., San Francisco   (415) 771-0600
The North Face   217 Alma St., Palo Alto   (650) 327-1563
The North Face   180 Post St., San Francisco   (415) 433-3223
REI   840 Brannan St., San Francisco   (415) 934-1938
REI   1119 Industrial Rd., Ste. 1B, San Carlos   (650) 508-2330

South Bay

REI   400 El Paseo de Saratoga. San Jose   (408) 871-8765
Western Mountaineering   2344 El Camino Real, Santa Clara
                                        (408) 984-7611

Internet Resources

(See Public Agencies and Outfitters for more listings)

Bay Area Hiker   www.bahiker.com
Bay Area Open Space Council   www.openspacecouncil.org
Bay Area Ridge Trail Council   www.ridgetrail.org
Bay Nature magazine   www.baynature.com

California Native Plant Society   www.cnps.org
Committee for Green Foothills   www.greenfoothills.org

Friends of Edgewood Natural Preserve
   www.friendsofedgewood.org/edgewood.htm

Greenbelt Alliance www.greenbelt.org

Marin Trails   www.marintrails.com
Mt. Diablo Interpretive Association   www.mdia.org
Mt. Tamalpais Interpretive Association   www.mttam.net

National Audubon Society www.audubon.org
National Geographic Maps/TOPO!
   http://maps.nationalgeographic.com/topo

Peninsula Access for Dogs   http://.prusik.com/pads
Peninsula Open Space Trust   www.openspacetrust.org
Point Reyes Bird Observatory   www.prbo.org

Save Mount Diablo   www.savemountdiablo.org
Sempervirens Fund   www.sempervirens.org
Sierra Club   www.sierraclub.org
Sonoma County Trails Council   www.sonomatrails.org/sctc

Tamalpais Conservation Club   www.tamalpais.org
Trail Center   www.trailcenter.org

National Weather Service   www.nws.noaa.gov
Weather.com   www.weather.com
Whole Access www.wholeaccess.org
   (to increase recreational opportunities for people with disabilities)
Wilderness Press   www.wildernesspress.com

Useful Books

Bay Area Trail Guidebooks

Heid, Matt, *Camping and Backpacking in the San Francisco Bay Area*. Berkeley: Wilderness Press, 2003.

Lage, Jessica, *Point Reyes*. Berkeley: Wilderness Press, 2004.

Lage, Jessica, *Trail Runner's Guide: San Francisco Bay Area*. Berkeley: Wilderness Press, 2003.

Margolin, Malcolm, *The East Bay Out*. Revised ed. Berkeley: Heyday Books, 1988.

Martin, Don, and Kay Martin, *Hiking Marin*. San Anselmo: Martin Press, 1995.

Martin, Don, and Kay Martin, *Mt. Tam*. San Anselmo: Martin Press, 1994.

Martin, Don, and Kay Martin, *Point Reyes National Seashore*. 2nd ed. San Anselmo: Martin Press, 1997

Rusmore, Jean, *The Bay Area Ridge Trail*. 2nd ed. Berkeley: Wilderness Press, 2002.

Rusmore, Jean, et al., *Peninsula Trails*. 3rd ed. Berkeley: Wilderness Press, 1997.

Rusmore, Jean, et al., *South Bay Trails*. 3rd ed. Berkeley: Wilderness Press, 2001.

Spitz, Barry, *Open Spaces*. San Rafael: Marin County Open Space District, 2000.

Spitz, Barry, *Tamalpais Trails*. 4th ed. San Anselmo: Potrero Meadow Publishing Co., 1998.

Stanton, Ken, *Great Day Hikes in & around Napa Valley*. Mendocino: Bored Feet Publications, 1997.

Wayburn, Peggy, *Adventuring in the San Francisco Bay Area*. Revised ed. San Francisco: Sierra Club Books, 1995.

Weintraub, David, *East Bay Trails*. Berkeley: Wilderness Press, 1998.

Weintraub, David, *North Bay Trails*. Berkeley: Wilderness Press, 1999.

Bay Area History Books

Lavender, David, *California*. Lincoln: University of Nebraska Press, 1972.

Richards, Rand, *Historic San Francisco*. San Francisco: Heritage House Publishers, 1999.

Natural History Books

Alt, David, and Donald W. Hyndman, *Roadside Geology of Northern and Central California*. Missoula: Mountain Press Publishing Company, 2000.

Barbour, Michael, et al., *Coast Redwood*. Los Olivos: Cachuma Press, 2001.

Burt, William H., and Richard P. Grossenheider, *A Field Guide to the Mammals, North America, North of Mexico*. 3rd ed. Boston: Houghton Mifflin Company, 1980.

Clark, Jeanne L., *California Wildlife Viewing Guide*. Helena: Falcon Press, 1992.

Coffeen, Mary, *Central Coast Wildflowers*. San Luis Obispo: EZ Nature Books, 1996.

Faber, Phyllis M., and Robert F. Holland, *Common Riparian Plants of California*. Mill Valley: Pickleweed Press, 1988.

Faber, Phyllis M., *Common Wetland Plants of Coastal California*. 2nd ed. Mill Valley: Pickleweed Press, 1996.

Kozloff, Eugene N., and Linda H. Beidleman, *Plants of the San Francisco Bay Region*. Revised ed. Berkeley: University of California Press, 2003.

Lanner, Ronald M., *Conifers of California*. Los Olivos: Cachuma Press, 1999.

Little, Elbert L., *National Audubon Society Field Guide to North American Trees, Western Region*. New York: Alfred A. Knopf, 1994.

Lyons, Kathleen, and Mary Beth Cooney-Lazaneo, *Plants of the Coast Redwood Region*. Boulder Creek: Looking Press, 1988.

National Geographic Society, *Field Guide to the Birds of North America*. 3rd ed. Washington, D.C.: National Geographic Society, 1999.

Niehaus, Theodore F., and Charles L. Ripper, *A Field Guide to Pacific States Wildflowers*. Boston: Houghton Mifflin Company, 1976.

Pavlik, Bruce M., et al., *Oaks of California*. Los Olivos: Cachuma Press, 1991.

Peterson, Roger T., *A Field Guide to Western Birds*. 3rd ed. Boston: Houghton Mifflin Company, 1990.

Schoenherr, Allan A., *A Natural History of California*. Berkeley: University of California Press, 1992.

Sibley, David Allen, *The Sibley Guide to Birds*. New York: Alfred A. Knopf, Inc., 2000.

Stebbins, Robert C., *A Field Guide to Western Reptiles and Amphibians*. 2nd ed. Boston: Houghton Mifflin Company, 1985.

Stuart, John D., and John O. Sawyer, *Trees and Shrubs of California*. Berkeley: University of California Press, 2001.

Maps

It would be nice if high-quality maps existed for each park covered by this guide, but that is not the case. The maps used to navigate these trails varied from topographic ones that were professionally drawn to sketch maps lacking contour lines and other features. In a few cases, no maps were available.

When you visit a park that has a staffed entrance kiosk or visitor center, check there for a map. Sometimes maps and trail guides will be found in dispensers near the trailhead. Not surprisingly, bigger, more well-known parks have the best maps. Check the Web site of the agency administering the park or open space you plan to visit to see if downloadable maps are available.

As an alternative, you can print your own customized maps using **TOPO!**, a computer program from National Geographic Maps, http://maps.nationalgeographic.com/topo. TOPO! uses USGS maps on CD-ROM combined with software that allows you to draw routes, insert text, measure distance, plot elevation gain and loss, and locate landmarks. An interface allows you to transfer data between your GPS unit and your computer, so you can load waypoints from a map into your GPS (so you can find them in the field), and also to take waypoints stored in your GPS during a hike and plot them on a map.

Getting to the trailhead requires some navigation too. The **California State Automobile Association (CSAA)** gives its members free road maps. Most useful for the routes in this book are San Francisco Bay and Monterey Bay, in the California Regional Series. **Thomas Guide's** Metropolitan Bay Area Street Guide and Directory is helpful for driving around the Bay Area.

North Bay Maps

The best map for Mt. Tamalpais, the Marin Headlands, and Muir Woods is the **Olmsted** trail map, available at REI and most stores. **Point Reyes National Seashore** trail maps are available at the visitor center. A **Point Reyes and surrounding area** recreation map is available from Wilderness Press. Maps for **California state parks** are problematic—sometimes they are available only at entrance kiosks or visitor centers, and these may be closed during the week. **Marin County Open Space District** has maps available by mail and from its Web site.

Lands of the **Marin Municipal Water District** are covered by Olmsted's Mt. Tamalpais map; there's also an MMWD brochure. The **Skyline Wilderness Park** map is available at the entrance kiosk and from the

Skyline Park Citizens Association Web site. Pease Press's *Trails of Northeast Marin County* map shows China Camp and Mt. Burdell.

East Bay Maps

A trail map of **Mt. Diablo State Park** is available at the park's visitor centers and from MDIA. **East Bay Regional Park District** has maps available at its trailheads, by mail, and from its Web site. **Olmsted** publishes maps for the **East Bay, Northern** and **Central** sections, available at REI stores.

South Bay Maps

Henry W. Coe State Park maps are available for sale at the visitor center. **Santa Clara County Parks** has maps at its trailheads and downloadable maps on its Web site; these are also available by mail. **Midpeninsula Regional Open Space District** maps are available at its trailheads, by mail, and from its Web site.

Peninsula Maps

Maps for **GGNRA's** Presidio of San Francisco and Phleger Estate are available at the Presidio's visitor centers and from the GGNRA Web site.

The **Trail Center** publishes detailed maps of the *Central* and *Southern Peninsula*, available from Wilderness Press and at REI. **Pease Press** publishes *Trails of the Coastside and Northern Peninsula*, showing San Bruno and Montara Mountains.

Midpeninsula Regional Open Space District maps are available at its trailheads, by mail, and from its Web site. Maps for **San Mateo County Parks** are available at trailheads and by mail.

Index

Author and Editor

David Weintraub

David Weintraub is a writer, editor, and photographer based in South Carolina and Cape Cod. A former long-time San Francisco resident, he has authored a number of books for Wilderness Press, including *East Bay Trails*, *North Bay Trails*, *Monterey Bay Trails*, and *Adventure Kayaking: Cape Cod & Martha's Vineyard*.

This year Wilderness Press will also publish David's *Afoot & Afield in the San Francisco Bay Area*, a comprehensive collection of hiking routes in the North Bay, East Bay, South Bay, and Peninsula. David's guide to the walking trails of Cape Cod and the Islands, also from Wilderness Press, is scheduled for release in 2005.

Joe Walowski Top Trails Editor

Joe Walowski's editing career begins with *Top Trails Los Angeles*. By day, Joe is a strategy consultant to magazine publishers. An avid hiker and climber, he has spent many pleasant days on the top trails throughout California. He makes his home in San Francisco.

Joe conceived of the Top Trails series as the definitive sampler of trails, the "must-do" hikes in the most interesting destinations. Feel free to e-mail feedback on Top Trails to joe@highpointpress.com